Prophets of the Apocalypse

Prophets of the Apocalypse

David Koresh and Other American Messiahs

Kenneth R. Samples,
Erwin M. de Castro,
Richard Abanes,
and Robert J. Lyle

Baker Books

A Division of Baker Book House Co
Grand Rapids, Michigan 49516

© 1994 by Kenneth R. Samples, Erwin M. de Castro, Richard Abanes, and Robert J. Lyle

Published by Baker Books
a division of Baker Book House Company
P.O. Box 6287, Grand Rapids, MI 49516-6287

ISBN: 0-8010-8367-2

Second printing, June 1994

Printed in the United States of America

This book is dedicated to the Davidian children who died on April 19, 1993, and to their young playmates who were released early on in the siege.

For those who perished, may their innocence never be forgotten. For those who now face an uncertain future in a world they've been taught to fear, may their emotional, spiritual, and psychological wounds soon be healed.

Contents

Preface

Within hours of the ATF's botched assault on David Koresh and his Branch Davidians, the Christian Research Institute International (an organization that monitors religious trends and movements) was bombarded by media inquiries. Who is David Koresh? Aren't the Branch Davidians part of the Seventh-day Adventist church? What do Branch Davidians believe? How long has the Branch Davidian "cult" been around? What *is* a cult? The steady stream of questions tied up the Institute's phone lines for hours.

As the siege continued, so did the inquiries. Hours became days. Days stretched into weeks, and still, the calls came. Eventually, the questions moved beyond the realm of Branch Davidianism and into the domain of other extremist groups, their leaders, and what could be expected from them in the future. "Cult-consciousness" in America had risen to a level unseen since the 1978 Jonestown tragedy.

For this intensified concern over "cults," we were grateful. Believers and nonbelievers alike have, for some time now, needed to become more fully aware of the darker side of religious devotion.

Unfortunately, the media circus produced by the Davidian siege also generated some rather erroneous information. On March 7, 1993, for example, *Philadelphia Inquirer* staff writer Cynthia Mayer referred to David Koresh as an "evangelical leader." And reporter Michael deCourcy Hines, in the April 20, 1993 edition of the *New York Times*, called the Branch Davidians "a group of fundamentalist Christians."

Mischaracterizations about evangelicalism, fundamentalism, and Christianity abounded. There was no shortage of faulty information about Koresh and the Branch Davidians. Inaccuracies were ringing in the public's ears and no one seemed to recognize it. Consequently, we decided to write *Prophets of the Apocalypse: David Koresh and Other American Messiahs* to help clear up the confusion.

Such an endeavor would not have been possible without the aid of some very special people. Our deepest thanks goes to ex-Branch Davidians David and Debbie Bunds, from whom we received a great deal of valuable, primary documentation. The historical information gleaned from them was extremely helpful. Their greatest contribution to the project, however, was the honesty, openness, and courage they displayed while working with us. We hope this book will confirm to David and Debbie that the experiences they endured under Koresh were not endured in vain.

Sue Johnson, who lost her brother Steve Schneider in the Davidian blaze, also receives our thanks. She provided important insights into Davidian attitudes, thought processes, and motivation. We pray that Sue and her family will soon recover from their tragic loss.

To Don Marion of KXXV (Channel 25) in Waco, we are grateful for supplying us with some very important and useful video footage.

A special acknowledgment must go to Baker Book House and its staff. Acquisitions Editor Kin Millen believed in the project from its very inception, and tirelessly worked to get the wheels of production started. The manuscript's editor, Maria denBoer, showed great patience and understanding as we endeavored to complete some very difficult and time-consuming research. Ultimately, it is Director of Publications Allan Fisher to whom we are the most indebted. His willingness to stand behind the project to its completion has been most appreciated.

One final word of thanks belongs to our families, along with our fellow staff members at the Christian Research Institute International, whose prayers and encouragement were of great comfort to us.

Taking a stand for truth is a difficult mission, but it is one that must never be forsaken. The price the world pays for unchecked deception is, as this book will show, much too high.

Kenneth R. Samples
Erwin M. de Castro
Richard Abanes
Robert J. Lyle

Introduction

This morning I am going to present to you what was presented to me. . . . It's unique, it's bizarre, and it's scary. Very scary. But I have had to exercise by many different ways, by the Spirit of God, to prepare for fear, anxiety, torment, torture. . . . The lessons are very clear.

—Vernon Howell, a.k.a. David Koresh

AGENTS MET BY BARRAGE OF GUNFIRE"; "UNWARNED, AGENTS RUSH INTO BULLETS"; "U.S. AGENCY RECORDS ITS BLOODIEST DAY." So read national headlines following February 28, 1993— D-Day for a search-warrant-serving mission launched by the U.S. Bureau of Alcohol, Tobacco, and Firearms (ATF).

"We had planned this operation for quite a while," said ATF special agent Ted Royster. "We practiced for it, we drilled over and over again, and had our plan down." But months of preparation still ended in disaster, as federal authorities lost what ATF deputy director Daniel Hartnett called their "element of surprise." (Eight months later Hartnett was suspended for "making misleading statements.")

The resulting tragedy played itself out just ten miles from Waco, on an isolated tract of East Texas flatland called Mt. Carmel, where over a hundred men, women, and children lived in a huge, L-shaped structure built with their own hands. Waco residents often referred to the dormitory-like compound as nothing less than a fortress. Their description proved all too accurate.

At 9:00 A.M. on what would eventually be nick-named "Bloody Sunday," nearly one hundred federal officers gathered on the outskirts of Mt. Carmel's property. Less than a half-hour later, ATF commanders gave their agents the green light to approach the site. Like lightning, ATF choppers descended from out of seemingly nowhere on the distant horizon and streaked toward the compound. On the ground, two cattle trucks filled with heavily armed law officers entered the property and slowly pulled up to the front door. The trucks had barely rolled to a stop when ATF officers began pouring out of their Trojan-Horse vehicles.

"Federal agents with a warrant!" they screamed.

The front door momentarily swung open and a voice from inside yelled, "What's going on here?"

Then, just as quickly, the door slammed. High-caliber-rifle-rounds from inside suddenly burst their way through the door and into the agents on the other side.

At the same instant, the rest of the unwelcome government intruders received a similarly brutal greeting—"heavy and sustained gunfire" from all directions. The catastrophe sent shockwaves all the way to the White House.

One thing in particular ignited controversy. The lethal shower of bullets that bathed ATF officers in blood that day didn't come from bootleggers, interstate tobacco smugglers, or drug traffickers, but from gun-toting members of an apocalypse-based religious group called the Branch Davidians.

The group's self-proclaimed "Son of God" leader, David Koresh, had often prophesied of just such a day. "They will take my life," he preached, "but I will arise and take theirs forevermore." Koresh and his disciples had begun preparation for that awaited occasion years earlier, stockpiling an assortment of military assault weapons, including explosive devices, AK–47s equipped with "hell-fire" switches (electrical devices that increase a semi-automatic rifle's rate of fire), and AR–15s modified into fully automatic weapons through M–16 conversion parts.

According to government officials, concern over this massive cache of weapons provided the impetus for checking out the remote stronghold. To the Davidians' prophecy-gorged minds, however, the ATF assault happened because of something much more significant: Armageddon.

When members of the group broke out their arsenal, stunned and disoriented law officers found themselves caught in a fierce gun battle the likes of which few of them had ever seen. One newsman said the Davidian compound "sounded like a war zone," and recalled how he could "hear people screaming with the agony of it." Another witness to the bloody confrontation recounted how "there were people dropping left and right."

After ninety minutes of all-out war, Branch Davidians and law-enforcement personnel finally negotiated a cease-fire to retrieve their casualties. But by then, two federal agents were already dead and twenty-two others lay injured (two of them with gunshot wounds so severe they died within a few hours after the incident). Never before had the ATF experienced such a devastating defeat. Thus began a fifty-one-day standoff—the second longest siege in American law-enforcement history.

In the ensuing weeks, national headlines expressed the gamut of American thought and sentiment: "RAID ON SECT IN WACO WAS FULL OF MISCALCULATIONS"; "A BELIEVER SAYS CULT IN TEXAS IS PEACEFUL"; "IN WACO, GOVERNMENT DECIDED TO THROW THE CONSTITUTION AWAY." On several occasions, the papers even tried to inject a little humor into the situation (perhaps to help ease the pain of the reality). There were, for example, such captions as "CULT LEADER CHALLENGES FBI TO PROVE HE'S NOT GOD."

Front-page stories about the "siege at Waco" eventually dwindled down to brief updates buried in the back sections of daily papers—partly due to statements issued by the Davidians' attorneys. During the standoff's latter period, the lawyers began giving assurances that the episode would soon come to a peaceful end. They were wrong.

On April 19, 1993 (day 51 of the siege), the world watched in horror as the Branch Davidian compound burst into a city-block-sized funeral pyre. David Koresh and somewhere between seventy-five and eighty-five of his loyal followers, including approximately twenty-five children, met their end in the all-consuming inferno. Although some died from the flames and smoke inhalation, gruesome coroner reports indicated that many Davidians,

among them Koresh, died from single gunshot wounds to the
head. The worst of Koresh's apocalyptic prophecies had finally
come to pass.

Why did the situation near Waco take a turn for the worse?
Some fault the ATF for staging an ill-conceived and poorly executed plan. Supporting this position are the findings released in
a 220-page Justice Department report on the assault. The investigation concluded that "The decision to proceed was tragically
wrong, not just in retrospect, but because of what the decision
makers knew at the time." The government report also mentioned "disturbing evidence of flawed decision-making, inade-
quate intelligence gathering, miscommunication, supervisory
failure and deliberately misleading post-raid statements."

Despite these blistering criticisms of the ATF, others put the
bulk of blame on either the FBI (in charge of the fifty-one-day
ordeal) or Attorney General Janet Reno (who ordered the FBI to
take action against the compound on the standoff's final day).

A few fingers have even pointed in President Clinton's direc-
tion.

And, of course, there are those who insist the incident was all
part of a secret government conspiracy against religious freedom.
(The authors have yet to see any credible evidence supporting
such an allegation.)

Yet throughout the entire affair, few seemed willing to consider
how the Davidian mind-set paved the way for their melee with
government agents and the subsequent fire. The following pages
will examine the stories and inner workings behind David Koresh
and the Branch Davidians, along with America's other "prophets
of the apocalypse." Taking a close and honest look at Waco's self-
proclaimed messiah and those he held spellbound may yield
some valuable insights into the questions that remain and prevent such a tragedy from happening again. As Koresh himself
stated, "The lessons are very clear."

1

In the Beginning

ANY PERSON experiencing an identity crisis or involved in a serious spiritual quest is theoretically vulnerable to the seductive outreach of the cults. . . . Persons who have recently gone through some kind of painful life experience or who find themselves in a state of unusual anxiety, stress, or uncertainty are far more susceptible. . . . When someone is feeling exceedingly anxious, uncertain, hurt, lonely, unloved, confused, or guilty, that person is a prime prospect for those who come in the guise of religion offering a way out or "peace of mind."

—Ronald Enroth, Sociologist

For thirteen-year-old Bonnie Clark the world wasn't big enough. *Carpe diem*! Seize the day! Live life to the fullest! Bonnie wanted to experience everything. And no one, not even her parents, could stop her. Every time they attempted to discipline the rambunctious teen, she'd simply run away from home—but only as far as the Howell residence, where her boyfriend Bobby lived.

"She was just a wild young girl," recounts Bobby. "We were both wild when we were young, did a lot of things we regret."

Less than two years later, in 1959, Bonnie's lifestyle finally caught up with her when she became pregnant. It didn't take long for her carefree ways to be replaced by anxious thoughts about the future. How would others react? Who would take care of the added expenses? What would Bobby do? Anxiety soon turned into downright panic. Bonnie simply couldn't bear the thought of being abandoned by her young beau.

But when twenty-year-old Bobby found out he was going to be a father, the best of all possible things happened: he asked Bonnie to marry him. She, of course, said yes. Even though Bonnie knew they would face hard times, she was sure they would somehow make it. Things couldn't have been better.

"We were going to get married," says Bobby. "Back then, you had to have a blood test in Texas and a check for venereal diseases. . . . We went and got all that done and went to get the license. And they told us that she would have to have her birth certificate."

At the tender age of fourteen Bonnie didn't even drive. Consequently, she had no identification for a marriage license. Undaunted, the young couple sent away for her birth certificate and continued making preparations for their marriage. Everything was going just fine—until Bonnie's wild streak flared up.

The impetuous teen went with an older girlfriend to one of Houston's downtown nightclubs and stayed out all night. Upon returning home the next day, Bonnie found her furious fiancé waiting. An explosive argument ensued, and words that cut too deep to be forgotten or forgiven forever changed the course of their future. They never got a marriage license nor even set a date for the wedding. At least, that's how Bobby remembers the incident.

Bonnie recalls an altogether different set of circumstances. She contends that a marriage license was indeed obtained, and a date for the ceremony definitely set. According to Bonnie, the marriage never took place because on the very day they were to be wed, Bobby "backed out."

After more than thirty years, both Bobby and Bonnie each defend their own side of the story. Regardless of who's right, Bonnie was heartbroken. Nevertheless, she realized she had to go on with her life. Just before turning fifteen, Bonnie gave birth to a baby boy and named him Vernon Wayne Howell.

The Early Years

After Vernon's birth, Bonnie alternately stayed with her mother and Bobby's mother. Whenever Bonnie stayed at the Howell residence, Bobby took care of his newborn son while Bonnie worked long hours at a nearby nursing home to meet her growing expenses.

Bobby remembers Vernon being "a smart young boy. Very intelligent for his age. . . . He was so energetic when he was young. . . . We nicknamed him Sputnik, after the Russian satellite. When he was little, he was all over the place. He couldn't be still; he was so energetic, hyper."

Although Vernon's young parents continued their relationship on and off for nearly two years, they were never able to fully get back together. The incident that had disrupted their marriage plans proved far too damaging. They simply couldn't forget the past.

Bobby eventually started dating another woman. Sensing it was finally over with Bobby, Bonnie also began dating someone else. Her newfound interest was Joe Golden, the man who subsequently became her first husband.

A Family Shattered

When Bonnie married Joe, things started to look up. Vernon finally had a full-time dad. But Bonnie's dreams of a happy life were soon dashed to pieces when, not long into the marriage, Joe allegedly became "very abusive." He often vented his rage at young Bonnie and her little boy. According to Bonnie, Joe frequently beat two-year-old Vernon "on his butt 'til he was black and blue." Joe even held the toddler's bare feet on a hot furnace grating.

After about a year of torment, Bonnie could allow no more. She obtained a divorce, headed for Dallas, and left the pain behind. She also left Vernon behind to be cared for by his grandmother in Houston, visiting him only occasionally.

Plans changed two years later, however, when Bonnie remarried and sent word that she wanted Vernon to live in Dallas with her and her new husband, Roy Haldeman. But by the time Bonnie took full custody of her son, Vernon had come to recognize his grandmother as his mother. "Don't take me from my mama," cried the boy to his real mother. "I don't want you to be my mama." His pleas did not change Bonnie's mind.

Soon after reuniting with Roy, the new Haldeman family moved to Richardson, Texas—a place of growth and change for the threesome, especially Vernon. But before little Vernon could bond with his estranged mother, Bonnie's attention was diverted from him again, this time by the birth of her second son, Roger.

Meanwhile, Bobby remained in Houston. Soon after Bonnie's divorce from Joe, Bobby tried to locate his former love. But by then, she had already gone to Dallas. When Bobby attempted to learn of her whereabouts, he was told nothing. "Nobody'd ever let me know where she was at," Bobby explains. "She had a brother in Houston. . . . I went to his house and he told me if I ever came back again he was gonna shoot me."

Approximately twenty years went by before Bobby was contacted by Vernon and the two were again part of each other's lives. By then, Bobby's estranged son had already envisioned a glorious end to human history. In Bobby's words, "Back then he [Vernon] had a belief that the first family should be together. . . . He thought his mother and I should go back together. . . . We should all go to Israel and stay and live in Israel until Armageddon." Vernon's dream of a reunited family never materialized.

Dark Memories

Perhaps one of the worst things that can happen to a child happened to Vernon: sexual molestation. One of the few individuals who heard Vernon talk about his ordeal says, "He was sexually abused—I know, specifically, at the age of five. It was one of his mother's male relatives. He never named who it was. He just said it was by a male family member. He never named names because he felt that it would hurt his mother too much."

The former follower recalls Vernon saying, "I was five years old, a little, innocent boy who didn't know anything."

Vernon mentioned his molestation only after hearing about how his young Davidian follower had herself been sexually molested by a relative. "I know what that's like," Vernon told the victimized girl. "I was sexually abused too."

The abuse suffered by Vernon reportedly lasted until he was nine. "For about four years there," continues the ex-Davidian, "he was consistently—he used the word 'raped'—by his male relative."

"Little children don't do this," Vernon said. "It's terrible that people do that to little children."

Long after becoming the leader of the Davidians, Vernon privately expressed to various members of the group the immense shame and embarrassment he felt about being abused, and how it continued to haunt him.

The year when the sexual abuse stopped, Vernon was formally introduced to the faith that would profoundly shape the rest of his life.

Growing Up an Adventist

A few years after settling in Richardson, Bonnie decided to rekindle her spirituality. She took nine-year-old Vernon with her and began attending a local Seventh-day Adventist (SDA) church, the denomination of Bonnie's upbringing.

According to Bonnie, Vernon loved to talk about God and read the Bible. Throughout his youth, he would spend hours listening to the radio preachers who thundered across the Richardson airwaves. Vernon also paid frequent visits to a nearby neighbor, a Baptist minister whose Sunday services he occasionally attended.

Of these varying streams of religious influence, Vernon's affiliation and involvement with the SDA church proved to have the most significant and lasting impact. Vernon derived from Adventism a foundation upon which he built his own religious system, which included a remnant mentality (the idea of one small band faithfully preserving God's truth throughout a period of apostasy), an unhealthy preoccupation with prophecy, and a belief in modern-day prophets.

Vernon ultimately memorized large portions of Scripture and was able to recite them effortlessly, quoting huge passages from such complex prophetic books as Isaiah, Ezekiel, and Jeremiah. He also consumed vast amounts of writings from two SDA giants: William Miller, the early nineteenth-century Baptist preacher who paved the way for Adventism, and Ellen G. White, the most prominent figure in SDA history and who many Adventists believe had the "spirit of prophecy."

In Search of Answers

"Inquisitive in his mind and searching for something" was how Bonnie described Vernon, especially during his formative years. He seemed determined to find answers to just about everything.

While still in his teens, Vernon became deeply puzzled about Adventism's stand on prophets. It wasn't because he had trouble believing in prophets. He could and did accept that readily enough. But "if Adventists accept the legitimacy of modern-day prophets," wondered Vernon, "then why is there a complete absence of such prophets in the denomination after the death of E. G. White in 1915?"

The lack of an acceptable answer from SDA leadership soon caused Vernon to start forming his own opinions. "Maybe Miller and White were not just isolated prophets, but were the first links in a prophetic chain that had continued all the way to the present," Vernon speculated. "Perhaps there were prophets *alive* somewhere. After all, even E. G. White herself said, 'The Lord will raise up men who will give the people the message for this time.'"

Yet there remained one huge problem with Vernon's theory: he didn't know of any living prophet. Still, he held fast, hoping that one day soon he would come face to face with his "missing prophet."

First Love

During the Haldemans' seven-year stay in Richardson, Vernon completed grades one to six at the Dallas Seventh-day Adventist Academy. When the family moved to the town of Sachse, Vernon continued attending the academy for one additional year. He then transferred to the Garland, Texas school system, where he completed the eighth and ninth grades. It was there that he met Linda, his first love.

Not much is known about Linda. She has given no interviews, has never spoken publicly about her relationship to Vernon, and has made no comments regarding the tragedy at Mt. Carmel. In fact, her connection to Vernon has never been widely circulated and remains largely unknown.

According to Bonnie, Vernon and Linda "had a child together," a daughter, when they were about seventeen years old. (Others say Linda was younger.) The situation was especially painful for Bonnie, as it brought back distant memories of a time when she had faced a similar predicament.

The two teens apparently loved each other very much. He was "crazy about this girl and was willin' to marry her," Bonnie conveys, "and her father was all for 'em, you know for a while. And then he sort of turned against Vernon."

The disapproval he met from Linda's father left Vernon emotionally destroyed. Then, a year after Vernon's and Linda's separation, the Haldemans packed up and moved from Sachse (in West Texas) to Chandler (in East Texas). But eighteen-year-old Vernon, distraught by the thought of never seeing Linda again, was determined to stay in the Garland area. He tried desperately to somehow convince Linda's father to change his mind. It didn't work.

Vernon lost the girl he loved, along with their newborn daughter. The two would never again be a part of Vernon's life. But he would never forget them. Years later, after becoming the leader of the Davidians, Vernon tried to convince the mother and child to join his group. Linda ordered Vernon to leave without even allowing him to see their daughter.

The Pastor's Girl

Bonnie could see no end to Vernon's despair. She tried to help ease her son's emotional grief, but was unsuccessful. During his regular visits to Chandler, Vernon often lamented over his dilemma with Linda and their little girl, sobbing in remorse for hours.

By then, a couple of years had passed since Vernon was an active churchgoer. But now, in hopes of finding some relief to his suffering, he decided to go back to church. While visiting his mother's SDA congregation in nearby Tyler, Vernon stumbled across the answer to his stricken heart. Her name was Sandy Berlin, and her father happened to be the new head pastor of Tyler's SDA church.

Bonnie remembers Sandy as an exceptionally beautiful, long-haired girl. Despite being only sixteen years of age, she reportedly "looked twenty-four and had a reputation following her." It wasn't long, said Vernon's mother, before Sandy fixed her sights on Vernon.

Vernon avoided the willowy blonde for months. He often complained, "Momma, I don't want another relationship, I love Linda. . . . And I'm not over it. . . . I don't want to get involved with this girl!"

Then one day Pastor Berlin asked Vernon to accompany him on a missionary trip to South Dakota. Vernon agreed, unaware that Sandy was slated to join them as well. They were, to use Bonnie's words, "thrown together."

Little by little, Vernon's heart softened and his sorrow over losing Linda was gradually replaced by his blossoming relationship with Sandy. Months of depression subsided and his passion to serve God burned hotter than ever. Vernon's active involvement with the Tyler church reached a high point in 1979, when he was officially baptized into the denomination. Vernon was alive again!

Costly Questions

Vernon's renewed interest in the Bible revived long-forgotten concerns and sparked new ones as well, prompting him to ask more questions than anyone cared to hear. Since no one seemed to have the answers he wanted, Vernon simply came up with his own. He came to believe that God had chosen him to speak about "certain truths" that, if accepted, would enlighten the church.

Disputes between Vernon and the church leaders over the proper interpretation of certain Bible verses soon became a regular occurrence. The disagreements caused so much disruption that something finally had to be done.

Bonnie claims that church authorities tried to "shut him up." But Lynn Ray, an elder who witnessed what happened, insists that church leaders treated Vernon with the utmost patience. They tried on numerous occasions to answer all his questions and lovingly correct his misguided thinking.

Yet Vernon simply would not relent. He continued to interrupt organized meetings, voicing his opinions on how the Bible should be interpreted. Vernon then went so far as to try swaying church members to his way of thinking—focusing especially on the youth, including Sandy.

When Pastor Berlin was apprised of Vernon's actions, he quickly put an end to Vernon's relationship with Sandy. Vernon countered by claiming God told him Sandy was to be his wife. But the pastor didn't buy it, and Sandy stopped seeing Vernon. Once again, Vernon was cut off from someone he loved. This time, however, his heartache was mixed with bitterness and anger.

To Vernon, it must have seemed like the whole world had turned against him—even Sandy reportedly began to taunt him. "What about all your prophecies now, Vernon? I thought God spoke to you?" Why Sandy reacted the way she did remains unclear. Vernon did, however, track down Sandy after he had established himself as the leading Davidian. Like Linda, she was asked to join his group; and like Linda, she refused.

Going over the Edge

Angry and dazed by the recent turn of events, Vernon launched an even more aggressive campaign against the church, making outbursts of "biblical truths" at every possible instance. During one Sabbath service, Vernon took advantage of an opportunity to share a brief testimony and delivered a seemingly endless sermon. The ushers ultimately had to remove him physically.

On another occasion, the church held a meeting to decide about the purchase of an organ. Vernon stood up and said that God spoke audibly to him and revealed that the church shouldn't buy the instrument. No one paid attention.

The situation grew increasingly volatile as Vernon frantically tried to prove he was special and worthwhile. Members of the congregation, however, simply viewed him as someone obsessed with showing off his knowledge and being the center of attention.

Vernon eventually stopped attending church services and was subsequently disfellowshipped for "his refusal to adhere to the principles of the church and not be disruptive" and for exerting a "bad influence on the young people of the church." His days as an Adventist were over.

Growing Pains?

Looking back, some think Vernon went to extremes partly because he wanted to prove something to himself—that he was good enough for Sandy and, before her, Linda. Those who remember Vernon as someone with "a definite inferiority complex" believe his emotional condition was more closely linked to his relationship with Roy Haldeman, his mother's second husband.

According to Bobby Howell, Roy constantly criticized Vernon, commenting how he never did do anything right and making him feel worthless. Former Branch Davidian David Bunds explains that tensions ran high between Roy and Vernon, and that Vernon was endlessly trying to prove to Roy (and everyone else) that he was "the best at everything."

Even after gaining full control of the Davidians, Vernon still sought recognition by trying to demonstrate that he could do everything better than anyone else, whether it involved fixing cars, shooting guns, playing music, or understanding the Bible.

"He did go through a lot growing up," remembers one of Vernon's former followers. "He always felt like he was ugly, and skinny, and stupid—always had problems with people. He was always lonely. He was never happy. He didn't know what happiness was. He didn't know what a real family was. He didn't grow up in a close family. He grew up in a very troubled family. He just grew up very unhappy, very lonely. He never felt like he was really loved by anybody. He felt like it was all his fault—that nobody could love him, nobody could like him because he was an unlovable, unlikeable person. He always wanted to have the power to make people like him."

Mt. Carmel or Bust

During his final year with the Adventist church, Vernon resided at the home of Harriet Phelps, a good friend of Bonnie and a member of the Tyler congregation. Around the middle of 1981 Vernon expressed his most pressing concern to her—his search for a living prophet.

"I see from the Bible that we need a current prophet but the Seventh-day Adventist church doesn't have one," he explained to her. "Their prophet died a long time ago, but I believe in current prophets and I'm looking for one."

Not only was Vernon seeking a prophet for religious reasons, but for emotional ones as well. His dismay over Sandy proved too much to bear. He needed a prophet with the latest "light" from God to help him through the pain.

"Oh, I know of this prophet in Waco," Harriet responded. "She's a prophetess." Her name was Lois Roden, the leader of a group called the Branch Davidians living at Mt. Carmel, a small commune located ten miles east of Waco.

Harriet's words were like a dream come true to Vernon. He could hardly believe that an actual prophet, teaching the latest and greatest truths of Scripture, lived just a stone's throw away! The very next weekend, Vernon got directions to the secluded site and drove over for a visit. Harriet had no idea what she had just done.

2

The Seventh Angel

David Koresh didn't get up one day, decide to have a message, and gather a following to himself. He came into an already established organization with a highly developed theology, with an established body of teachings, and a group of people there who had already for years and decades been doing this. But then he came over and successfully took over and molded it into his own vision.

—David Bunds, ex-Branch Davidian

The Branch Davidians were born out of the 1959 fracture of a much larger sect called the Davidian Seventh-day Adventists,* which in turn had broken away from the mainline Seventh-day Adventist denomination thirty years before.

Though differing in many ways, all three groups shared one thing in common: an intense preoccupation with Bible prophecy. The Branch Davidians were especially taken by the prophetic and used it as the basis for almost all their doctrines. When Branch Davidian founder Benjamin Roden died in 1978, his wife Lois

*Although more than one "Branch Davidian" group would emerge from this 1959 splintering, *Prophets of the Apocalypse* only deals with that particular faction that evolved into David Koresh's "Branch Davidians."

assumed leadership and kept the group on an unwavering course to Armageddon. Like Ben, she placed heavy emphasis on "the last days" and prophesied frequently about "the end."

The Davidians claimed that humanity stood on the threshold of the apocalypse and didn't even know it. History was winding to a close and mass destruction lay just around the corner. But Davidians weren't fearful in the least. As God's "remnant," they were scheduled to finish the great task they'd been assigned. And while a heavenly reward awaited them, everyone else had nothing to look forward to but doom.

Unfortunately, "the last days" seemed to be lasting a bit longer than the faithful had anticipated. In fact, 1981 marked nearly twenty-five years of waiting for the eagerly anticipated "end." As one ex-member put it, "These people had lived there year after year with their drudgery, in their boring little pitiful insignificant lives. I mean, ho-hum."

Little did they know that the "the end" was just about to drive around the bend, and history would shortly descend upon them with a fury.

Enter Vernon

As Rachel Jones and Debbie Kendrick talked beneath the blinding Texas sun, a battered old car raced by them and screeched to a halt in front of Rachel's house. Neither of them recognized the driver. They were both perplexed since strangers didn't make a habit of visiting Mt. Carmel unannounced, especially during the high holy days of June. But their curiosity soon faded, and after a few minutes the two twelve-year-olds made their way to Debbie's house.

No sooner had they stepped into the Kendrick home when the phone rang. It was Perry Jones, Rachel's father who served as Lois Roden's right-hand man. "Listen Rachel, I got somebody down here who wants to meet you two girls," he said enthusiastically. "Why don't you come on over?" They obliged his request.

Perry wasted no time introducing Rachel and Debbie to the mysterious guest, who had apparently struck the right chords.

"Rachel and Debbie, this is Vernon. He said he wanted to meet 'those two pretty girls' standing in front of the administration building."

The two girls greeted Vernon politely, but were not at all impressed by his appearance. "He just looked like one of those guys on the street," relates Debbie. "His hair wasn't brushed; it didn't look like he washed it regularly. He was kind of dirty. Everything was old and stained and kind of smelled."

"You girls sure are pretty," chimed the twenty-one-year-old stranger. "What's your names?" Rachel and Debbie knew right away they didn't like Vernon, and after fifteen minutes the two friends were practically "begging to leave."

Later that afternoon, Vernon met Lois Roden and heard her teach for the first time. He finally found what he'd been looking for: a modern-day prophet who claimed to be the successor to William Miller and Ellen G. White. Vernon knew this was the place for him.

A Breed Apart

Vernon relocated to Mt. Carmel a few months after his initial visit. Once there, he actively participated in the group's day-to-day routines. He took out people's garbage, painted fences, repaired cars, and did numerous other chores no one else wanted to do. Vernon actually seemed to enjoy life in the commune, unlike most of the members who were both spiritually and emotionally jaded.

Many Branches (as Davidians refer to themselves) would go for days without uttering a word. The group had been isolated and out of touch with the rest of the world for so long that there was little to discuss. Life just dragged on uneventfully. No one thought they would still be there. "The end" should have happened years ago. All they could do now was to keep on waiting . . . and waiting . . . and waiting.

Even Lois Roden's studies had grown lifeless. She taught the same topic over and over, and every day she would draw the identical "seven-year prophecy chart" on the board. Her followers could see it with their eyes closed.

For Vernon, however, virtually everything was new and exciting. He constantly talked and asked questions during Lois's studies, absorbing every word and voraciously gobbling up every morsel of spiritual insight he could get. Vernon was at last beginning to get his questions answered.

Vernon was quite emotional and would often burst into tears. "Most of the studies for probably the first year he was there were interrupted by him crying," recounts Debbie (the girl Vernon met during his initial visit to Mt. Carmel). These crying episodes, it seems, were not limited to public displays.

Debbie lived next-door to Vernon, and from her bedroom had an unobstructed view of Vernon's curtainless room. She observed that Vernon "would get down and just throw himself across his bed with his arms flailing, and he wouldn't just cry; he would be going into convulsions practically. He did this every single day."

Dietary Hang-ups

"When you got to know Vernon, his faith in God and his eating went together," adds Debbie. "Either he didn't eat or he just totally 'pigged out.' And if he ate, then he thought he was going to hell because of *how much* he ate or *what* he ate or *that* he ate."

In fact, immediately after moving to Mt. Carmel, Vernon stopped eating as a means of purging his sins. For weeks his diet consisted of nothing more than herbal tea. Vernon lost so much weight during that period that his bones became visible.

Vernon believed that food exerted a corrupting influence over people and therefore needed to be monitored carefully. During a taped conversation with fellow Davidians in 1987 (long after he had already assumed leadership), Vernon made the following comments when the discussion turned to noodles:

> Think how much money in the name of God you've been spilling out over these past few years and what food value is in that stuff? I mean, just to get this feeling of these little squishy, little round,

little long, little wormy, little things always through your mouth going slurp! "I love spaghetti, I love spaghetti!" Right? But really, what are you eating? Dead, cooked, starchy, little, funny, little, long pieces of bread is what you're eating, called a noodle. . . .

The *Lord's* counsel is that we don't need that kind of stuff like that. You see? . . . Potato chips are a sin. It's part of the Mark of the Beast. You know, the Mark of the Beast is man's tradition. A Hostess Twinkie is the Mark of the Beast. . . . Yeah, the Mark of the Beast is Snicker's candy bars and soda pop.

Once in control, Vernon imposed rigid and unusual dietary regulations. Ex-member David Bunds, for example, was restricted for an extended period of time to a regimen of a small bowl of corn meal mush for breakfast, an apple and two slices of bread for lunch, and a handful of popcorn and/or a banana for dinner.

It seems, however, that Vernon's rules did not remain fixed. "Once, [Vernon] Howell ordered followers not to eat any fruit except bananas," said one former Davidian. "Then Howell would not let anyone eat oranges and grapes at the same meal. They could, however, eat oranges and raisins."

Vernon habitually violated his own rules. "First, he was the only one allowed to eat meat," relates ex-Davidian Marc Breault. "Then he was the only one allowed to drink Coke.® Then he was the only one allowed to drink beer. The thing I noticed about Vernon is that whatever he was tempted with, eventually God would get around to saying it was all right for him to do." David Bunds explains how Vernon conveniently rationalized his hypocrisy:

> Vernon saw himself as having inspiration. He always felt that he had the right to eat foods forbidden to other people. . . . He would eat meat that other people were forbidden to eat just because he was the prophet. . . . Vernon stood up in front of the congregation while we were fasting and he ate an apple in front of everybody. And he said, "Well, I can eat this apple because I have more knowledge than you, knowledge that you guys don't have. And if you have the knowledge that I have, you learn what I know, then you can eat too."

Strange Appeal

Shortly after moving to Mt. Carmel, Vernon exhibited another one of his peculiar paranoias: personal sin. "He cried for everybody," remembers one former member. "He would cry for his sins. He cried because he thought he was lost. . . . In fact, he was so paranoid that he was afraid that the ground was going to open up and swallow him because he was such a horrible sinner."

Unfortunately, Vernon's fear often turned into condemnatory sermons that were leveled against everyone, especially the children. He also made it his business to delve into everyone else's private affairs. One former follower claimed that Vernon was

> always nosin' into other people's business. He could never keep his mouth shut, ever! I mean, you turned around and he was tellin' you what your sin was, and he would just go into people's private things. He used to go up to Lois Roden's house and go through her cupboards and refrigerator, and throw things away because he didn't think that she should be eating them. And then he'd go down to Perry Jones's house and do the same thing.

Ironically enough, Vernon's peculiarities actually enhanced his mystique among the members of the compound. "It was exciting," says one ex-Davidian. "We had a reason to get up and something to do, something to think about, something to talk about every day. . . . Vernon came along and like, 'Oh, finally something's happening!'"

Vernon also wowed the Davidians with his music. By then, he had become an accomplished rock guitarist and even composed his own songs. Tunes such as "Happy Sabbath Day," "By the Rivers of Babylon," and "Happy New Moon" revitalized the weary and renewed their hopes. As David Bunds put it, "Vernon breathed new life into a dying message and a bored people."

Endorsed by the Prophet

Vernon brought much excitement to the Davidian commune, but it was Lois Roden's "helping hand" that gave him the credibility he would need to eventually assume leadership. Many former members recall how "Sister Roden wanted him to move there" and how "she took him under her wing."

"It was because of Lois Roden that everybody ended up following Vernon Howell," Debbie Bunds [formerly Kendrick] comments. "When he first started out, she was the one that told everyone to listen to him. 'Give him a hearing, listen to him, sit down, don't be judgmental.' And so, basically, people were already starting to go his way because they thought, 'Well, he must have a message if Lois Roden says he does. He must have something to say.'"

Eventually, Lois allowed Vernon to lead a few studies, in some instances going so far as to sit down to listen to his teaching. The impact her actions had upon the other members cannot be over-estimated. After all, she set the standard. Although not impressed by Vernon at first, David Bunds admits he was stopped "dead in his tracks" when he heard that even Lois was heeding his words. "I thought, if Lois Roden was listening, then what right do I have to *not* listen?"

By and large, former Davidians agree that Vernon owed much of his power to Lois. "He could have stood upside down; there's nothing he could have done," claims one former member. "It was Lois Roden who gave him the 'in' that he got. He never could have done it."

It seems that the elderly prophet gave preferential treatment to the strange and unusual young man because she was romantically attracted to him from the moment he first stepped into the compound. Lois even went after Vernon to bring him back to Mt. Carmel when he left the commune a year after joining the group. (Apparently, Vernon felt too confined by the commune's general rules, such as mandatory attendance at all meetings, obtaining clearance for daily routines, etc.).

Throughout the summer of 1983 Lois continually gave Vernon additional opportunities to teach. And the more he was given, the more he took. She may not have realized it, but Lois was gradually building up in the eyes of her followers another prophet—one who would soon replace her.

Early Warning Signs

During that same summer, Vernon began giving guitar lessons to Rachel Jones, one of the two girls he had met two years earlier when he first stepped foot in Mt. Carmel. Although Rachel's good friend, Debbie, tagged along as a chaperone, Vernon still persisted in asking the most intimate and private questions.

"Have you ever thought about what sex would be like?" "Have you ever had sex with a boy?" For nearly a month, the two fourteen-year-olds endured sexually oriented questions on an almost daily basis. But it didn't stop there.

Vernon was also interested in their thoughts about marriage. "Have you ever thought about marrying me? When you get married, would you want to share your husband?" he would inquire of them. At one point, Vernon even asked the two friends point-blank whether it would bother them to "share" *him*.

Nobody knew what went on during Vernon's "guitar lessons" because the girls felt it would do no good to report Vernon's behavior. They believed they had no one they could turn to for help. In fact, mentioning the incident could have actually made the situation worse. Debbie Bunds elaborates:

> I never told anybody because I had a mother who didn't even care if I was raped by my father. I mean, why would she care about this? . . . I didn't trust her to tell her anything. . . . There were no adults there that we kids trusted. They didn't listen to us. We were just—we were non-humans to them. . . . They didn't really look at us as human beings, as people with feelings and rights and minds. They just looked at us as their little clay. Lumps of clay I guess to mold and do with as they wished. . . . Perry Jones [Rachel's father] . . . his own sons used to attack his daughter and he was totally oblivious to it. He knew that my father had raped my older sister and was trying to get at me. And you know what he did? He blamed us! He blamed us girls! It was our fault! . . . He decided that it was our fault. We were whores and we were seducing our father at the age of like eight. At the age of eight we were seducing him. . . . My father's doing this, and my mother knows about it and also doesn't care. I mean, what grown-ups were there to tell?

With the passage of time, the abusive treatment of younger Davidians at Mt. Carmel would only get worse.

Paving the Way for the Seventh Angel

The Davidians believed Victor Houteff's teaching that the seven angels mentioned in Revelation 1–3 symbolized seven modern-day prophets within the Davidian lineage. The angels' messages, in turn, prefigured each prophet's special teaching. William Miller, the father of American millennialism, held the position and preached the message of the "First" and "Second Angel."

Ellen G. White, the galvanizing leader of the Seventh-day Adventist church, fulfilled the role of the "Third Angel."

Victor Houteff, who broke away from the Adventists in 1929 to start his own group (the Shepherd's Rod Seventh-day Adventists, later renamed the Davidian Seventh-day Adventists), was the manifestation of the "Fourth Angel."

Benjamin Roden, the head of the largest faction (the Branch Davidians) originating from the 1959 split of Houteff's group, claimed to be the "Fifth Angel."

Upon his death, Benjamin's wife, Lois, assumed leadership of the Branch Davidians and labeled herself the "Sixth Angel."

One final "Angel" remained: Vernon Howell.

Setting the Stage

In early 1983 Mt. Carmel's administration building, the hub of the commune, burned to the ground. (Some say Howell privately admitted to having started the fire.) The Davidians lost their printing press, their records, and vast amounts of valuable teaching material. Their loss, coupled with the inescapable truth that long-awaited prophecies of "the end" had failed to materialize, dampened morale and generated a degree of apathy so strong that the very survival of the movement seemed threatened.

Vernon came to the rescue by claiming that the fire was God's judgment on the Davidians for failing to adhere to prescribed dietary laws. They had not lived up to God's Word and had been punished for it. Furthermore, Vernon declared that it was their spiritual laziness and disobedience that had prevented those long-awaited prophecies from coming to pass. A quarter of a century had come and gone uneventfully, and 1983 was doomed to a similar fate unless the Davidians quickly got their act together.

Vernon's scathing rebuke hit like a sledgehammer. Someone had finally given a credible explanation for the Davidians' long wait. After so many years of eager anticipation they knew something was wrong. Surely, they couldn't have committed their lives to a lie. That would have been too much to face—over twenty years of suffering and sacrifice for nothing. It was much easier to press on than to start over again.

The Branches should have figured it out long ago: *they* were at fault. Having realized that "truth" the members were now determined to work even harder and tighten discipline further so they could usher in "the end." Vernon's "revelation" drew everyone closer together.

He promised that God would breathe new life into their movement if everyone stood united and participated in reforming the group. Of course, since Vernon had discovered the need for reform, it would naturally fall on him to implement the necessary changes—which he tackled with fervor.

Vernon immediately instituted an entirely new list of dietary rules and regulations. He also strengthened his authority and began issuing direct orders. Lois's grip over the group was starting to loosen and Vernon knew it. He couldn't have picked a more opportune time to make his move.

A Budding Relationship

September of that year witnessed twenty-four-year-old Vernon moving in with Lois, who was sixty-seven at the time. It was then that Vernon pronounced himself, and officially became recognized as, the "Seventh and Final Angel."

The following month, Vernon and Lois went to Israel together. Everyone knew by then that the two were living together, but no one really dared think the obvious. As one ex-member put it, "It was just so weird and uncomfortable."

Theresa Moore, Lois's close friend, however, admits Vernon and Lois were actually married shortly before their trip. She claims the wedding was conducted by Lois in a private, nonlegal ceremony. Though Theresa's account has not been confirmed to date, one former Davidian observed that the couple "appeared to be man and wife" when they returned from their trip.

Ex-members clearly recall that soon after the Israel trip, Lois gave Vernon an even greater measure of control. Looking back, some speculate that Vernon may have led Lois into thinking they were going to rule Mt. Carmel together as joint-prophets. If so, she was in for a big surprise.

Taking a Fourteen-Year-Old Bride

In January 1984 Vernon borrowed Lois's van to run some errands. Later that day, he returned with bad news. The old van had acted up again and broken down on a dirt road near the commune. Vernon was forced to leave it. He felt terrible for causing such an inconvenience. But Lois, as always, was understanding and told Vernon not to worry.

While Lois lay asleep that very night, Vernon quietly got dressed and made his way to Perry Jones' house. "Perry," Vernon muttered, "I've been told by God that Rachel is to be my wife."

After recovering from the initial shock of the revelation, Perry talked the matter over with Vernon. It didn't take long to remove whatever doubts Perry had. After a short discussion, he was convinced God had indeed instructed "the Seventh Angel" to marry fourteen-year-old Rachel. Surely, Vernon wouldn't lie about such a thing? After all, Lois said he was "special" and confirmed he had a message from God.

The two men quickly woke the sleeping teen. "Rachel, you're gonna be my wife, okay?" Vernon gently whispered. "But don't be afraid, we're gonna just be married in name only. We're gonna live together like brother and sister."

"All right, Vernon, if it's okay with my daddy," responded the sleepy-eyed girl. Rachel, according to Debbie, never crossed her father's wishes. As soon as Perry gave his nod of approval, Vernon and his child-bride snuck through Mt. Carmel's gates, across a darkened field, and onto the dirt road where Lois's "broken down" van was parked. The couple then drove off to town.

While Lois was waking up to an empty bed, Vernon and Rachel were busy signing their marriage license. Later that day, the aged prophet found out from Perry what had happened. She "freaked out emotionally and had a breakdown," says one witness. War was about to erupt.

A Woman Scorned

Lois Roden's eldest son, George, was not the kind of man Vernon would want to anger. He was big and reputedly had an extremely bad temper. George also dreamed of one day succeeding his mother as the leader of the Branch Davidians, which may explain why he wasn't particularly thrilled about Vernon's rapid ascent.

When Lois told George about her romantic involvement with Vernon, he exploded. In George's eyes, Vernon raped his mother. Although George restrained himself from physically attacking Vernon, he did not remain silent. No sooner had the newlyweds returned to the compound when George reportedly began harassing and threatening Vernon. The enraged son relentlessly stalked and hounded the couple.

To make matters worse, Lois allegedly gave George license to bully whomever he pleased—which he did. Then Lois herself apparently lost control, displaying fits of anger. "She acted like a jilted teenager," explained one witness. "A spurned woman—she was irrational, she was violent, and she attacked everyone. She decided it was everyone's fault. She got a pregnancy test, and she went around and showed it to all the people at this meeting, and showed them all that she was pregnant."

If Lois had only stayed calm, her seniority would have probably won the members to her side. But she didn't. "Because of the way she acted," relates a former member, "the people just decided that her time had come to step down, and that it was Vernon's time to take over."

A Real Crowd-Pleaser

In the midst of all the chaos and turmoil, Vernon underwent a most amazing transformation. He changed into an incredibly nice and normal person. The more Lois "lost it," the calmer Vernon got. Debbie describes the metamorphosis in the following way:

> He stopped all the weird things he'd been doing. He turned into a very nice, very normal, very clean-cut young man. He started acting very sweet. He started dressing very nice and very clean . . . speaking better, calmed down, stopped the crying fits, and started treating people better, stopped hounding them and attacking them every time he met them. He like totally changed and that is what drew me in. . . . I thought, only God can change somebody this much because he changed from being this wacko to being normal. And Lois Roden changed from being the Lois Roden that we knew into this totally crazy, nasty woman.

Ironically, Lois's "seven-year prophecy," which she had drilled into her followers since 1977, may have contributed to her undoing. Lois predicted something momentous would occur in 1984—which her followers later interpreted as Vernon's succession.

Lois also taught that 1981 would be the start of something big—that was the year Vernon arrived. In the words of someone who lived through those events at Mt. Carmel, "the dates were just totally perfect for him [Vernon]."

The Final Conflict

The conflict between Lois and Vernon finally came to a head during the Davidians' ten-day Passover celebration in April. It started peacefully enough, with Vernon delivering his "Seventh Angel's message" (a generic term given to whatever he taught) at his father-in-law's house. Among those in attendance were Lois Roden, a number of long-standing Branches, and several prospective converts.

Vernon's message dealt with the eighth chapter of Isaiah, concerning a female prophet who had conceived. Everything was proceeding normally enough when, suddenly, the place went wild.

Without warning, Lois stood up and began disclosing the sexual escapades she had had with Vernon. She claimed she was repeatedly propositioned by Vernon to have sexual intercourse, and that after an extended period finally gave in to the pressure. She then went on to describe the sordid details.

"Oh, Sister Roden, Sister Roden, why are you doing this?" Vernon pleaded. "Oh, Sister Roden." That was all he could say.

Lois continued. "Like you said, Vernon, 'The Emmanuels shall know the truth,' so I decided to tell the truth."

Vernon just stammered and stuttered. The woman operating the tape machine was shaken. Eighteen-year-old David Bunds, who was visiting from California, was in shock. The crowd was left speechless.

But Lois's story failed to shake the faith of those who believed in Vernon. Instead, they blamed their one-time prophet-leader. She'd been acting ungodly and strangely, anyway. Obviously, the present fiasco was simply more of the same. And even if her accounts were true, they reasoned, Vernon must have been either tricked or led by God into it.

Rachel was not present at the meeting, but eventually learned about it days later. She was sickened by what she heard. "If I'd have known he did that," Rachel cried, "I never would have married him."

After a week marked by accusations, gossip, and fits of rage, George managed to force Vernon and Rachel off the commune. They retreated to the city of Waco. And after lodging a few months at an apartment rented by Rachel's father, Vernon was able to rent a house of his own.

A King in Palestine

Lois's continued hysteria, coupled with George's violent conduct (like pointing his Uzi at Branches every time they entered the commune), steadily caused the members to leave Mt. Carmel. The old prophet's hold on the flock was quickly deteriorating as the Davidians looked elsewhere for guidance. Vernon, the "Seventh Angel," became their new leader.

Throughout the following year, Vernon continued to solidify his teachings along with his base of power. After returning from his trip to Israel with Rachel, in March 1985, Vernon declared himself to be the antitypical Cyrus. He claimed his appearance was prefigured by the ancient Cyrus spoken of in the Old Testament. Vernon also believed, as did his followers, that the biblical account of Cyrus destroying ancient Babylon was actually a foreshadowing of the Seventh Angel's destruction of modern-day Babylon (or the world).

In May of the same year, Vernon purchased a small tract of land in Palestine, Texas, and set up camp for his loyal band of followers. They lived in tents, buses, and plywood shacks. There was no heat, no running water, and no indoor plumbing. In fact, each make-shift shack's bathroom consisted of nothing more than a plastic bucket.

Vernon's group also began purchasing and stocking arms. It certainly wasn't against the law, and they felt it was the wise thing to do since they had no other means of protecting themselves in the wilderness they called home. They also wanted to be prepared just in case George, who by the close of 1985 had virtually run everyone out of Mt. Carmel at gunpoint, decided to pursue them with violent intentions.

Despite such rugged circumstances, the men, women, and children of the group were all content. And why shouldn't they be? After all, *they* had the truth; *they* had the prophet; and among all the people in the world, *they* were God's special remnant.

3

Prepare
to Meet Thy God

I want to show you about a God that you haven't yet known. You've all been spoon-fed. You've all been diaper-padded. And now it's time for this cloak to be thrown off, and you're going to go through the fires. You're gonna see whether you believe this message. I'm ready to be delivered. I'm ready to go through the portals of darkness and death, and you're not. Let's see if you believe the message after so many years.

—Vernon Howell

GET READY! GET READY! GET READY!" opened Vernon's February 28, 1986 letter sent to all Branches. "If you want to learn how to stand, you had better make definite plans to come for a second Passover, April 24 through 30." The pitch apparently worked.

Within days, Branches from as far away as Hawaii, Australia, and Great Britain began gathering in Palestine to hear the Seventh Angel's message. Even Lois Roden (who would only live for another six months) arrived unexpectedly. Her reasons for attending, however, were more political than spiritual: she wanted to make one last bid for the leadership of the Davidians. She failed miserably.

In terms of controversy, the friction between the two rivals took a back seat to another issue: Vernon's personal act of polygamy (the practice of having more than one wife).

Take Number Two

As the ten-day-long celebration began, everyone couldn't help but notice Karen Doyle. The thirteen-year-old was always sitting next to Vernon, on the side opposite Rachel. To a few "in the know," however, the arrangement didn't seem unusual at all.

Only one month earlier, Vernon had taken Karen as his second wife. It happened shortly after Vernon's return from California, where he had been spreading his message. There was no ceremony or celebration. Vernon simply interpreted his sexual rendezvous with Karen as being equivalent to a marriage.

At first only residents of Palestine were aware of what Vernon had done, and many reacted adversely. One former Davidian recalls, "Everybody was just going through all kinds of emotional ups and downs." Yet Vernon merely ignored the group's sentiments and responded by hammering them with hours of Bible studies.

Branch Davidian Wayne Martin, a Harvard-educated attorney, reportedly considered committing suicide; he feared being charged with accessory to statutory rape. Stan Silvia, one of Vernon's reputed "enforcers," apparently thought Vernon's interests would eventually strike close to home. He reportedly told the prophet, "I knew you always wanted to do this; you want to get my wife!"

Still, Vernon remained unmoved. Rather than repent for his immorality, Vernon simply turned the vocal opposition to his advantage. "I just had this 'new light,'" he related to the California Branches, "and it was so awesome that Stan was saying things like he wanted to kill me, and Wayne was wanting to commit suicide, and Novelette [another member] was thinking that maybe the Bible was deceiving her."

The prophet claimed he was about to unfold a doctrine so profound that only the spiritually minded could understand and accept it. "He was trying to bait us with it," one of the Californians later confirmed. "He would say, 'I can't tell you yet. You have to pray about it and seek God and get ready to hear such a great truth.' When he eventually told us, we had been built up to accept it."

Vernon deliberately chose the Passover celebration to make his announcement. "He wants to have you right there when he tells you something," explains one ex-member. "He doesn't want you to be away . . . where you can be out of his influence. He wants to have you right in front of him so he can pressure you."

Delivering the Pitch

Those who attended that landmark Passover of 1986 recall Vernon beginning his saga about Karen by saying something like, "I remember Karen when she was a little girl. Then, after I came back I noticed that she had filled out, and looked pretty nice." Predictably, his words raised some eyebrows and produced a sense of discomfort. Sighs of relief broke the tension only after Vernon gave assurances that God had helped him restrain his unwanted and sinful feelings. But the young prophet's ordeal wasn't over yet.

Vernon continued the story by describing how, after his lustful desires had abated, he started looking over a prophecy chart created by former Davidian leader Victor Houteff, the "Fourth Angel."

While studying the diagram, Vernon made a most incredible discovery. The drawing of the woman in the chart (an artist's rendition of a figure described in Revelation 12) appeared to be a cross between Karen and Rachel, Vernon's first wife!

Just then, a voice boomed, "Give seed to Karen." Somehow, Vernon knew it was God telling him to impregnate the young girl. Vernon told the audience he was struck with horror and immediately cried out the names of his wife and child: "My Rachel! My Cyrus!"

Suddenly, a vision appeared. In it Vernon saw Rachel being formed in her mother's womb, then Cyrus forming inside Rachel. Once again, the voice interrupted, "No! *My* Rachel! *My* Cyrus!" The congregation was on pins and needles.

The meaning of the vision, Vernon declared, was obvious: Rachel and Cyrus didn't belong to him, but to God. This meant Vernon could no longer point to them as an "excuse" for disobeying the Lord's directive.

Vernon tried to remain outwardly calm, but his mind was reeling and his spirit lay in despair—so he claimed. Vernon spent a sleepless night desperately trying to find a solution to his dilemma. When morning finally rolled around, the weary Seventh Angel concluded he had no alternative but to follow God's command.

But before he was able to carry out his mission, Vernon heard the voice once again. This time it told him the entire episode was nothing more than a test of his obedience and faithfulness. He never really had to "give seed to Karen" after all! At least, not just yet.

A few hours later the voice returned, saying, "Give seed to Karen." Vernon knew this wasn't just another test; this time it was for real. "I had made up my mind," Vernon told the Passover crowd, "to do what God said, even though I could only see destruction and ruin." He captured their sympathy.

Convinced of what he had to do, Vernon immediately looked for Karen and, after locating her, shared the divine command he heard. "Karen, you know we have to do what the Lord says, don't you?" he asked gently. The thirteen-year-old nodded in agreement. She was prepared to do whatever God required. Karen became Vernon's "wife" that very day and had since remained obedient to God's decree. So ended Vernon's account.

Tying Up Loose Ends

Over the course of the Passover celebration, Vernon tried to wipe out any remaining apprehensions about his practice of polygamy. He referred inquirers back to the prophecy chart he brought up previously and pointed to another one, also by Houteff, picturing two women and one man in a small hut. The Seventh Angel vigorously argued that the women represented Rachel and Karen, respectively. Of course, the man in the middle was supposedly Vernon.

Vernon also tried legitimizing his "marriage" to Karen by claiming that God prophesied the two would have a baby girl, named Shoshonna. According to Vernon, God declared that Shoshonna would marry Cyrus (Vernon's son from Rachel), and that the half-siblings would rule the world side by side.

Vernon's revelation was indeed remarkable, for Karen was physically incapable of bearing children. A terrible bicycle accident she had suffered at the age of ten had left her infertile. When Vernon announced that God would miraculously give Karen a child by him, many saw it as sure sign that Vernon acted in a righteous and God-pleasing manner. The prophecy, however, never came to pass.

Still, Vernon's smooth rhetoric and persuasive personality successfully convinced the members to accept their leader's unconventional marital arrangement. Marc Breault, an Australian, was swayed by Vernon's apparent frankness:

> To have the guts to blatantly say something that people might see as weird, knowing how people would react, he had to have some sort of conviction. . . . The way I was looking at it then was that your TV evangelists pretend to be average, normal people. They keep the bad things in the closet. When they come out, they fall. But this guy was saying it straight out.

Others, such as David Bunds from California, bought into Vernon's scheme for entirely different reasons. He approached the situation with the following attitude:

> I don't understand it. I don't see it in the Bible. But it doesn't affect me personally. He's the prophet. God speaks to him. He must know what he's talking about. As long as it doesn't affect me personally, I'm not going to worry about it. In other words, I had my own wife. I wasn't worried about him taking my own wife. She was mine.

What of Rachel?

Vernon's second "marriage" may not have affected most of the Davidians directly. The same cannot be said for Rachel, however.

Shortly before the "divinely inspired marriage," she and little Cyrus were accompanying Vernon on a missionary trip to California. Then Vernon, allegedly on God's orders, drove back to Palestine by himself. On the day he "married" Karen, Vernon placed a long-distance call to Rachel to tell her what had transpired. She was crushed by the news.

Upon her return, Rachel tried to express her grief and anguish on several occasions, but Vernon simply walked away each time. "Vernon claimed that God told him to just leave Rachel alone because she needed to be tough," explains an ex-member who had tried to comfort Rachel. "He would get up to leave and she would cry and say, 'No, don't leave!' And he would just leave anyway. . . . He didn't want to deal with her crying and complaining."

The distraught teen eventually came to accept Vernon's second wife, apparently because of a peculiar detail in one of Houteff's prophecy charts. She noticed that the woman who supposedly looked like her and Karen combined had toes identical to Karen's! It seemed that was all Rachel needed to go along with Vernon's arrangement. A former Davidian who lived through the incident, however, believes Rachel just caved in to Vernon's pressure.

Adding to the Mix

After clearing up the controversy with Karen, Vernon began to change the tenor of his messages. More so than before, his Bible studies took on an increasingly sexual flavor, and the twists he put on certain biblical words reflected it. For example, Vernon explained that the Old Testament word for "horn" referred to the male sex organ and the term "oil" meant vaginal secretions.

Vernon also began to elaborate on his polygamy doctrine, using the Song of Solomon as his basis. According to Vernon, the book's main character foreshadowed the Seventh Angel's life. Thus, whatever the poetic narrative said about its protagonist applied to Vernon as well. And since the story's leading man had "threescore queens and fourscore concubines and virgins without number," Vernon explained he should have likewise—translating to sixty wives, eighty concubines, and a whole lot of other women waiting in the wings.

Vernon's assertions and teachings remained unchallenged, and understandably so. After all, who would dare question the word of the Seventh Angel, the living prophet of God? It seemed Vernon was in full control and could do virtually anything he wanted. He was, and he did.

Near the end of 1986, just months after "marrying" Karen, Vernon secretly took Michelle Jones (Rachel's younger sister) as his third "wife." Only a handful of individuals knew what had taken place until Vernon boastfully made the disclosure a year later during a Bible study.

Late one night, Vernon snuck quietly into Michelle's room and gingerly slid underneath the sheet with the sleeping twelve-year-old. Awakened by the movement, Michelle recognized there was no need for alarm. It was only Vernon. Perhaps he was just cold and simply wanted to get warm, Michelle reasoned. Vernon was amused by her naiveté. He wanted much more.

Vernon was determined to have his way with Michelle. At first, he tried seducing her with sweet talk. It wasn't enough. Vernon realized he had to take another course of action. Gentle persuasion soon gave way to physical force, as the twenty-seven-year-old prophet wrestled with a girl less than half his age. Michelle resisted as the Seventh Angel struggled to pull off her underwear, but her efforts failed. She finally succumbed and became "wife" number three.

Interestingly enough, Vernon actually admitted his passion for Michelle a year *before* their late night encounter in 1985. He said he wanted everyone to know about his struggles. "Vernon confessed that during a drive he and Michelle had taken from Texas to California, he was severely tempted to take her somewhere and just molest her and rape her," recounts an ex-Davidian. "He said he fought his desires during the whole trip and kept praying."

After making his confession, Vernon praised God for rescuing him from his sinful intentions. The prophet claimed that God was testing him. It is highly probable that Vernon was merely testing the water to see how his disciples would react. "We thought," reveals David Bunds, "'Well, you know, he's a man. You know, he's got to go through these experiences. But he got the victory.'"

For Vernon, more "victories" lay ahead.

"Wife" Number Four

Although her parents and brother were staunch followers of the Seventh Angel, Robyn Bunds remained somewhat of a rebel. She simply couldn't stand Vernon. She thought he was an arrogant jerk and had no qualms telling anyone about it. Robyn apparently minced no words when it came to Vernon, referring to the prophet on one occasion as an "a—h——." Her parents strongly disapproved.

Vernon, in turn, considered Robyn to be a brat and rebuked her parents for rearing such a "spoiled" girl. He further disrupted her domestic retreat whenever he stayed at the Bunds' residence (during his missionary trips to California). The tension and strife in the household grew so intense that Robyn finally decided to leave. She moved in with her relatives in Massachusetts.

Robyn quickly discovered that her new home on the east coast was far worse than California. Her New Bedford relatives were huge televangelist fans, particularly of Jim and Tammy Bakker, and incessantly pushed her to "accept Jesus." Though well-intentioned, they drove Robyn crazy with their persistence. Robyn hoped for some peace and quiet away from California; instead she got nagged.

Robyn's relatives interpreted her lack of response as a sign of demon possession. Practically every night they would form a "prayer circle" outside Robyn's bedroom door and loudly command the demons inhabiting Robyn to "Come out, in the name of Jesus!" Robyn was miserable—not because she was demon-possessed, but because she was treated as though she were.

No longer able to endure the situation, Robyn placed a long-distance call to California. "I want to come home," Robyn told her parents over the phone. Their answer, in obedience to Vernon's counsel, was "No." She could not come back home. However, upon the prophet's advice, they gave Robyn a choice: stay in New Bedford or go to Palestine, Texas, to learn how to be a faithful Davidian. Left with nowhere else to go, she chose Palestine.

Isolated in the Texas wilderness, Robyn was at the mercy of the Seventh Angel. Much like the three girls before her, the feisty seventeen-year-old aroused the prophet's interest. Consequently, she became Vernon's fourth "wife" and eventually bore him a son, named Wisdom.

The House of David

After conquering the strong-willed Robyn, Vernon's appetite for women became even more insatiable. Using as a pretext the reference to "threescore queens" in the Song of Solomon, Vernon declared every unmarried woman in the group to be his "wife." He called his harem "The House of David."

Women longed to be part of Vernon's "entourage." They would bear God's children who were destined to rule over a Kingdom of Righteousness. At least, that's what Vernon told them. "It's like he cooks women," said ex-member Lisa Gent in an interview for the *Waco Tribune-Herald.* "He prepares them for the fire by the way he gives his studies. It's mind manipulation."

When Vernon made a missionary journey to their region in Australia, Lisa and her husband Bruce (also an ex-member) experienced firsthand the prophet's power of persuasion. One evening their teenage daughter, Nicole, approached them and said, "Vernon wants me to be his teddy bear for the night. Will you give me your permission?" Who were they to deny the Seventh Angel?

"Nicole had spent four days with him being convinced of the message," recalled Bruce. "It wasn't for me to say yes or no. . . . She was going to have children for the Lord. I shudder when I say that now."

Thirteen-year-old Aisha Gyarfas was another Australian who caught the prophet's eye. (She was reportedly brought over to America for the express purpose of joining Vernon's harem.) In the same crude manner in which he related his initial sexual contact with twelve-year-old Michelle Jones, Vernon bragged about his first sexual encounter with Aisha.

During a Bible study, Vernon told everyone Aisha's heart was beating so hard during sex that he could actually hear it. "You know when an animal's scared, how its heart just pounds? . . . That's how Vernon said her heart sounded," relates Robyn Bunds. "Like when you're hunting something is how he put it. That's how he said the heart of all the girls sounded when he's with them for the first time."

Both Aisha and Robyn had, on separate occasions, been "favorites" of Vernon's. "It's not like he says that you're his favorite. It's just obvious. He isn't with anyone else," Robyn explains. "It's more like a flavor-of-the-month thing. It was like a beauty contest—all of us battling against each other to be this woman that God thinks is the greatest. It was like a fairy tale. . . . Back then, I was still dreamy-eyed. I wasn't into reality."

For those "into reality," Vernon had the words of the "Second Angel," prophetess Ellen G. White: "Let me tell you that the Lord will work in this last work in a manner very much out of the common order of things and in a way that will be contrary to any human planning." It was Vernon's perfect rationale.

According to David Bunds, "Anytime Vernon wanted to do something really weird or strange he would use this [explanation]. He'd say, 'Well see, it's out of the common order of things. I'm having sex with girls. That's weird. That's out of the common order of things.'" Vernon's point proved sufficient.

Showdown at Mt. Carmel

Vernon spent a good portion of 1986 and 1987 consolidating his power and "wives" in Palestine. George Roden, on the other hand, gained nothing but weight and empty houses. The Mt. Carmel he ended up inheriting had become a virtual ghost town. A year after Lois died, the population of the once thriving commune had dwindled down to George, a few elderly Davidians, and some buzzards.

But George was born of a mighty prophet and was not about to fold, especially since discovering in the latter part of 1987 that he was God. However, the self-proclaimed deity faced a most serious dilemma: he had no followers. George saw himself as the rightful heir to the Davidian throne. Vernon merely snatched his subjects.

After contemplating the matter, George thought he had found the perfect solution, one that would forever settle the issue of who should lead the Davidians. A resurrection contest would determine the one true successor! And so, with shovel in hand, George went off to the commune's cemetery to hunt for someone worthy enough to get a second shot at life.

Anna Hughes had been a faithful Davidian, and when George came across her twenty-year-old grave he knew she was the one. He immediately began to dig. After placing the casket inside an old shed, George then issued his challenge to Vernon. Whoever raised Anna from the dead was the legitimate prophet-leader of the Branch Davidians, George declared.

George was confident he would come out on top. But, still, he wasn't about to take any chances. He wanted to make sure he was in peak form when it came time for the contest. And so, to prepare himself for the showdown, the would-be combatant proceeded to place the corpse inside the commune's chapel and began practicing.

Vernon may have been psychologically disturbed and sexually deviant, but he certainly wasn't stupid. Rather than accept the challenge, the reigning prophet decided that getting George arrested was the best course of action. Vernon and his group filed a complaint against the husky challenger, charging him with abuse of a corpse.

Lieutenant Elijah Dickerson of the Waco Police Department stated in an April 1988 interview with the *Waco-Tribune Herald* that one Davidian who claimed to have seen the body described it as having "no skin" and "just bones and hair on the head." The police, however, needed more than a testimony. They refused to go to the property until they had some evidence—such as a photograph—that a body had indeed been illegally exhumed.

On the afternoon of November 3, 1987, Vernon and seven of his followers threw on their camouflaged hunting outfits, loaded up their military assault rifles, and headed for Mt. Carmel. Their mission: to get the snapshot the police said was necessary to press charges.

When George caught Vernon's party in the compound, he fired his trusty Uzi. Rounds were exchanged, and in the wild gunfight that erupted, George barely survived. "They didn't come here to get a picture," he protested. "They came here to kill me."

Waco police arrested the eight Davidians and charged them with attempted murder. "They had more ammunition than a patrol would have in Vietnam in their possession at the time of their arrest," commented Lieutenant Dickerson.

"I figured if he [George] could see . . . that we have as much firepower as he has, he'd back off," Vernon countered. While out on bail, the Seventh Angel and his disciples reburied the corpse that was the center of all the controversy.

George, in the meantime, argued during a local television news interview that he was merely "moving the cemetery from the front of the property to the back of the property." He explained that during the process his equipment broke down, forcing him to temporarily "put the coffin in the church in a respectable place." He was never charged with abuse of a corpse.

After a ten-day hearing, Vernon and his bunch were acquitted. (Some of the guns returned to them were used against federal agents five years later.)

George, on the other hand, was handed a six-month sentence for contempt of court. A few weeks before the actual trial, the fiery gunman filed a legal motion asking God to inflict AIDS and herpes on members of the Texas State Supreme Court. With George out of the way, there was no one to stop Vernon from reclaiming Mt. Carmel. Vernon "proved" he was the Davidians' true leader. (George is currently incarcerated at an Odessa, Texas state mental institution for the criminally insane. He was placed there after being judged incompetent to stand trial for allegedly committing a 1989 unrelated murder.)

Home Sweet Home

By the time Vernon gained control of Mt. Carmel, it had become little more than a collection of garbage-laden, dilapidated houses.

The compound required serious renovation and rebuilding, and Vernon's followers provided the necessary manpower.

Of course, such an ambitious project required money as well. For years (as far back as the reign of the Rodens), the Davidians thrived on the tithes and offerings that poured in from fellow members outside the commune. The same source was used to restore Mt. Carmel to full health. A number of the compound residents also added to the funds by working odd jobs in the local area. Vernon, for one, turned a hefty profit from dealing musical equipment and guns. There was never a shortage of things to be done.

For the residents of Mt. Carmel, the day always began at half-past five in the morning. The members were rewarded with a small breakfast after completing a prescribed exercise routine that included a run through the compound's obstacle course (designed by Vernon). The rest of the day was then devoted solely to one thing: work.

Vernon, apart from everyone else, regularly got up as late as two in the afternoon. Nobody seemed to mind, though, because the prophet regularly held all-night teaching sessions. Unfortunately, the individuals forced to get up at the crack of dawn were usually the same ones required to listen to Vernon's all-night sermons.

Vernon's evening Bible studies had no fixed schedule. They started and ended at his whim, sometimes lasting as long as eighteen hours. Marc Breault observed that Vernon usually conducted teaching marathons when everyone else was fatigued.

At times Vernon would keep everyone up until the early morning hours, depriving them of much needed rest, before launching off into one of his long, drawn-out lectures. He was, for example, fond of playing his guitar at full volume until two or three in the morning and then initiating a Bible study. In another instance, Lisa Gent recounts, "We managed to get to bed at 11:00 P.M. At 1:00 A.M. Vernon ran through the camp ringing the food bell, making an awful racket. We had to come and eat, as he himself had not had food that night. We then were compelled to study with him until 5:00 A.M."

The conditions made it very difficult for the Davidians to stay alert, ask questions, and consider the validity of what they were being taught. "You don't have time to think," recalls one former member. "He doesn't give you time to think about what you're doing. It's just bang, bang, bang, bang, bang!"

Beat the Children Well

In 1988 tiny eight-month-old Tarah Tom committed one of the worst of sins: she started to cry after being placed on Vernon's lap. Vernon reportedly exploded in anger, grabbed the child, and brought her to the front of the meeting room. He then exposed the baby's bottom and, using a large wooden spoon, beat her for almost forty minutes until her badly bruised buttocks bled. That evening's Bible study turned into an object lesson on "properly" disciplining a child.

Vernon long held that children eight months and older ought to be disciplined by having their bottoms beaten with some type of paddle. (Vernon eventually replaced his wooden spoon with a paddle of an oar, which he dubbed "the Helper.") Parents were never to use their hands and the beating ought to continue until the child stopped crying. The beatings lasted thirty to forty-five minutes.

When ten-month-old Wisdom (Vernon's son with Robyn Bunds) refused to go to Daddy, he was severely beaten, just like Tarah. "His bottom was hit so much that the skin was raw," Robyn painfully recollects. "It's not like a scrape. It's just where the skin is hit so much that it bruises and can't take anymore and bleeds."

Cyrus, Vernon's son from Rachel Jones, suffered what may have been the worst case of abuse within the group. The details of his ordeal were later revealed in court and subsequently reported in the *Waco Tribune-Herald* as follows:

> Once, Cyrus refused to call Nicole Gent "mommy," [Mark] Breault told the Michigan court. She [Nicole] had been babysitting the boy. [Vernon] Howell ordered his son to sit next to Gent . . . one of his "wives." When Cyrus, then about 3 years old, refused, Howell forced him to sleep on the kitchen floor and go without food.
>
> After a couple days, Howell told Nicole Gent to feed Cyrus, who was so weak he could not eat by himself, Breault testified.

That night Howell made Cyrus sleep in the garage of the cult's house in Pomona, Calif. Howell told the boy that large rats prowled the garage, and they ate naughty boys, according to former Branch Davidian James Tom.

Tom said Howell ordered him to take Cyrus to the garage. "I told Vernon that it wasn't a good idea, because there were rats there. . . . Vernon made me take him anyway and told me to make sure I told Cyrus that there were rats. The child was terrified. Cyrus was made to sleep on a hard bench . . . and was beside himself with fear."

During a 1986 Bible study in Palestine, Texas, Cyrus, then about 1 year old, began crying, Bruce Gent said.

The baby had been left alone inside a bus.

Howell, irritated at the disruption, made several trips to the bus to strike his son. . . . "You could hear the spanks from where we were." Neither Cyrus' mother Rachel Howell nor any other member . . . left to comfort the baby. . . . "It's hard to understand if you've never been there," Breault said. "But we're talking about a man who was supposed to be a prophet. He was giving the words of life. You were not supposed to miss out."

Vernon expected, if not downright commanded, every parent to follow his example and discipline their children in the same manner and degree he did.

"Yeah, I spanked him [Wisdom]," Robyn admits. "I'm not proud of it. . . . There's no way to take it back. But I was told to. . . . All I can say is I was in a certain frame of mind. Vernon said that even if a child died from a spanking they would go to heaven."

To the Davidians, Vernon was uniquely qualified to talk about heaven. After all, he was "the Lamb."

"The Lamb"

One of the most important doctrines ever taught by Vernon involves the "the Lamb," mentioned in Revelation 4–5. Christians have traditionally viewed "the Lamb" as a symbolic representation of Jesus Christ. In 1988, however, Vernon began identifying "the Lamb" with someone else. In a formal letter to the Seventh-day Adventist church, he wrote, "All the prophets of the Bible speak of Me. I Am The Branch . . . *The Lamb.*" David Bunds explains how Vernon arrived at his conclusion:

> The way he [Vernon] became the Lamb is a long story. Isaiah 16 [in the Old Testament] talks about a lamb, it's a prophecy. . . . He [Vernon] takes it out of context, twists it around, comes out with the idea that the Lamb is an actual person. . . . So he ended up being "a" lamb with a little "l". He was "a lamb" . . . like a follower, like a lamb of God, like a symbolic lamb. And then from that point he progressed. . . . He came to the point where he was teaching that he was "*the* Lamb" of the Book of Revelation.

Vernon had already claimed he was the antitype of King Cyrus in the Old Testament, hence setting the precedent for his ruling authority. Then Vernon claimed he was prefigured by the Song of Solomon's male protagonist, thereby providing the rationale for his collection of "wives." Now Vernon was claiming to be "the Lamb" of the New Testament, thus establishing the foundation for his declaration to be the ultimate source of truth.

The full significance of this doctrine would not be realized until a year later, when Vernon used it to justify his "new light" revelation of 1989. This revelation caused nothing short of a Davidian civil war. It was a battle of insults, lies, cover-ups, and death-threats spanning at least five countries, including the United States, Canada, Great Britain, New Zealand, and Australia.

Vernon's adversaries were well organized, highly motivated, and intelligent. Previously allied with Vernon, they locked horns with him under the inspiration of Marc Breault, formerly one of Vernon's top lieutenants. Breault realized Vernon was no prophet of God upon hearing the Seventh Angel's "new light." For Breault, it was a wake-up call: the people had to be warned, the children had to be saved, and Vernon had to be stopped.

4

Faithful to the End

Since Vernon teaches that it is wrong to use one's own mind, one's own reasoning power, it is highly unlikely that you Branches will make any attempt to absorb, discuss, study, or analyze any opposing viewpoints. . . . Vernon will not save you in the day of trouble. . . . When you all feel confident that you have the knowledge that will see you through, you WILL BE RUDELY SURPRISED. *Take note, for I have given you fair warning.*

—Marc Breault, Ex-Branch Davidian

August 5, 1989 found Vernon and a handful of followers at the California home of Don and Jeanine Bunds (two of Vernon's many "in-laws"). "It was an ordinary sort of day," commented Marc Breault, "and no one really had any idea that the course of the Branch movement would change." Then Vernon unloaded a doctrinal "bomb" of megaproportions—but not without some warning.

During the previous day's lecture, Vernon explained that all women ought to want his "seed" within them. Allison Manning, who sat through the session, was greatly disturbed by the comment. She asked Vernon if he meant what he said literally. Of course not, the prophet replied in anger. It was all spiritual.

The "seed" represented God's truth; and it only made sense that women desirous of such truth should seek out the only one capable of dispensing it—Vernon. Only he could plant truth or "seed" in their hearts, thus satisfying their deepest needs. Twenty-four hours later, Vernon's explanation no longer applied.

Let There Be Light

Vernon's "new light" of 1989, as the Branches referred to it, made its debut around the fourth hour of a nine-hour-long Bible study. It was, to put it simply, all of Vernon's previous teachings rolled together with a few sinister new twists.

According to the "new light," marriage was nothing more than glorified adultery. Vernon felt that as "the Lamb" he alone had the right to procreate; hence, all marriages within the group were "annulled," and wives were required to separate themselves from their husbands in order to join Vernon's harem, the "House of David."

Vernon built this new doctrine around the number seven which has special significance in the Bible; it almost always represents completeness, fullness, or perfection. In the Book of Revelation, "the Lamb" is depicted as having seven horns that are symbolic of authority. Combined with the number seven they stand for perfect, total, or complete authority, something Vernon claimed for himself as the Lamb.

But the horn to Vernon, in addition to being a sign of authority, also represented the male sexual organ. Consequently, "If the Lamb has seven horns," explains David Bunds, "then the Lamb has complete procreational ability and authority to procreate, and the only one who has authority to do so. That's where he [Vernon] gets the doctrine that he can have all the women."

A House Divided

By the time Vernon finished his message, everyone was reeling. Australian Marc Breault had been harboring doubts about

Vernon's "message" for months. That evening's session confirmed
his worst suspicion: Vernon was a false messiah.

As he prepared to leave the room, Marc felt Vernon's arms
around him. "So Marc, how does it feel now that I'm stuck with
Elizabeth [Marc's wife]?" the prophet asked with a smile and hug.
"Are you ready to do the Lord's will?"

"I don't know," muttered the perplexed disciple.

"Well, at least that's an honest answer."

For the duration of the evening, Marc couldn't help but ago-
nize over what he should do next. His wife had already left for
Australia a few weeks earlier due to immigration problems, and
there was really no one else around he felt he could trust. For
Marc, there was no other choice: he simply had to get in touch
with Elizabeth. Restless and unable to sleep, the dissident Davidian snuck off to a nearby store and placed a long-distance call.

News about the "new light" left Elizabeth stunned. But after
recovering from the initial shock, she agreed that they had to find
out what Vernon's revelation held in store for the group. "I went
back and sat in on most of the studies," recounts Marc. "Vernon
gave studies night after night and he put a great deal of pressure
on me. . . . Everyone knew I was set against this doctrine."

After weeks of Vernon's grueling sermons, Marc had all the
information he needed and headed for Australia to join his wife.
He was only able to do so because the visa he applied for had
finally been granted. Meanwhile, Elizabeth was busy filling the
Australian Branches in on the "new light" and what it meant for
members of the group. According to Marc, by the time he got back
"the place was in an uproar."

As soon as he learned about Marc and Elizabeth's actions, Vernon ordered all Branches to cut off communication with the couple. They were shunned by family and friends. Vernon also told
the Australians that no "new light" had ever been taught. Marc
and Elizabeth looked like complete liars.

Not willing to merely stand by, the husband and wife struck
back with a letter-writing campaign. First, they targeted the Australians who were the closest to them and the farthest from Vernon. If these Branches could be convinced to leave Vernon, others might follow. Then they bombarded Mt. Carmel. But their

letters reached the commune too late. Vernon had already returned and the "House of David" was growing.

The Mating Game

Vernon's first order of business when he got back to Mt. Carmel was to separate the men from the women—for their own good, he claimed. It's impossible for men and women to be friends, Vernon taught. Men are never motivated by "pure" love, just lust. They'll always want to have sex with their female friends. In fact, according to Vernon, not even husbands could love their wives properly.

During one of his studies the prophet decided to prove his point. He ordered one of the women to get up in the middle of the session and physically expose herself. The woman did as she was told, pulling up her skirt and standing in silence as all eyes gazed toward her. Vernon then turned to the men and asked how many were sexually aroused. Almost all the men raised their hands.

Vernon, however, didn't rationalize his "new light" doctrine simply by using bold examples. He also asserted that his divinely revealed doctrine could be seen in the Bible. Alluding to the Book of Genesis, Vernon explained how everyone's perfect spouse would come from their own side in the same manner that Eve, Adam's perfect mate, came from Adam's side.

Vernon taught that everyone has a mirror person of the opposite sex living within. Following the Day of Judgment, this "inner self" will emerge as a perfect mate from the side of every faithful Davidian—an eternal wife for each man and an eternal husband for each woman. "That is what these men in that camp are waiting for," said David Bunds on the willingness of male Davidians to give up their wives. "They have something to look forward to."

According to Vernon, men who refused to surrender their wives would have a male emerge from them instead of a female. Vernon further threatened that God would then force the men to commit homosexual acts in public with their newly birthed male

counterpart. As for the women, they were destined to either submit to Vernon for procreation or suffer the torments of a burning hell.

"Sometimes, to illustrate what hell would be like, how the
people would scream, he'd start screaming," Marc said of Vernon.
"He once said it would be worse than someone flaying off your
skin with nail clippers. It was certainly graphic. It got your attention." It also worked.

Prophet of Persuasion

One of the first "married women" Vernon took was fifty-year-
old Jeanine Bunds (mother of David and Robyn). Vernon had
apparently prophesied to Jeanine that she would bear a child if
she had sex with him. They had sex, but she never conceived.

"I wanted to be in the House of David," remembered Jeanine.
"He made it sound so wonderful. I did, I did believe. I couldn't
tell you why now. The children in the group are so beautiful, they
really are. You think, 'These must be God's children. They're so
beautiful.'"

Despite his elaborate explanations, Vernon failed to convince
all the women and young girls to "marry" him. Nor did every man
see eye to eye with his pronouncement to have their wives turned
over to him. But the prophet persisted, responding with prolonged teaching sessions his loyalists pointed to as a sure sign of
his authority.

Vernon also employed various intimidation tactics to insure
compliance, including verbal abuse, condemnations to hell, and
threats of losing one's salvation. "You're a bitch because you don't
want to make babies for God!" Vernon yelled at fourteen-year-
old Misty for hesitating to have sex with him. She eventually gave
in, as did most of the others.

For stubborn individuals who remained skeptical and eager to
leave, Vernon lined up another means of persuasion: physical
violence. So that everyone got the message, Vernon occasionally
made nightly rounds in the commune, sporadically firing off his
assault rifle into the air or at tin cans lying on the ground.

The prophet made it clear that he was ready and willing to put his weapon to actual use. "I could shoot everybody right now and God wouldn't be mad at me," declared Vernon. One Davidian named Trudy claimed that Vernon waved a gun at her head and said that if she or anyone else said anything he'd send people after her and kill her.

Life at Mt. Carmel had become very different.

Widening the Gap

As tension mounted at Mt. Carmel, Marc Breault continued his campaign against Vernon in Australia. In one instance, he confronted the prophet's right-hand man, Steve Schneider (Marc's replacement), about his conversation with an Australian member.

"Steve, I just want to know something," Marc began. "I understand that Oliver talked to Vernon, you, and Judy [Steve's wife]. He told me that you and Judy denied that the ["new light"] doctrine ever came up. You said it was never taught. . . . Did you and Judy tell him that Vernon never brought up the doctrine nor taught the doctrine of Judy and the other wives going to bed with him?"

"Yes, we did," admitted Steve.

"It was explicitly taught," replied Marc in disbelief. "You know that. Why did you deny it had?"

Steve answered, "We can't just tell them the truth or otherwise they will freak out and leave the message before they've heard the evidence."

Marc finally understood. "So you're trying to calm them down by denying everything until you guys can get here [Australia] yourselves and teach them."

"You know that's true, Marc."

"So the doctrine is still the same as when I was there?" Marc continued.

"You know it is, Marc," replied Steve.

Marc realized Vernon was willfully deceiving his followers. But as the months passed, more and more Australian members began to see the truth and disregarded Vernon's communications ban against Marc and his wife. The prophet was steadily losing followers.

Vernon countered Marc's charges by circulating a taped message titled "The Foundation," which finally introduced the Australians to his "new light" doctrine. In defense of the newest revelation he stated, "Only the Lamb is to be given the job to raise up the seed of the House of David." But Vernon's strategy proved ineffective and he had to respond to his challenger in person.

When Vernon flew to Australia in the early part of 1990 he almost instantly launched into one of his marathon studies at the home of Lisa and Bruce Gent. The prophet failed to impress the crowd, however, and was subsequently asked to leave.

Undaunted, Vernon immediately made his way to the home of Michelle and James Tom, Lisa Gent's daughter from a previous marriage and son-in-law. There Vernon challenged Marc to come over for a face-to-face debate. The outspoken critic arrived sooner than Vernon expected and a war of words quickly ensued.

Break Point

Witnesses to the confrontation saw that Vernon was outgunned. Marc pointed out contradiction after contradiction in Vernon's teachings and demonstrated how Vernon had twisted countless biblical passages. At a loss for a response, Vernon suddenly began to speak as though he were Jesus—the *real* Jesus—bemoaning his betrayal by Judas! By then, Marc had enough. He left with Elizabeth.

Shortly after the couple departed, there was a knock on the door accompanied by a voice warning that the police were on their way. Vernon, still shaken by his encounter with Marc, darted out the back door, hopped onto a bicycle, and pedaled off into the darkness. That was the last the Australians ever saw of Vernon.

Within a year after the introduction of Vernon's "new light," all the Australians had turned away from the "Sinful Messiah." Most joined the effort to convince other Davidians around the world to support their cause. They soon found allies within neighboring New Zealand. Vernon was furious and threatened to retaliate with violence.

Troubled by Vernon's intentions, Marc wrote a letter to Sherri Jewell, a close friend who also happened to be one of Vernon's "wives" at Mt. Carmel. His October 1991 letter claimed that

> Vernon has instructed some of his minions to inflict bodily harm on my person, and such an attempt was even tried. . . . He threatened to send people to New Zealand to kill Leslie. He threatened to kill James, stab Michelle, and smash Tarah to pieces!! He has threatened to kill my wife Elizabeth. . . . He has called me a f———, dead jack-——f, f———g a—h——and d——head. He has called my wife a bitch and a whore. . . . I have received a phone call from one of his minions threatening to come over and "kick my balls in." Ian Manning and all the Australians have been told by Vernon, "If Marc comes over, kick him in the balls and slam the door in his face." Vernon has drafted an actual hit list. . . . He has even bragged that he knows a mercenary friend who will help train the guys to carry out that list.

Despite such threats, Marc and his band forged ahead with their mission. They wrote letters, distributed taped messages, made phone calls, sent telegrams, and did whatever else they could to reach as many of Vernon's disciples as possible.

Since the Davidians believed strongly in the Bible, the army of dissenters decided to use the Scriptures as their primary weapon. Unfortunately, one of the biblical arguments they used to expose Vernon also became a catalyst for the prophet's most grandiose claim: that he was Jesus Christ.

Vernon, the Christ

Since 1988 Vernon had taught he was "the Lamb" in the Book of Revelation. He used the title to justify his supreme rule over the Davidian sect. It meant that only he could open up the "seven seals" spoken of in the Book of Revelation, the only one who could teach the Bible perfectly, and that all the women belonged solely to him.

However, Vernon was apparently unaware that the term he chose for himself, "the Lamb," is actually a reference to Jesus Christ! Revelation 4, 5, 19, and 20 clearly show this to be the case. And in the first chapter of the Gospel of John, Jesus is described as "the Lamb of God who takes away the sins of the world." It couldn't have been more plain to see.

Marc and other dissenters hammered the point home to numerous Davidians, among them Steve Schneider. If the Bible is to be interpreted consistently, Marc argued, then "the Lamb" could only refer to Jesus Christ. Vernon couldn't possibly be saying he's actually Jesus Christ, could he? Steve remained silent.

When the issue was brought up to Vernon, he went into a tailspin. The basis of his authority was summarily refuted in black and white by a single formula: "the Lamb = Jesus Christ." The implications for Vernon were devastating. The cornerstone of his empire was being demolished. He had to move swiftly. David Bunds explains:

> Vernon was pressured, forced to make a decision. He either had to deny he was the Lamb or say he was Jesus. See, he couldn't stay where he was. But what he did was he said he was Jesus. . . . He wasn't gonna deny it. . . that means he wouldn't have been able to have the wives. The entire justification for him taking the women was that he was the Lamb. . . . If he wasn't the Lamb, then that whole thing fell apart.

Those who saw the obvious and had the strength to accept it, packed up and left. As for the rest, time was quickly running out.

Enter David Koresh

For years Vernon had declared himself the antitype of two kings mentioned in the Old Testament: David, the Israelite who killed Goliath and united the tribes of Israel under one kingdom; and Koresh or Cyrus the Great, leader of the Medo-Persian empire who encouraged the Jews to return to Palestine and rebuild their temple after conquering their Babylonian captors. Consequently, Vernon Howell legally changed his name to David Koresh in 1990.

Thinking himself to be the antitype of such powerful and regal figures, Koresh naturally figured he could best anyone at anything. He claimed God even said so. "When he was giving his new light, he said over and over, 'I am the best because God says I am,'" comments Marc Breault. "I believe he fears that married men are more attractive to their wives than he is. Therefore, he is not the best. Hence, this new doctrine. Now he is the ultimate male, along with everything else."

It wasn't unusual for Koresh to make comments during Bible studies such as: "I'm a real professional in bed," "You have only one seed that can deliver you from death," and "There's only one hard-on in this whole universe that really loves you and wants to say good things about you."

In Koresh's eyes, he was the ultimate. "I'm a winner! I'm a winner!" proclaimed the "divine" prophet. "The Psalms do not talk about Marc Breault, except in the negative. . . . Where I'm at, they can never touch me. . . . Do you know who I am? God in the flesh. . . . I will be exalted amongst the heathen. Stand in awe and know that I am God."

"I am the Son of God . . . The Immanuel," he wrote in a letter addressed to Seventh-day Adventists. "My Name is the Word of God . . . I Am all the prophets: all of them. . . . I only can open up the prophecies of David and Solomon. . . . I have come in a way contrary to your preconceived ideas. . . . I Am the Word and you do not know Me."

Such bold assertions weren't always easy to swallow, even for the most loyal of followers. But somehow the faithful invariably found a reason—or felt one.

Experiencing Truth

For many Davidians, personal experience became the measure of truth, and they relied heavily upon it to justify their faith in Koresh. "The older Branches, like Katherine [Schroeder], Clive

[Doyle], and Perry [Jones] always fall back on their past experience," relates one former member. "They've lived under three prophets, Perry under four. . . . They have an experience."

In a letter dated August 29, 1990, Davidian Myrtle Riddle tried explaining the reasons behind her acceptance of the "new light" doctrine. She wrote the following words to Ian and Allison Manning, a couple who had by then left the group:

> We shared our experience as present truth believers. . . . We internalized the message that was 'sweet in the mouth but bitter in the belly.' . . . We expressed our hopes for Lisa and Bruce [Gent]. . . . Now you deny your experiences over the years to cling to your fleshly ignorance of the marriage relationship. You see the messenger of God as just a man. . . . I cannot deny my experience! . . . We are not giving up marriage. We are overcoming our ignorance of it. It is amazingly clear and simple.

On the contrary, the reality of Koresh's "new light" really wasn't all that "amazingly clear and simple." It transformed Mt. Carmel into a hotbed of anger, bitterness, and sorrow. "When I was there . . . guys were in tears about it—that God wanted them to give up their wives," reveals a former resident. "They were heartbroken."

Even Steve Schneider, Koresh's newest right-hand man, was torn by the teaching. "It's really hard," he told Marc over the phone. "I'll tell you the truth—there have been times when I've wanted to kill Vernon, but I hang in there every day." Steve and others like him hung on to the fiery end.

Alerting the Authorities

Many of the married women quickly became pregnant. Babies were being born nonstop. To keep the authorities from getting suspicious, Koresh ordered the women not to fill out the portion of the birth certificate asking for the father's name. Mt. Carmel soon looked like a day-care center.

Meanwhile, the Australians decided to put some legal teeth into their assault. In 1990 they hired private detective Geoffrey

N. Hossack to deliver volatile information to federal, state, and local law-enforcement officials in Waco. However, the September 18 meeting between Hossack and five officials (U.S. Attorney Bill Johnston, then-McLennon County District Attorney Paul Gartner, his top aide Ralph Strother, Sergeant Terry Lee of the Texas Department of Public Safety, and McLennan County Sheriff's Department officer Lieutenant Gene Barber) brought no action. In fact, the complaints were virtually ignored.

But 1992 saw much more success for the Australians. The legal system that had disappointed them two years earlier became the very instrument they used to rescue eleven-year-old Kiri Jewell from becoming a part of Koresh's harem.

Apparently, Robyn Bunds (who at that point had already left the group) alerted Breault that Kiri was dangerously close to joining Koresh's "House of David." Acting on Robyn's information, Breault quickly contacted the girl's father. Kiri's father, in turn, filed a suit against Kiri's mother, Sherri Jewell, for legal custody of their daughter.

A number of Australians flew to the United States to testify at the hearing. Finally, the court resolved that the parents would have joint custody provided that Koresh would be nowhere near the little girl. Sherri, however, decided to return to Mt. Carmel at once and resume her role as one of Koresh's "wives." As a result, Kiri wound up in the sole custody of her father in Niles, Michigan.

One of the littlest Branches had been saved. But not many more would follow.

Trapped in Terror

Life in the commune had gone from bad to worse to frightening. There was, as one ex-member put it, "an evil in the Branch." One story in particular involved a young girl from New Zealand (we will call her "Eileen"), whose experiences were related by her ex-Davidian sister Angela (name also changed) and Marc Breault.

It all began when disembodied voices awakened Eileen one early morning. "Go to the prophet's room," they told her, "for you alone are worthy of him and deserving to bear his children." She did as she was told.

Unfortunately, the prophet was in bed with Nicole Gent when Eileen entered the room. Still, she couldn't very well disobey the voices. She disturbed Koresh and related the message.

Koresh called a meeting, pounded Eileen with question after question, and finally pronounced her crazy. She was locked up on June 6, 1991, following the cruel inquisition.

One of Koresh's enforcers (we'll refer to him as Frank) was assigned to guard Eileen. He was to keep a watchful eye on her twenty-four hours a day. At first, Frank treated his young detainee fairly well. But soon he started making advances toward her and even began spying on Eileen whenever she took a shower.

Then came the beatings. With trusty paddle in hand, Frank made sure that Eileen was bruised after each session. Maybe this was God's way of cleansing me and making me pure, Eileen thought to herself. She desperately tried to find a reason for the punishment, but found none.

"I don't deserve this," Eileen would scream out the window. "Let me out of of here!" Her demands were ignored. To make matters worse, even her supervised exercise privileges were taken away. It was the only time she was permitted to go outdoors, the only time she experienced a sense of relief and freedom. And now it was gone.

Eileen went crazy. She threw fits of violent rage and anger. At times several men had to be called in to restrain her. But Eileen didn't care. "F———me!" she would yell at them. The next time she says something like that, Koresh instructed Frank, do it!

Frank followed through on Koresh's orders and repeatedly assaulted Eileen. At times, Eileen even willingly gave in to Frank's sexual demands, just so he'd stop beating her.

The prophet slapped her around as well, never hesitating to mock and ridicule her. "So you want to f———me? Maybe you better f——— me," he would screech. For Eileen, Mt. Carmel became hell itself.

Demon Possession?

Eileen remained in confinement for three months until her visa, which was only good to the third week of September, saved her. She, along with her sister Miriam (name changed), had to leave the cult and return to their South Pacific home of New Zealand.

Almost as soon as the two girls boarded a flight to California, the voices returned and Eileen began talking to herself. Her agitation slowly mounted as the trip continued. Upon landing in San Francisco, Miriam made a huge blunder—she left Eileen unattended. Miriam soon realized her mistake. Her sister was nowhere in sight.

Eileen found herself in the city streets, walking in a daze toward no particular destination, until the police picked her up and took her in for questioning. They got nothing. Eileen was stricken with fear. All they could do was send her to a nearby hospital. It took one week, but she finally revealed her parents' phone number.

Angela, who by then had left Koresh's group, was elected by her family to fly from New Zealand and escort her sister Eileen back home. She was also advised to counsel Eileen from the Bible to show that Koresh wasn't who he claimed to be. That's when the situation took a very strange turn.

Angela quickly made her way to the hospital in San Francisco where Eileen was being detained. As soon as Angela began to reason with Eileen from the Scriptures, the enclosed room suddenly turned icy cold from a gust of frigid air that seemed to come from nowhere. A very deep and guttural voice spoke through Eileen. Angela swears it wasn't Eileen. The voice made prophetic utterances, quoted Bible verses, and cursed Angela. "David Koresh will come to kill you and your husband," the voice threatened.

"Who are you?" Angela asked.

Rather than give an answer, the voice simply laughed. "Who do you think you are?" the voice said as Eileen's head violently cocked back and froze, with eyes bulging from their sockets. Angela had no idea what to do and decided it was time to get her sister home.

Back in New Zealand, whenever Angela and James (name also

changed) tried to show Eileen that Koresh was a deceiver, the voice would manifest itself. Eileen sometimes became so violent that several men were needed to hold her down as she screamed and yelled out profanities.

Such episodes have drastically subsided over time and the voices have ceased completely. But to date, Eileen's trauma has not fully gone away. She continues to struggle with the nightmare of her ordeal.

"The Last Days"

By 1993 Mt. Carmel had degenerated into a madman's carnival. Child abuse had skyrocketed, as did the number of pregnancies due to Koresh's sexual escapades. The men had become little more than eunuch enforcers sworn to protect the prophet and his harem at any and all cost.

The tenor of Koresh's prophecies and apocalyptic visions had also taken a more ominous and violent tone, which had previously called for a complete remodeling of Mt. Carmel almost overnight. Koresh ordered the commune's multiple houses to be converted into one huge L-shaped compound. Features of the newly modified structure included separate dormitories for men and women, a handful of storage barns, numerous underground tunnels, and a four-story lookout tower.

Koresh had also implemented commando-like drills and exercises. They needed to be ready for "the end," so they were told; and according to Koresh the end was very, very near. He was right. Others outside the group also feared the final countdown, but not the way Koresh had envisioned it. On April 30, 1991, Marc Breault wrote a chilling letter to David and Debbie Bunds. In it he said:

> One night I had a dream. In this dream I saw Vernon was heading down the course Jim Jones followed. . . . I saw that if left unchecked, Vernon would eventually hurt and kill his own followers. . . . In Vernon's mind, he is God. At the same time he is constantly confronted with his own fallability and mistakes. . . . The more people who

leave Vernon, the more his mind has to deal with his failure. . . . While he may believe he is supreme, he must battle the
problem that so many are leaving. . . . He was defeated in Australia. . . . He lost Robyn and failed to recapture her. . . . Now he is
apparently penned at Carmel. The more who leave him, the higher
[the] probability that the authorities will have enough to nail him.
If you were Vernon, what would you do? . . . You could, like Hitler,
hope that something will turn out right and remain in your
bunker. . . . But when Hitler realized he was. . . truly defeated. . .
he killed himself, his children, and a few others besides. . . . So
we're dealing with human beings. Vernon is, in effect, in his bunker.
We must stop him before he does a Hitler. Vernon is (I guarantee
this) confronted with his humanness and I do not believe Vernon
is strong enough to resign or bow out in a sportsman's checkmate.
Vernon has always had to be the best, the ultimate. He has grabbed
for the gold and his fall will be much more unbearable for him.

Two years later, these warnings came to pass. The Davidian
messiah "pulled a Hitler."

5

The Final Option

For the great day of his wrath is come; and who shall be able to stand?

—Revelation 6:17

Marc Breault's fears were confirmed on February 28, 1993, when agents from the Bureau of Alcohol, Tobacco, and Firearms (ATF) tried serving Koresh a warrant. The hail of bullets that ignited the ninety-minute war between the government agents and members of the commune marked the beginning of an ordeal lasting nearly two months.

The FBI immediately took over and tried to bring the matter to a peaceful close, but prolonged negotiations with Koresh seemed to go nowhere. Confusion, rather than expertise, dominated as FBI negotiators and their advisors butted heads with FBI tacticians over how to resolve the conflict. The cost of the stand-off soon rose well into the millions as hundreds of law enforcement personnel remained tied up. (One estimate put the siege's cost at $6.6 million.) Finally, acting on orders from Attorney General Janet Reno, the government forces made a decidedly bold and controversial move.

In the early morning light of April 19, M–60 tanks were mobilized
to punch holes into the walls of the Davidian domicile. Tear gas was
then injected through the newly made gaps.

Six hours after the daring maneuver was launched, tiny puffs of
smoke began to seep through one of compound's numerous second-story windows. Within minutes the wisps of white turned into
great billowing clouds of thick, black smoke. Half an hour later the
Davidian structure was reduced to ashes. Only nine members survived.

Conflicting Claims?

The survivors claim that one of the tanks knocked over a kerosene
lamp, igniting bails of hay and transforming the place into an
inferno in mere seconds. Debris from the collapsing building
blocked most of the exits, preventing most from escaping. Only a
handful of members were fortunate enough to find a route to safety.

The Davidians' account of the unfolding of events seems plau-
sible enough. But is that how it really happened? Was the fiery car-
nage the result of an accident? The FBI claims otherwise. The fire,
they maintain, was deliberately set by Koresh and one or more of
his disciples.

FBI officials argue that the facts clearly favor their side of the story.
At least two fires broke out simultaneously at different locations in
the complex. Sharpshooters observing the compound through tele-
scopic lenses noticed at least one person spreading some kind of
liquid throughout the compound. The marksmen also witnessed,
through a second-story window, a man dressed in black igniting
something cupped in his hands.

Based on their information the government ruled the April 19
tragedy a mass suicide. However, Davidians consider suicide to be
a sin. Consequently, it couldn't have been an option for them. Furthermore, suicide did not fit into Koresh's endtime scenario involving a battle or violent confrontation during which he and many of
his followers would die.

There is, however, another explanation that can account for such
discrepancies while at the same time reconciling both the testi-

monies of the survivors and the agents. The keys to the puzzle are notes contained in ex-member Robyn Bunds' Bible, which we obtained approximately three weeks before the siege's end. Her written comments, gleaned from Koresh's lectures, seem to foretell the events of April 19.

The Sixth Seal

The "seven seals" mentioned in the Book of Revelation were a central theme in Koresh's eschatology, or view of the endtimes. The opening of each seal signified periods of time during which the Lamb would unleash specific judgments upon the world. Koresh, it seems, attempted to carry out the judgment contained in the sixth seal.

On April 13 the *Los Angeles Times* reported that "Negotiators were told that the cult leader was awaiting signs 'from God' and 'certain *cataclysmic events* to take place, either *fire, earthquakes* or other events of nature.'" That description closely resembles the events coinciding with the opening of the sixth seal in Revelation 6:12, 17:

> And I beheld when he [the Lamb] had opened the sixth seal, and, lo, there was a *great earthquake*; and the *sun became black as sackcloth of hair*, and the *moon became as blood*; . . . For *the great day of his wrath has come*; and who shall be able to stand? (KJV)

Another description of the same event (commonly known as a "parallel passage") is found in the Old Testament Book of Joel, which states: "The *earth shall quake* before them; the *heavens shall tremble*; the *sun and moon shall be dark*, and *the stars shall withdraw their shining*" (2:10 KJV). Next to that verse in her Bible, Robyn had written, "6TH SEAL."

"If we do not listen we will be *devoured by fire* or destroyed by other means," warned FBI agent Bob Ricks in an April 13 interview with the *Los Angeles Times*. Interestingly enough, Joel 2:1–5 speaks of a similar occurrence:

Blow ye the trumpet in Zion, and sound an alarm in my holy mountain: let all the inhabitants of the land tremble: For *the day of the Lord
cometh*; for it is nigh at hand; A day of *darkness and of gloominess*, a
day of *clouds and of thick darkness*, as the morning spread upon the
mountains: *a great people and a strong*; there hath not been ever the
like. . . . *A fire devoureth before them; and behind them a flame bur-
neth* . . . and nothing at all escapes them. . . . *they leap, like the noise
of a flame of fire that devoureth* the stubble, as *a strong people set in
battle array*. (KJV)

The passage depicts God releasing his people, "great" and
"strong" and "set in battle array," as an instrument of judgment
upon the land. As indicated by the final verses, their actions are
likened to devouring flames of fire. Could it be that Koresh took this
to mean that he would send forth his followers as a flaming judgment of destruction on the "day of his wrath"?

The Cleansing Fire

Quoting Jeremiah 50:22, Koresh wrote in his April 9 letter to the
FBI, "The sound of battle is in the land, and of great destruction."
The significance of that verse to the events of April 19 is once again
brought out by the notes Robyn scribbled in her Bible. Above the
Book of Joel, she had written: "Joel 1 & 2 = Jer[emiah] 50."

Koresh apparently recognized his confrontation with the government agents as part of the events surrounding the sixth seal
judgment, which would ultimately culminate in a battle "of great
destruction." Jeremiah 50:24, 32, from which Koresh drew his quote,
reads as follows:

I have laid a snare for thee, and thou art also taken, O Babylon, and
thou wast not aware: thou art found, and also caught because *thou
hast striven against the Lord. The Lord hath opened his armoury*, and
hath *brought forth the weapons of his indignation.* . . . I will *kindle a
fire* to his cities, and it shall *devour all round about him.* (KJV)

Based on his allusion to this portion of the Bible, Koresh may
have well thought that the government agents (part of the "world

order" the Davidians identified with Babylon) were merely acting out their prophesied roles. They were playing their parts perfectly and didn't even realize it. All that remained was for the Lord (Koresh himself) to "kindle a fire" that would "devour all round about him."

The image of imminent fiery destruction is also present in Isaiah 13:6–9, which Robyn's notes also link to the passage from Jeremiah. These verses in Isaiah indicate that the Lord's purpose was to exterminate the sinners (which Koresh identified with the government "intruders") who inhabited the land:

> Howl ye; for the day of the LORD is at hand; it shall come as destruction from the Almighty. . . . every man's heart shall melt. . . . they shall be amazed one at another; *their faces shall be as flames.* Behold, the day of the LORD cometh, cruel both with wrath and with fierce anger, to *lay the land desolate*: and he shall *destroy the sinners thereof out of it.* (KJV)

Aside from Jeremiah 50, Robyn had referenced Joel 2 with two other prophetic books in the Old Testament that graphically portray the Lord carrying out his fiery judgment—Daniel 7:9–10 and Amos 1:2. The first of these, Daniel 7:9–10, contains the following description: "his throne was like the *fiery flame*, and his wheels as *burning fire. A fiery stream issued and came forth before him*" (KJV).

The second passage mentioned in Robyn's note is Amos 1:2, which says, "The *Lord will roar* from Zion . . . and the *top of Carmel shall wither*" (KJV). In the succeeding verses the phrase, "*I* [the Lord] will send fire," is repeated several times, indicating the form of judgment pronounced upon the wicked. It was indeed to be, as Robyn had written next to verse 7, "The fire that will cleanse"—both sinners and believers alike.

Living Flames of Destruction

Following the "I will send fire" passages of Amos 1, Amos 2:5 explains that God's people, Judah, would also be subject to fiery judgment. In light of the fact that the Davidians identified themselves with "Judah," could it be that Koresh and his followers thought that they, too, would be consumed by the impending inferno? Did Koresh believe that his followers were fated to die?

Once again, Robyn's Bible appears to hold the solution. First, Robyn drew a line connecting Amos 2:5 to Joel 3:14–17, which pertains to the sixth seal judgment. This would seem to indicate that Koresh expected Judah's (i.e., the Davidians') fiery ordeal to take place during the time of the sixth seal. Robyn had further referenced the sections in Joel with the account of the Lord's judgment in Isaiah 4:

> When the Lord shall have *washed away the filth of the daughters of Zion*, and shall have *purged the blood of Jerusalem* from the midst thereof by the *spirit of judgment*, and by the *spirit of burning*. And the LORD will create upon every dwelling place of mount Zion, and upon her assemblies, a *cloud and smoke by day*, and the shining of a *flaming fire by night*: for upon all the glory shall be a defence. (KJV)

Next to the portion that reads, "washed away the filth of the daughters of Zion," Robyn had scrawled, "CHANGE THE DNA." Alongside the part stating "the LORD will create upon every dwelling place," she had written that "dwelling place" simply means "person." Beside the clause, "a cloud and smoke by day, and the shining of a flaming fire by night," she had scribbled, "FACES OF FLAMES."

What did Robyn mean by her cryptic notes? Although somewhat puzzling, these clues provide important insights into Koresh's thinking that led to the fiery tragedy of April 19. They give an answer as to why he wouldn't have considered it an act of suicide to set the compound on fire after ordering his faithful followers to remain inside the building.

To understand the full significance of Robyn's comments, we need to recognize that the figurative expression "the daughters of Zion" refers to the inhabitants of Jerusalem, whom the Davidians identified with themselves. That fact, coupled with Robyn's words, "CHANGE THE DNA," strongly suggest that Koresh expected the Davidians to undergo some sort of genetic mutation during the sixth seal judgment.

What the Davidians were to be transformed into is hinted at by Robyn's equating the phrase "dwelling place" with the word "people" in the passage from Isaiah quoted above. The substitution meant, at least in Koresh's mind, that God was going to create fire on the "people." In other words, Koresh believed that he, as the Lord, would loose fire upon the faithful, killing off their old nature and transforming them into flaming, glorified individuals. This idea is further supported by Robyn's comment, "FACES OF FLAMES," written at the end of the passage.

Finally, Robyn had referenced Revelation 6:17 (part of the key sixth seal passage) to another portion of the Bible (Isa. 34:1–4) that describes the destruction of God's enemies. Verse 2 of this passage is particularly revealing. It reads, "For the indignation of the LORD is upon all the nations, and *his fury upon all their armies*: he hath utterly *destroyed them*, he hath *delivered them to the slaughter.*"

Next to that verse, Robyn had scribbled, "Because we're cloven tongues of fire," indicating that Koresh expected to transform the Davidians into living instruments of fiery judgment whose mission was to slaughter the armies of the world. With the FBI and ATF launching a concerted assault upon the compound, the self-appointed messiah probably figured that the time to let loose the fire was finally at hand!

Judgment Day

If Koresh had indeed kindled a fire to transform his followers into flaming beings of judgment that would consume and cleanse the land of foreign invaders, why did he choose April 19 to do so? The answer is once again hinted at in the notes Robyn had written.

Robyn had marked "6TH SEAL" next to Nahum 1:6, which states: "Who can stand before His indignation? and who can abide in the fierceness of His anger? His *fury is poured out like fire*, and the rocks are thrown down by him" (KJV). Nahum 2:3–4 reads:

> The shield of his mighty men is made red, the valiant men are in scarlet: the *chariots shall be with flaming torches in the day of his preparation*, and the fir trees shall be terribly shaken. The *chariots shall rage in the streets*, they shall justle one against another in the broad

ways: they shall *seem like torches*, they shall *run like the lightnings*. (KJV)

Robyn, in her Bible, had written the word "TANKS" over the reference to "chariots," in Nahum 2. On April 19, when the government's "chariots" crashed through the compound, Koresh must have thought that Nahum's prophecy was right on schedule. If so, the time had finally come to make his move.

Nahum 2:5, in Koresh's mind, came off like clockwork: "He [the Lord] shall recount his worthies: they shall stumble in their walk; they shall *make haste to the wall* thereof, and the *defence shall be prepared*" (KJV). What further indication was necessary? The time for action was now, as verse 13 had predicted: "Behold, I am against thee, saith the LORD of hosts, and I will *burn her chariots in the smoke.*"

Koresh, it seems, did what he thought was the biblically prescribed response to the prophecies coming to pass. He proceeded to "kindle a fire" (as mentioned in Jeremiah 50) to destroy the faithful's mortal nature and transform them into fiery beings of judgment—"cloven tongues of fire"—to cleanse the land by destroying the enemy.

Several weeks into the standoff, Koresh had asked the FBI for some batteries. The FBI complied, unaware that Koresh and his right-hand man, Steve Schneider, were planning to use the batteries to power a cellular phone. Once the batteries were delivered, the two men placed a long-distance call to Sue Johnson, Steve's sister in Wisconsin.

"When are you coming out?" Sue asked them. "Very soon," replied Steve, assuring her numerous times not to worry and that suicide was not part of their plan. "But when is the group going to come out?" she kept pressing her brother. "It's a lot more complicated than you think, Sue," he said. "Read the Book of Nahum."

Steve was right. There was more involved than his sister could have imagined. Without realizing that the chariots mentioned in the Book of Nahum stood for tanks—which Koresh waited for and planned to burn—she couldn't have understood why Steve instructed her to read Nahum. Little did she know, it would be the last time she'd hear her brother's voice.

Koresh mentioned the fiery confrontation scheduled to take place during the sixth seal judgment in a sermon titled, "Study on the Assyrians." In that taped message, recorded on January 10, 1987, he made the following remarks:

> Revelation tells us in the sixth chapter that . . . it's a day of the Lord, a day when the Lord is going to consume all things off the land. . . . That sounds a lot like Joel 2, doesn't it? Exactly like Joel 2. Joel's prophecy tells us about an army, doesn't it? It's going to come into the land of Judah, into the land of Israel in the last days, and totally waste the land. . . . God is going to consume all things off the land, the Bible says. All things—nobody is going to be there. It's going to be hot. . . . Sister [Ellen G.] White, in her writings, keeps telling us that Jerusalem will not be God's holy place until it is cleansed by fire.

Koresh continued, quoting the Book of Zephaniah: "Neither their silver nor their gold shall be able to deliver them in the *day of the* LORD's *wrath*; but the whole land shall be *devoured by the fire of his jealousy*: for he shall make even a *speedy riddance of all them* that dwell in the land." Koresh then proceed to quiz his followers to make sure they understood what he had said.

"So, you see, those who dwell in the land during this time are going to be what?" Koresh started.

"Consumed," responded Marc.

"Burned . . . 'the whole land shall be devoured by the fire of his jealousy: for he shall make even a speedy riddance of all them that dwell in the land'—Zephaniah 1:18," reiterated Koresh. "Going to be devoured by what?"

"The fire of his jealousy," answered the class.

But why didn't the fires ignite as soon as the tanks began rolling onto the Davidian compound at 6:00 A.M.? Again, it appears that Koresh was trying to follow the timing set forth in one of the Bible's prophetic books. Amos 8:9 states, "And it shall come to pass in that day, saith the LORD God, that I will cause the sun to go down *at noon* and I will darken the earth in the clear day."

Next to the words, "the sun to go down at noon," Robyn had written Koresh's final prophecy: "DEATH OF CYRUS." The fires didn't break out until somewhere between seven minutes before, and five minutes past noon. Koresh was apparently waiting for the proper time to fulfill Amos 8:9. He waited until the appointed time to carry out his plan of destruction and transformation.

It's highly probable that only Koresh's inner circle, along with a few others, really understood what was happening. The complexity of Davidian doctrine often confused the group's members—so much so that they often weren't even able to articulate what they believed. Thus, the surviving Davidians' statements about not starting the fire or committing suicide are completely true from their point of view.

Sorting Through the Ashes

In looking back at the closing moments of the tragic drama in Waco, the circumstances strongly indicate that Koresh saw the advancing tanks as the awaited sign marking the opening of the sixth seal. An hour before the fire, Koresh disappeared—survivors of the conflagration have told conflicting stories not only about where he was and what he was doing, but about the entire episode. (Some recall having seen Koresh upstairs shortly before the fire started.) Koresh's disappearance may very well have marked the period when he, and select members of his inner circle, began making preparations to start the fire that the Lord (Koresh himself) would "kindle," as foretold in Jeremiah 50.

Most of the Davidians who died had probably forgotten about the relevant prophecies they once studied. Hence, they didn't even really know about the unfolding prophetic drama in which Koresh had cast them once the tanks moved forward. Even for those aware of the Scriptures burning in their prophet's mind, his order to "kindle" a fire would not have been viewed by them as anything but the biblically prescribed means of transforming the faithful into fiery beings of divine judgment.

In fact, during a June 16, 1993 conversation with one of the authors, long-time Branch Davidian Edna Doyle confirmed that those Davidians who "died" had actually *not* died. They had been "transformed."

The evidence seems to indicate that the Davidians did not "commit suicide." By the time the majority of them realized their fortress was burning, it was simply too late. Only those near open windows or the rear of the building were able to escape. All other exits were blocked by debris that had fallen from the roofs and walls during the preceeding tank assaults. Davidians fleeing toward the front of the building had nowhere to go and were quickly engulfed by the smokey darkness that filled the structure within seconds.

Confused and trapped, most of the terrified Davidians retreated into a cold storage room and covered themselves with wet blankets. As the fire's intense heat closed in, most either shot themselves or were shot by other members of the group. To endure the inferno until fully consumed by the searing flames would have been excruciatingly painful.

In one room, thirty-two bodies were recovered. Most had been melded together by the 2000°–4000° temperatures of the blaze. One woman was pulled from the rubble with a handgun at her side, a rifle on her back, and a baby in her arms. Several individuals may never even be identified because only portions of their torso and limbs remained.

Some reports say the charred bodies of Koresh and his top lieutenant Steve Schneider were found only a few feet from each other in the communications room. Other reports place the bodies in front of the room containing the above mentioned Davidians. Family members of those who perished say they've been told that the two Davidian leaders were upstairs when they died. The truth may never be known. It is certain, however, that both had been shot in the head at close range: Koresh in the forehead, and Schneider, either in the back of the neck, the back of the head, or under his chin. The reign of the Seventh Angel had finally ended.

After making the discoveries in Robyn's Bible, we learned of a letter sent to the FBI on April 8, 1993. The note came from Frank Leahy, the husband of one of the social workers who took part in an investigation involving child abuse charges against the Davidians.

Shortly after the ATF's failed raid on February 28, Leahy spent countless hours listening to Koresh's teaching tapes. He then wrote his thoughts about the situation and sent them to the FBI. According to special agent Jeff Jamar, the FBI received the letter, which read:

> David Koresh is currently on the fifth seal. . . . In order to progress to the Sixth Seal, David and some of his followers must be killed for their beliefs. The end must be a fiery conflagration. Suicide is not an option as, according to David, "it is not written in the book. . . . The standoff, as it now exists, will end after Sunday, April 18. . . . It must be a fiery ending, and David and a number of his followers must die. . . . there will be some aggressive action by the Federal law enforcement officials. . . . even if the final conflagration is caused internally, it must be because of some sort of act of the law enforcement officials.

Leahy watched as the tanks rammed through the compound, wondering how the federal agents could have played so neatly into Koresh's plan. "Why in God's name," he asked, "did they pick that date, the exact date?"

Other notations in Robyn's Bible suggest that a course of action other than the one taken by the FBI may have averted the destructive outcome of the siege. But for those who have lost relatives and friends to the inferno, such a solution means nothing.

In spite of the disastrous aftermath of the seige, a handful of Davidians in Waco still remain faithful to Koresh. These remnant disciples continue to look forward to the day when their messiah and his slain followers will return in glory. Only then, they believe, will justice be finally served to those who opposed them and God's earthly kingdom be established.

How did all this begin? Who initiated this mad race toward Armageddon? For the Branch Davidians, along with a host of other American "endtime" groups, the doomsday clock began ticking with a man named William Miller.

The fountainhead of American millennialism, William Miller.

Ellen G. White, nineteenth-century prophetess of the Seventh-day Adventist church.

Victor T. Houteff, founder of the Shepherd's Rod Seventh-day Adventists (renamed the Davidian Seventh-day Adventists in 1942).

Ben Roden, founder of the "Branch" Davidians.

Big George Roden, arch-rival of Koresh.

Lois Roden when she was still the undisputed leader of the Branch Davidians.

Vernon defending himself and his followers soon after their 1987 shoot-out with George Roden: "I've owned a BB-gun once in my life, maybe twice. You see? None of the guys in this group have ever been busted for anything."

The six Davidians arrested with Vernon in 1987. In the foreground are Peter Hipsman, Floyd Houtman, and Stan Sylvia. In the background and barely visible are David Jones, Greg Summers, and James Riddle (from left to right). Only Sylvia, who was in California at the time of the ATF raid, remains alive. The others died in the blaze that destroyed the Davidian compound on April 19, 1993.

Rachel Jones, Koresh's first (and only legal) wife, perished with her husband.

Eleven-year-old Michelle Jones (Rachel's little sister) just before she turned twelve and became Vernon's third wife. Michelle did not survive the Davidian fire.

Two of Vernon's child brides: sixteen-year-old Karen Doyle (right) and her sister, thirteen-year-old Shari Doyle (left). The ATF raid took place while Karen was in California. Shari was not as fortunate—she perished in the Davidian fire.

Koresh "married" Nicole Gent after the teen's parents gave their permission.

Robyn Bunds (Koresh's fourth wife) and Cliff Sellors at their Las Vegas "wedding." This marriage of convenience was arranged by Koresh so that Sellors, a native Canadian, could stay in America. Sellors and Bunds never lived together as man and wife. When Robyn left the group, Sellors divorced her. He died in the April 19 fire.

A 1986 photo of Steve and Judy Schneider before their involvement with Koresh. Prior to becoming Koresh's second-in-command, Steve often preached at his Adventist home church in Hawaii (note the church's announcement board).

A postraid photo taken by the ATF. The two cattle trucks used by ATF agents to approach the site can be seen still sitting in front of the compound.

This seven-year prophecy chart (drawn by Lois Roden in 1979), which marked 1981 and 1984 as significant years, greatly influenced Davidians to follow Koresh, whose arrival at the commune and grab for control coincided with the prophesied years of importance.

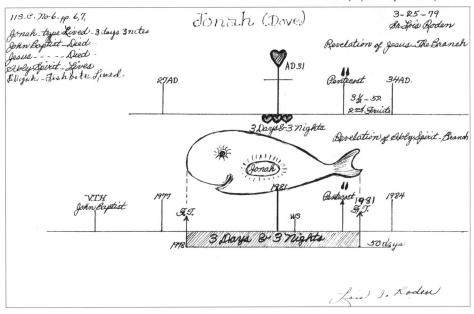

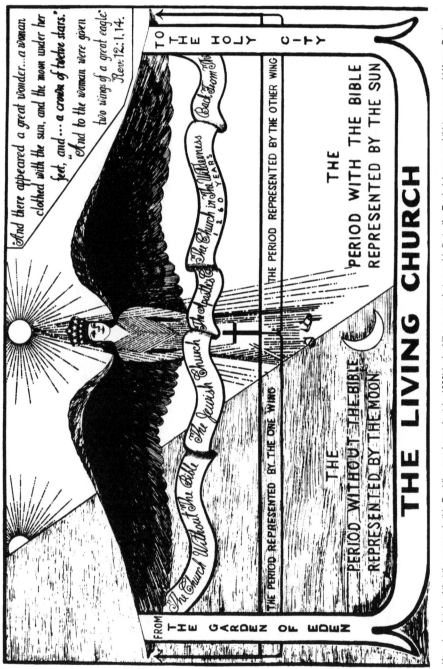

Koresh maintained that the woman in this Davidian prophecy chart (c. 1930) looked like a cross between his first wife, Rachel Jones, and thirteen-year-old Karen Doyle. He used the alleged resemblance to justify taking Doyle for his second wife.

Koresh claimed that his polygamous union with Rachel Jones and Karen Doyle was prophesied by this 1932 Davidian prophecy chart. According to Koresh, he and his two young wives were prophetically represented by the "hut" drawing in the lower left-hand section of the central circular image.

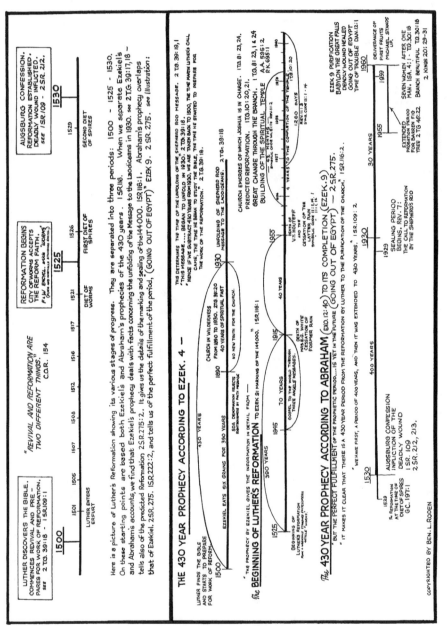

A pre-1960 prophecy chart by Ben Roden in which he predicted that the end of the world would occur in 1960.

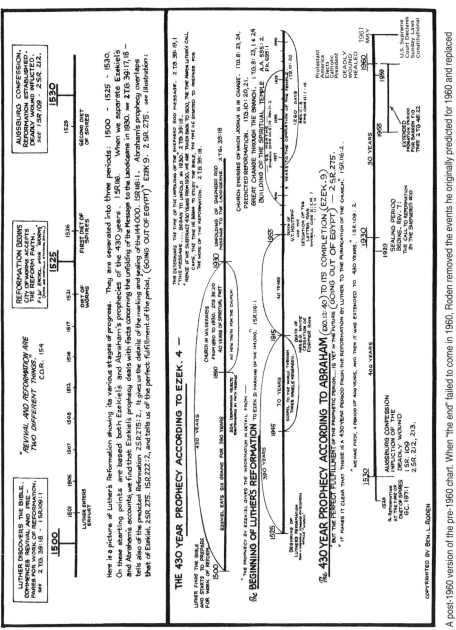

A post-1960 version of the pre-1960 chart. When "the end" failed to come in 1960, Roden removed the events he originally predicted for 1960 and replaced them with the events that had actually taken place.

I personally witnessed sex between Vernon Howell and Nicole Gent who was my roommate at Mt. Carmel, Waco, Texas. I also witnessed the birth of their baby, Dayland Gent on July 22, 1989.

I saw Vernon spank my daughter for forty minutes because she did not sit on his lap. (Another baby was spanked because she wouldn't smile at him.) My baby was eight months old at the time and when he finished, her bottom was badly bruised and bleeding. I tried to keep her away from him as much as I could because nearly every time he saw her, he would spank her.

I was threatened with eviction because I did not spank my daughter enough. On that occasion, my daughter was very ill and I didn't want to spank her for crying in pain. It was generally understood that it didn't matter if a child was ill. He spanked his own son when the child was very ill. Vernon also told another woman and me if he ever saw us giving our children a pacifier, he would kill the children by smashing them against a wall.

Vernon's son, Cyrus, was spanked all the time. Joshua, the young son of another member, was thrashed. Vernon ordered people to go out and do the thrashing.

Signed affidavit of Michelle Tom, whose daughter was beaten by Koresh.

A portion of page 848 in Robyn Bunds' Bible. Next to Isaiah 34:2 (a verse describing how God will destroy wicked armies) Robyn noted Koresh's teaching about the means through which God would bring such destruction: "because we're hot cloven tongues of fire."

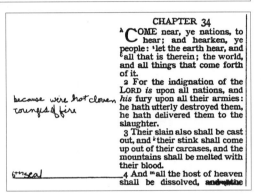

In an August 29, 1990 letter to a dissenter from the cult, Davidian Myrtle Riddle gives a rebuke and defends Koresh's "new light" doctrine: "You deny your experienc[e] over the years to cling to your fleshl[y] ignorance of the marriage relationship. You see the messenger of God as just a man. . . . We are not giving up marriage. We are overcoming our ignorance of it" (pp. 1–2).

6

Prophet of the End

This year, according to our faith, is the last year that Satan will reign in our earth.

—William Miller, 1844

Though they splintered off from Adventism, the Branch Davidians departed radically from the ways of their "spiritual ancestors." The group's most notorious trademarks—including their later view of marriage and sex, the widespread instances of intimidation and abuse, and the military-like conduct and activities governing the rank and file—have never been part of the broader Adventist tradition.

The Davidians' most-publicized doctrines and practices find their origins in David Koresh's bizarre thinking, abusive personality, and deviant behavior. Yet even the prophet's religious ideas did not emerge in a vacuum. Koresh took key Adventist themes and twisted them into his own configurations. The results were deadly.

The responsibility for the tragedy that played itself out in Waco must ultimately rest upon Koresh and his misguided followers. But even so, it should be recognized that the Davidian leader's troubled outlook was greatly influenced by the prophetic and apocalyptic focus of Adventism's rich theology which, in turn, grew out of a nineteenth-century movement spawned by William Miller.

A Genuine Self-Starter

On February 15, 1782, Pittsfield, Massachusetts witnessed the birth of a child who would significantly shape the character of America's religious landscape. The oldest of sixteen children, William Miller grew up in a poverty-stricken household in the frontiers of Low Hampton, New York.

Receiving little more than a rudimentary education, young Miller made up for his lack of formal schooling by devouring books borrowed from nearby neighbors. Few activities were as enjoyable to Miller as reading at night beside a warm, crackling fire. His passion for study steadily built up his storehouse of knowledge, and by the time he reached his teens Miller landed a job as a community scribe.

As much as he loved to read, Miller learned his longest-lasting lessons from his mother, a pious woman whose father and two brothers served as ministers. A devout Baptist, she instructed her son to believe the Scriptures and to love the Christian faith. Together with her husband, who had served as an army captain during the American Revolution, she trained Miller to live an upright and honest life.

Christianity suited Miller just fine until he married Lucy P. Smith and moved to Vermont in 1803. In the town of Poultney, where the young couple settled, Miller's faith was critically damaged. Disillusioned by the hypocrisy he saw among professing Christians, and dissatisfied with the conflicting answers he received from local ministers, Miller became increasingly uncertain about his own beliefs.

Miller's tumble was greatly accelerated by his new circle of friends and acquaintances. They were educated, articulate, and refined. Hume, Voltaire, Payne—all skeptics—served as their role models. Won over by his associates' "rational" approach to religion, Miller abandoned his faith in the Bible and the church. He, like them, turned to Deism, which, during that period, was in vogue.

Deists believed in God but denied that the Almighty continues to involve himself with his creation. God, they claimed, simply wound up the universe, set it on its course, and then waved goodbye—never again to dabble in its affairs. The world of the Deists was governed strictly by natural laws, leaving no room for the miraculous or the supernatural. Hence, they rejected the Bible as divine revelation.

Though Miller experienced a change of faith, his moral outlook remained very much the same. A respected figure and recognized leader, Miller at various times served as the community's constable, justice of the peace, and deputy sheriff. When America found itself engaged in war in 1812, Miller joined the militia and became a captain in the infantry.

By then, Miller had already been struggling with his Deistic outlook. Morality and reason, the cornerstone of Deism, couldn't seem to fill the spiritual void left by his abandonment of the Christian faith. Years of religious upbringing had left its indelible mark. Something had to give.

The Turning Point

The fatal blow to Miller's Deism was delivered at the battle of Plattsburg, where he and about 5,000 other Americans squared off against a reported 15,000 British troops. Miller believed that unless God lent a helping hand they were doomed for a devastating defeat. Nothing short of a miracle would do.

After rounds of grueling skirmishes at both land and sea, the American forces scored a decisive victory over the British fleet on September 11, 1814. Without the support of their navy, the British army had little choice but to retreat. Plattsburg ultimately spelled disaster not only for the king's invading units, but for Miller's flagging Deism as well: Did God actually step in and perform a miracle?

After the war had ended, Miller went back to Low Hampton with his family and took up farming. However, he couldn't forget the events at Plattsburg, and he was deeply troubled by what the future held in store:

> The more I thought, the more scattered were my conclusions. I tried to stop thinking, but my thoughts would not be controlled. I was truly wretched, but did not understand the cause. I murmured and complained, but knew not of whom. I knew that there was a wrong, but knew not how or where to find the right. I mourned, but without hope.

Miller regularly attended the local Baptist church pastored by his uncle. Though not an official member of the congregation, Miller was asked on several occasions to perform sermon readings. The reading on one occasion focused on Isaiah 53, describing Jesus' suffering and dying for the sins of the world. Miller was so moved by the words he recited that he simply had to sit down:

> I saw that the Bible did bring to view just such a Saviour as I needed. . . . I was constrained to admit that the Scriptures must be a revelation from God. They became my delight; and in Jesus I found a friend. . . . [T]he Scriptures, which before were dark and contradictory, now became the lamp to my feet and light to my path. My mind became settled and satisfied.

Miller's spiritual search culminated in his reverting back to Christianity in 1816. His religious journey had come full circle. But he still had to face his Deist associates. As expected, they didn't hesitate to level the same criticisms Miller had previously foisted among his newly made brethren. He resolved to find answers to their questions.

Beginning with the Book of Genesis, Miller embarked on an intensive two-year study of the Bible. Seeking to avoid what he believed to be preconceived biases, the determined convert sought only the help of a Bible concordance (a book grouping verses by key words) to guide him through his literary trek.

Miller pursued his studies with great diligence and sincerity, taking a keen interest in prophecy like so many of his countrymen. Along the way, however, he encountered many portions of the Bible that were particularly difficult to interpret—especially in light of his neglect of scholarly resources (such as Bible commentaries), his lack of formal training, and his limited linguistic skills.

Unable to fully uncover the historical and grammatical context of various prophetic passages, Miller arrived at a staggering conclusion: "I was thus brought, in 1818, at the close of my two year study of the Scriptures, to the solemn conclusion, that in about twenty-five years from that time [1818] all the affairs of our present state would be wound up."

The world, Miller claimed, would end around 1843 with the return of Jesus Christ to earth.

The Time Is at Hand

Anyone of reasonably normal intelligence can decipher the Bible's prophecies, Miller insisted. There were rules that governed such an undertaking, but they were well within the grasp of the untrained layperson who took the time and care required to achieve success. So confident was Miller in the abilities of other Bible students to unlock prophetic passages that he encouraged them to compare his system with theirs.

Miller challenged the sequence of endtime events held by the majority during his day—namely, that the church would bring about a millennium or thousand-year period of peace and prosperity that would usher Christ's return (postmillennialism). Not so, said Miller and the small band of others like him who believed that only after Christ's return will peace be established on earth (millennialism or premillennialism).

That awaited time, he proclaimed, would soon be at hand.

Using the past as the key to unraveling the future, Miller explained that he "found that predicted events, which had been fulfilled in the past, often occurred within a given time." If that has indeed been the case with past predictions, Miller reasoned, then the same must be true for predictions yet to occur, including Christ's second coming.

Miller had some fifteen different historical and biblical arguments for arriving at 1843 as the terminal year for human history. However, two key Bible passages provided Miller with the date he was after: "unto 2300 days, then shall the sanctuary be cleansed" (Dan. 8:14) and "Seventy weeks are determined upon thy people . . . to make an end of sins . . . unto Messiah the Prince" (Dan. 9:24–27).

Using the interpretative principle that a prophetic day equals a literal year, Miller claimed that Daniel's 70 weeks (490 days) represented a 490-year period that began in 457 B.C.—with the Persian king Artaxerxes' decree to rebuild Jerusalem (Ezra 7:11–26). Going 490 years forward from 457 B.C. brought Miller to A.D. 33, the year, according to a number of believers, that Jesus was crucified. Christ's first coming, in Miller's eyes, was perfectly fulfilled at the end of Daniel's 70 weeks.

As for the cleansing of the sanctuary mentioned in Daniel 8:14, Miller believed that the passage was a unique reference to Christ's second advent. Applying the same principle as before, Miller computed 2,300 years from the same starting date of 457 B.C. His calculations brought him to the target date A.D. 1843.

Miller anticipated that all sorts of negative criticisms would be hurled against his pronouncements. He knew he had to be ready to refute and answer all such objections head-on. To prepare for the impending confrontations, Miller spent five additional years in personal Bible study to confirm his conclusions.

As many Bible scholars have pointed out, Miller's calculations suffered from serious problems of interpretation and chronological assumptions. Nevertheless, relying upon his understanding of the English King James Bible, Miller sincerely believed that the world would soon come to an end.

Knowing that the apocalyptic day of the Lord was just a few short years away created inner tension for Miller. It brought him both great joy and personal consternation.

On the one hand, Miller was moved by a sense of urgency and great responsibility. Believers and unbelievers alike had to be warned that the end of the world was dangerously near. The people needed to be told that unless they embraced the gospel of Jesus Christ, there would be no forgiveness of sins or eternal life.

But having had no formal public speaking training, Miller felt extremely unqualified to carry out this mission. He tried at first to share his insights privately with those close to him. Yet inside him he knew all too well it wasn't enough:

> When I was about my business, it was continually ringing in my ears, "Go and tell the world of their danger." . . . I felt that if the wicked could be effectually warned, multitudes of them would repent; and that if they were not warned, their blood might be required at my hand.

All the reasons Miller offered himself to not "go tell the world"—too old, not a preacher, no training—ultimately proved unsuccessful in extinguishing the conviction that burned fiercely in his heart. On the morning of Saturday, August 13, 1831, the fifty-year-old farmer promised God that "if I should have an invitation to speak publicly in any place, I will go and tell them what I have found."

Little did Miller know that even as he was making his covenant with God, his nephew was en route to deliver an invitation for him to preach the next day at the Baptist church in neighboring Dresden. The news of the invitation so took Miller by surprise that he felt the need to go to a nearby grove and pray. As has been aptly put, "Into that grove went a farmer; out came a preacher."

Tell It to the World

Miller's preaching engagement turned out to be something bigger than he had envisioned, as he was asked to speak throughout the entire week. His sermons on prophecy were received with great enthusiasm, and he was soon deluged with invitations from churches in New York and throughout the northeastern part of the United States.

Miller started as a simple country preacher sharing his views with those willing to listen but quickly developed into a power-

ful and engaging orator. It wasn't long before he began attracting
large crowds and gaining recognition as an itinerant evangelist.
On numerous occasions spiritual revivals even broke out in the
churches and towns following his dramatic presentation of apocalyptic truth.

Miller became so popular that he was able to respond to only
about half the invitations he received from Baptist, Methodist,
and Congregational churches. After much success, in 1833 Miller
was granted a license to preach by the Baptist Church.

During that same year, Miller put out a sixty-four-page pamphlet titled, *Evidence From Scripture and History of the Second
Coming of Christ About the Year A.D. 1843, and of His Personal
Reign of 1,000 Years.* It consisted of a series of eight articles Miller
had previously written for the *Vermont Telegraph,* a local Baptist
periodical.

Miller was later assisted by others in producing various
prophecy time charts with a bevy of winged-lions and leopards,
bears, and dragons. The pictorial images relating the predictions
set forth in the books of Daniel and Revelation to past, current,
and future events captured the interest of a nation tantalized by
Bible prophecy.

For more than a decade Miller criss-crossed the east coast and
parts of Canada, preaching about "the time of the end" and the
imminent second coming of Jesus Christ. Miller later stated that
he had delivered in excess of 4,500 lectures over a twelve-year
span to more than a half million people.

At first, the clergy viewed Miller with an eye of skepticism. But
gradually a number of leading ministers embraced the evangelist's message. With the help and support of such preachers as
Josiah Litch, Joshua V. Himes, Joseph Bates, and Charles Fitch,
Miller's views became more widespread than ever.

Himes, in particular, was a gifted organizer and promoter. A
convert to Miller's cause in 1839, Himes played a key role in
Miller's move from standing in front of small, rural audiences to
preaching before huge crowds in large cities. He was in large measure also responsible for introducing Miller's concerns via the
front page of several national newspapers.

In addition, Himes also established two significant periodicals to further spread Miller's advent teachings. In March 1840 he started the *Signs of the Times* (which would later be called *The Advent Herald*). Then, in November 1843, he put out the *Midnight Cry*, what Himes dubbed Miller's message.

Millennial madness had swept America under the banner of the Millerite movement.

Millerite Momentum

Millerites—that's what William Miller's followers were called in 1842. To the dismay of several established churches, the movement was by then full-blown. While determining the exact number of Millerites has proved elusive, conservative estimates range from fifty thousand to well over one hundred thousand.

The Millerite movement crossed all denominational boundaries, drawing primarily from the Methodists, but also including among its ranks Baptists, Congregationalists, and Presbyterians. This rare sense of unity and identity amidst diversity fueled the movement even further, and through formal conferences, camp meetings, and various publications, a new sect was born.

Miller never intended to form a new sect. But as the terminal date of history drew inevitably closer, the "adventists" became increasingly intense and divisive, isolating themselves further from others outside their circle. They soon started denouncing churches that rejected their message of the fast-approaching end. The churches, in turn, became even more scornful toward the apocalyptic messengers, expelling and excommunicating scores of ministers and lay members.

During the movement's last days, the Millerites classified all other Christian churches (both Catholic and Protestant) with Babylon (the false religious system Millerites believed would pervade Christendom in the final days before Christ's second coming). In Millerite thinking, the fact that the other churches rejected the imminent advent message was a sure sign of their association with Babylon.

Miller had always been somewhat vague about the exact date of Christ's second advent, simply saying that it would occur around the year 1843. But on January 1, 1843, he stated, "I am convinced that somewhere between March 21st, 1843 and March 21st, 1844, according to the Jewish mode of computation of time, Christ will come."

His message was plain and simple: "The hour of God's judgment is at hand—prepare to meet thy God." The year 1843 brought great excitement and enthusiasm among the Millerites as they awaited the return of Christ. For the faithful, earthly concerns no longer seemed to matter.

The papers pounced on practically any and all acts of fanaticism at Millerite tent meetings: fainting and yelling, throwing away of all possessions, fleeing from cities. A number of these reports were later proved to be highly exaggerated. Nevertheless, the numbers of Millerites continued to swell as the date drew closer, their expectation reaching an almost feverish pitch as March 1843 turned around the corner.

The unexpected appearance of a blazing comet in February seemed a sure sign that the anticipated event was truly at hand. Yet March 21 came and went, and nothing happened. Still, the Millerites had one whole year to wait for the glorious second advent. In the meantime, against Miller's wishes, Charles Fitch began urging adherents to "come out" of their denominational churches and form their own.

The Great Disappointment

The Millerites experienced stark disappointment when their leader's one-year time table passed without seeing the coming of the Lord. "I confess my error, and acknowledge my disappointment," conveyed a dejected Miller in May 1844. "[Y]et I still believe that the day of the Lord is near, even at the door."

Miller later made a public apology at a general conference meeting in Boston. Despondent and disillusioned, some decided to abandon the movement altogether. Opponents expected Miller's following to dissolve completely. Yet in spite of the disappointment and defections, a large number continued on in their anticipation of the Lord's soon coming.

The movement was given a much needed shot in the arm when Samuel S. Snow, a committed Millerite, claimed to have found the explanation for Miller's miscalculation. According to Snow, Jewish chronology indicated that Christ would return in the fall of 1844, rather than in the spring of 1843 as Miller had indicated.

According to the Jewish computation of time, Snow explained, Christ would return on the tenth day of the seventh month, or October 22, 1844. Millerite expectations were raised once again as people prepared for the new date, dubbed the "seven month message" and the "new midnight cry!"

Initially reluctant, Miller finally accepted the date and aligned himself with the renewed movement. Tension continued to mount as the awaited moment drew ever closer. One Adventist historian describes the mood as follows:

> As the 22nd of October approached, people prepared to leave the world bodily, just as someone going on a long trip gets his business affairs in order. Moreover, there was a sense of the utter lack of the value of possessions. Farmers refused to harvest their crops, merchants closed their stores, mechanics abandoned their shops, and laborers deserted their employers. People paid their debts, and those who had money left over freely shared it with fellow believers so that they too might settle up and owe no one anything. Large amounts of money were brought in, received, and disbursed without any accounting.

Tremendous excitement surrounded the arrival of the final day. There was shouting everywhere: "Last hours of time!" "Last moments of time!" "We're living on the brink of eternity!" But joy and enthusiasm soon turned to overwhelming disappointment because, as one person put it, "The day came—but the Lord didn't!"

The Millerite movement suffered a mortal blow, and there was no reviving it. October 22, 1844 went down in history as the day of the "Great Disappointment."

"You can have no idea of the feeling that seized me," wrote Joseph Bates to a friend the following day. "I had been a respected citizen, and had with much confidence exhorted the people to be ready for the expected change. . . . If the earth could have opened and swallowed me up, it would have been sweetness compared to the distress I felt."

"Our fondest hopes and expectations were blasted, and such a spirit of weeping came over us as I never experienced before," reflected Millerite Hiram Edson several years later. "It seemed that the loss of all earthly friends could have been no comparison. We wept till the day dawned."

As for Miller, he eventually removed himself from active ministry and died in 1849—still looking for the apocalyptic appearance of Jesus that he had so longed to see.

Despite its collapse, many Millerite beliefs and methods of Bible interpretation found their way into the modern era—thanks primarily to a young disciple named Ellen Gould Harmon who, after marrying James White, gained recognition as Ellen G. White. Under her leadership arose a group of individuals from whom the Branch Davidians would one day emerge: the Seventh-day Adventists.

7

Torchbearers to Armageddon

The Lord God will do nothing until he reveals his secret unto his servants, the prophets. . . . One thing we're trying to emphasize is that we need a living voice in the church today.

—David Koresh

When the world didn't end on October 22, 1844, the Millerite movement fractured into several groups of Adventists. Three of these groups eventually united under one name: the Seventh-day Adventists (SDA).

SDAs looked to three former Millerites for leadership: Hiram Edson, Joseph Bates, and Ellen G. Harmon (later Mrs. James White). Each of these leaders made their own distinct contributions to what would eventually blossom into a new denomination.

Hiram Edson introduced a doctrine he claimed originated from a vision he had received while walking in a corn field. In a private diary he wrote, "while passing through a large field I was stopped about mid-way of the field. Heaven seemed to open to my view." This heavenly "view" revealed to Edson something that both astonished and comforted those who had lived through "The Great Disappointment." Miller's predicted date had been right all along. However, the event expected by the faithful had been wrong. The "cleansing of the sanctuary" that took place in 1844 was not an earthly occurrence, but a heavenly one.

This new doctrine stated that Christ had changed locations in the heavenly realms in order to actually blot out the sin of those he judged worthy of eternal life—what Adventists presently refer to as the "investigative judgment."

Despite the complete absence of such a doctrine throughout the entire history of Christianity, it was still readily accepted by numerous Adventists as a way of cushioning their despair over the "Great Disappointment."

Joseph Bates, meanwhile, began teaching the need for Christians to observe the seventh-day Sabbath. Citing Revelation 14:12 (where the third angel speaks of "they that keep the commandments of God"), he declared that Saturday, not Sunday, should be the designated day of rest and worship. According to Bates, these commandments included the fourth commandment, which referred to the keeping of the Sabbath.

Ellen White emphasized the "spirit of prophecy," a gift of divine inspiration many believed had been given to White. Adventists based this belief on the numerous visions White claimed to have had after Miller's failed prediction, visions that assured her and others that Adventists would eventually triumph over the "Great Disappointment."

White's message of hope catapulted her to a position of leadership—even among followers of Edson and Bates. Having divine inspiration for the purpose of imparting truths from God placed her in an altogether higher category than the other Adventist leaders. White gained even more prominence than did William Miller.

The Millerites learned all too well that mere humans were fallible. White's claim of inspiration, however, was an ideal motivator and comforter. Having divine "inspiration" meant that God himself was actually doing the leading and guiding. Hence, the possibility of a future prophetic blunder was removed (if not in reality, at least psychologically).

By 1860 some of the Millerites had coalesced into a group that adopted the name Seventh-day Adventists. Eventually, Ellen G. White became this group's central, though unofficial, leader.

The Spirit of Prophecy

Ellen G. Harmon (later White) was born on November 26, 1827, in the tiny village of Gorham, Maine. Reared in an apocalyptic atmosphere, her first exposure to prophecy came from a scrap of endtime literature she found one day while walking to school. Upon reading the slip of paper that predicted "the end," ten-year-old Ellen "was seized with terror," she later wrote.

According to various biographies of White, this episode kept her tossing and turning without sleep for several nights because she was worried that she might be one of those who would not be saved.

The next most significant event in White's life almost killed her. While walking with her twin sister Elizabeth, Ellen was struck in the face with a rock thrown at her by an angry schoolmate. The attack knocked her unconscious and left her in a coma-like state for three weeks. Although she lived, she never fully recovered and experienced lifelong poor health. Many believe this incident, coupled with its subsequent ill effects, contributed greatly to White's keen interest in diet and other health-related issues.

White's preoccupation with health matters helped her blend in quite easily with other religious leaders of that same period. In fact, the prophetess had much in common with such leaders. Like many of them, she grew up in a religious home, had difficulties in school, and rose to prominence through visions.

Similar experiences played a significant role in Koresh's life as well. Also like Koresh, White suffered from horrible guilt over what she considered sins. She would often fear that she was not even saved. In his book, *Prophetess of Health: Ellen G. White*, Ronald Numbers wrote of White:

Even her conversion and baptism failed to bring lasting peace to Ellen's troubled mind. . . . She felt certain no forgiveness could be granted. . . . She began feeling terrible feelings of guilt over her timidity to witness. . . . Her burden of guilt grew to such proportions that even her secret prayers seemed a mockery to God. At night she would . . . crawl out of bed and silently pour out her heart to God. "I frequently remained bowed in prayer nearly all night," she wrote, "groaning and trembling with inexpressible anguish, and a hopelessness that passes all description."

White had some rather peculiar views on sexuality that could hardly be called divinely inspired truths. In her first pamphlet on health, titled *An Appeal to Mothers: The Great Cause of the Physical, Mental, and Moral Ruin of Many of the Children of Our Time* (1864), White tackled the delicate issue of masturbation, or to use her words "solitary vice."

According to White, an angel showed her the results of masturbation in a June 5, 1863 vision: "Everywhere I looked I saw imbecility, dwarfed forms, crippled limbs, misshapen heads, and deformity of every description." Because of "solitary vice," she also maintained that "a large share of the youth now living are worthless."

Sometimes White would blend her strange sexual ideas with her obsessions with food. She taught, for instance, that one of the best ways to control the urge to masturbate was to eat bland foods. White maintained that foods like "Mince pies, cakes, preserves, and highly-seasoned meats, with gravies" created "a feverish condition in the system, and inflame[d] the animal passions."

For more than half a century White led the Adventist denomination and wrote over forty-six books totally more than 25 million words, dealing with virtually every facet of Adventist beliefs and social issues including fashions for women. Her works still serve as standard reading material for modern-day Adventists.

It should be mentioned here that, unlike other religious figureheads of the nineteenth century, Ellen G. White's doctrinal guidance served to bring the Adventist church closer to, rather than farther away, from orthodoxy. For example, White clearly directed Adventism's once unorthodox view of Christ back to a more biblically sound position. The Adventist denomination also accepted the doctrine of the Trinity under White's teachings. Furthermore, if it had not been for White, Seventh-day Adventism may never have embraced the orthodox Christian doctrine of salvation (justification by faith alone through grace alone).

Although White taught several aberrant and rather peculiar doctrines from which evangelicals would distance themselves, the positive contributions she made to her denomination cannot be overlooked. Because of her, Adventism's foundation is now basically orthodox. Consequently, well-informed evangelical scholars have rightly refused to label the denomination a cult. Dr. Walter Martin, Kenneth R. Samples, and other experts on the history and doctrines of Adventists recognize the vast chasm that doctrinally separates Seventh-day Adventism from groups like the Mormons, the Christian Science Church, and the Jehovah's Witnesses. In fact, Seventh-day Adventism is the only nineteenth-century established sect that has actually become more orthodox with the passage of time, rather than more aberrant. For this, it is Ellen G. White who must be commended.

When Ellen G. White died in 1915, Adventists suffered a terrible shock—they were without a prophet. Even after White died, however, she continued to speak to Adventists through one hundred thousand or so hand-written pages that contained her prophetic utterances, Bible interpretations, and words of counsel.

Such writings, for most Adventists, served as more than an adequate continuation of her prophetic voice. But to some Adventists, having White's thoughts and beliefs on paper was not enough. They missed the spiritual high of receiving words of "new light" from a living prophet on a daily basis. This was especially true of those who would one day splinter off from Adventism to become Davidians.

They would be drawn to a young Bulgarian named Victor Tasho Houteff. The course he paved would prove to be far deeper and even more destructive than Miller's early date-setting.

Davidian Beginnings

Victor T. Houteff was born in 1886 in Raikova, Bulgaria, and reared as a member of the Eastern Orthodox Church. According to Baylor University professor Bill Pitts, Houteff's family "engaged in the perfume business." Houteff's natural acumen at selling merchandise apparently enabled him to "undercut his business competitors who, in turn, damaged his shop." Pitts says that when Houteff asked for help from local church authorities, "they were reluctant to intervene." "This episode," adds the Baylor professor, "prompted Houteff's decision to emigrate." His destination would be the land of opportunity—America.

In 1907 Houteff settled in Milwaukee, Wisconsin, but soon made his way to the tiny midwestern town of Rockford, Illinois, where he operated a small hotel. Having disassociated himself from the church of his upbringing, Houteff's search for spiritual truth drew him for the first time toward the Christian denominations of the Western world.

To Houteff, truth had never been presented in a clearer way than during a 1918 tent-meeting sponsored by the Seventh-day Adventist church. He joined the church almost immediately, and was officially baptized into the denomination on May 10, 1919.

Houteff moved to Los Angeles, California, in 1923. Soon after his arrival he contracted an illness that led to a noteworthy experience. Pitts explains:

> The Adventists ran sanitariums in many places in the U.S., including California. As a Seventh-day Adventist, he [Houteff] applied for admission and expected good care. Instead, hospital officials asked for his twenty-five dollar admission fee and waited for the check to clear before they let a doctor see him. This story is told with enough passion to suspect that Houteff harbored resentment over this episode for many years.

After recovering, Houteff rose through the church's ranks to the position of assistant superintendent of the Sabbath School of the Olympic Exposition Park Seventh-day Adventist church, a job that consisted of reviewing weekly lessons. For many years all went well. Members of the Los Angeles church not only liked him personally, but also appreciated his teaching abilities.

But in 1929 Houteff started doing something he was not commissioned to do: he changed the established curriculum for the Sabbath classes he was teaching. More specifically, he began expanding on the officially accepted Adventist interpretations of the books of Isaiah, Ezekiel, and Revelation.

When Adventist leadership learned that Houteff, an unordained lay teacher with no formal education, was not following the standard curriculum, they clamped down hard and fast. Houteff was removed from his teaching position.

Such an action, however, didn't dissuade the Bulgarian from teaching what he thought were inspired truths. Inspired because he believed himself to have the prophetic gift of inspiration. Fortunately for Houteff, a church member who believed in what he was teaching happened to live across the street from the Sabbath school and made her home available for Victor to continue his teachings.

Adventist leadership became furious and tried desperately to stop Houteff, even making an attempt to get him arrested and deported. Church officials went so far as to threaten with excommunication anyone who read Houteff's literature, studied with him, or went to his meetings. The straw that broke the proverbial "camel's back" for Houteff reportedly occurred when "a ruffian posted outside the church knocked him [Houteff] down, and a doctor present in the congregation refused to treat him."

Despite all attempts to silence the Bulgarian teacher, his classes grew exponentially until he had a bonifide following. By 1930, any Adventist wanting a living prophet had one.

The Shepherd's Rod

Eventually, Houteff crystalized his "divergent views" and presented them to the public in *The Shepherds Rod Vol. 1* (1930) and *The Shepherd's Rod Vol. 2* (1932). The purpose of Houteff's first book was "to reveal the truth of the 144,000 mentioned in Revelation 7" and "bring about a reformation among God's people"

(Adventists). Houteff described his second volume as "a complete symbolic revelation of the entire world's history, both civil and religious." These two works served as the basis of his theology.

The Shepherd's Rod also served as the original name for Houteff's new sect. In a 1975 interview, George W. Saether (a longtime follower of Houteff's) recalled that the name Houteff chose for his group was based "on the idea of hearing the 'rod' (Micah 6:9) and on the notion of Moses' rod as the instrument of an emancipation."

In 1935 the Bulgarian prophet led twelve of his followers (comprising seven families) to Mt. Carmel, a 189-acre tract of lakeside land located two and one half miles from Waco, Texas. The state of Texas was chosen because Isaiah 19:24 reads: "In that day shall Israel be in the third with Egypt and Assyria, even a blessing 'in the *midst* of the land.'" To Houteff, who loved finding hidden meanings within Scripture, "in the midst of the land" meant Texas— because Texas is in the "midst" of North and South America.

Houteff tried to maintain some degree of affiliation with Seventh-day Adventism until 1942, when he decided to make a clean break from the mainline denomination by officially calling his group the Davidian Seventh-day Adventists. The name "Davidian" came from Houteff's belief in the imminent restoration of David's kingdom in Palestine, a belief that found its way all the way to Koresh.

Several other similarities exist between Houteff's communal sect and Koresh's group. For instance, Houteff was a rather harsh disciplinarian who enforced strict rules of conduct and dress. He didn't even allow little girls at the commune to have dolls. No ball games or other games of competition were allowed either—Ellen White had condemned such activities. "On one celebrated occasion," relates Pitts, "Davidian teenagers asked for a roller rink. Houteff dismissed them and their parents from the group."

Houteff, again like Koresh, was obsessed with keeping himself and his followers totally separate from the world. Association with "unbelievers" was permitted only for business purposes and other unavoidable contacts that occurred on the "outside." He even controlled the amount of worldly information that touched Davidian ears. One of the teachers at the commune's school was designated to inform Houteff's followers of important world developments by reading selected newspaper reports during the noonday meal.

Several individuals in Houteff's commune had divorced unbelieving spouses. This, too, was done by several in Koresh's group.

The sexual abuse that took place at Mt. Carmel under Koresh was also reminiscent of the sexual molestation that took place at the Mt. Carmel of Houteff's era. In fact, the man Houteff appointed as principal of the commune's school (M. J. Bingham) seduced many of the young girls he presided over. Allegations were so substantive that the classrooms were closed and the children were forced to go to public schools.

Failed Expectations

Houteff and his followers intended to stay at Mt. Carmel for less than a year. Their ultimate destination was Palestine, where they believed they would not only direct the final work of the gospel prior to the second coming of Christ, but also assist in establishing the new kingdom of God, a kingdom "just around the corner." But God's kingdom failed to materialize, and suddenly, for those at Mt. Carmel, there was no "end" in sight.

During the following twenty years under the leadership of Houteff, the sect's membership reportedly reached nearly 10,000 with as many as 125 members living at Mt. Carmel.

In 1955 Houteff died and the mantle of prophetic leadership fell to his wife Florence who, from a prophetic point of view, made a fatal mistake: she set a date for the establishment of God's kingdom on earth. The very year Victor died, Florence issued an official call for the faithful to gather at Mt. Carmel during the week of April 16–22, 1959.

According to Florence, April 22 would mark the end of the 1,260 days mentioned in Revelation 11 as well as the beginning of the judgments in Ezekiel 9. The day was furthermore supposed to witness an outbreak of war in the Middle East, God's clearing out of all Jews and Arabs from Jerusalem, the purification of the Seventh-day Adventist church, the ushering in of the Davidic kingdom, and eventually, the second coming of Christ. Many Davidians hinted that their beloved prophet, Victor T. Houteff, would also be resurrected from the dead as a "sign" that the ushering in of the kingdom of God was near.

In response to Florence's announcement nearly one thousand "true believers" sold all their possessions, gave their money to the church, and gathered at Mt. Carmel. Their only reward was to see April 22 come and go.

The result of Florence Houteff's failed prophecy was the disillusionment of many believers who either left the Davidian movement altogether, or joined one of the several factions that broke off from the main sect. The largest faction resulting from this disintegration of Houteff's group remained near Mt. Carmel and was led by a fifty-seven-year-old Davidian named Benjamin Roden.

Roden, former head elder of an Odessa, Texas Adventist church, became a Davidian in 1946. He claimed that his arrival at Mt. Carmel on April 22 was the "sign" for which Houteff's followers had been waiting. He named his faction the Branch Davidians and declared himself to be the one sent by God to deliver the message of the fifth angel spoken of in the Book of Revelation.

The "Branch" part of the group's name apparently came from a 1955 episode in which Roden allegedly heard God's "audible voice" say "Jesus' new name is Branch." Ben Roden also claimed to be the antitypical David of the Old Testament. Consequently, he kept the name "Davidian."

The Branch

Like Victor and Florence, Ben Roden capitalized on the Adventists' desire for another prophet who would bring forth "new light." But Roden took his followers even further from mainline Adventism. Roden's new doctrines included a mandatory observance of the Old Testament Jewish feast days, and dietary rules beyond the Adventist ones already being observed by the Davidians.

When Ben died in 1978, Branch Davidian leadership was assumed by Ben's wife Lois (the one who would deliver the message of the sixth angel of Revelation).

Lois's most noteworthy addition to Branch doctrine was her

concept that the Holy Spirit was a female personage. She arrived at this novel bit of "new light" through a 1977 vision that happened while she was studying Revelation 18:1 at 2 A.M. one day. In her words, she looked out her bedroom and saw a "vision of a shining, silver angel fly by."

In one newspaper interview, she maintained that she knew that "the angel represented the Holy Spirit Mother." Lois made a great deal of headway spreading this message. She even managed to publish a monthly newsletter entitled *SHEkinah*, after the "SHE" part of God.

Lois's unorthodox views were clearly not in line with those of the Seventh-day Adventist church, from which her group traced its roots. Nor would they have fit in with the theology of William Miller, the founder of the Adventist movement.

Some may speculate that without Miller's intense pre-occupation with date-setting—which gave rise to the Adventist sect and later the Davidians under Houtef and subsequently the Rodens—Koresh wouldn't have gotten to the place he did and, consequently, would not have enacted the horrors at Waco that climaxed in a fiery holocaust. In all fairness, however, we need to understand that Miller was not too different from other Americans of his generation—nor ours.

Since the establishment of the church, biblical prophecy has played an important role in every Christian's life. Down through the ages it has remained an area of keen interest and a topic of serious study by individuals from all walks of life. Yet many today are unaware of the significant role it has played throughout Western history. Popular interest in the endtimes is hardly a modern-day phenomenon. On the contrary, it has and continues to be part of the cultural landscape of Western civilization in general and the United States in particular.

8

The Land to End It All

As we read about the Branch Davidians the obvious questions that come to mind are "How could this happen?" and "Why did this group get so out of control?"

To answer these questions and others like them we need to remember some important facts. Controversial religious groups are not a new phenomenon to the United States. Nor is their confrontation with the general public or their friction with the government. Mormons, Jehovah's Witnesses, Christian Scientists, and others have had confrontations with outsiders.

Historically, America has been known as the land of religious tolerance and experimentation. In order to properly understand the American "cult" phenomenon we need to gain a broader perspective of the American religious experience. This chapter will investigate the religious background that America has inherited from its foundation and show how various American "messiahs" have exploited its ideals.

Religious groups do not develop in a vacuum. For example, Mormonism developed in response to a specific historical setting. It embodies the ideals of the nineteenth century—personal moral reform, perfectionism, communalism, millennialism, and extremism. Many of these ideas, however, did not originate in nineteenth-century America. We must go back even further to the earliest days of the church.

The Prophets of the Early Church

Though the Bible sets no date for the return of Christ (indeed, Jesus himself remarked that no one knows precisely when this event will take place), the history of the church shows that date-setters have been active from the very start. Professing to be a prophet of God as well as the Holy Spirit in the flesh, Montanus, in the late second century, proclaimed that the New Jerusalem mentioned in the Book of Revelation was about to descend on Phrygia along with the impending Day of Judgment.

Others, such as Augustine (354–430), the preeminent Christian thinker from North Africa, attempted to do away with speculations about the date of the coming millennium and the endtimes. He argued that the description given by the apostle John in the final book of the New Testament does not refer to some literal event slated to take place in the future. Rather, Augustine explained, it served as a metaphor of the faithful's ongoing struggle against the unbelievers of the world.

For the most part, Augustine's view—which wielded enormous influence over the Catholic Church—discouraged much of the earlier streams of millennialism. Yet the Middle Ages experienced no shortage of self-styled soothsayers of the second advent who wandered the European countryside spreading their own messages of the end.

Prophecy Meets Politics

Considering the endtime scenario that the old order of things will give way to the new, it's hardly surprising that the rich apocalyptic imagery of biblical prophecy has been liberally used (or misused) to criticize existing establishments and to promote a number of causes. Of course, this doesn't mean that all individuals applying the Bible in such a manner are seeking to further their own personal agendas. It may well be that they are truly convinced that certain prophetic descriptions do, in fact, foretell the situation at hand.

The series of Crusades conducted during the Middle Ages (1097–1270) were sparked and kept aflame by the fervor to recapture the Holy Land from Islamic conquerors. European nobility and commoners alike thought that retaking Palestine with Christian forces would bring them one step closer to the New Jerusalem. The belief that both Jews and Muslims were agents of the Antichrist led not only to bloody clashes with the Muslim army but also to the persecution and murder of European Jews.

One of the most celebrated figures of this period was a monk named Joachim of Fiore. Being the foremost prophecy scholar of that time, Joachim was consulted by King Richard the Lionheart before he embarked on the Third Crusade in 1190. Joachim wrongly told Richard that he (Richard) was destined to rout the Muslim leader Saladin—said to have been the Antichrist—from the Holy Land.

Joachim wrote profusely about biblical prophecy. His *Book of Figures* resulted from his followers compiling the vast amount of illustrations he drew encapsulating his view of prophecy. According to Joachim, history is made up of three successive stages, as indicated by the Trinity. First is the Age of Law, associated with the Father. Next came the Age of Grace, marked by the Son's entrance into the world. Yet to come is the Age of the Spirit, linked to a future millennium.

Joachim's understanding ran counter to Augustine's nonfuturistic view of the millennium which, by then, had been adopted as the official position of the church. That, along with his views about the Trinity, ultimately spelled trouble for the monk, who was finally condemned as a heretic in 1215. Though Joachim previously found favor in the eyes of three successive popes, his prophetic teachings later served as a basis for a barrage of criticism leveled at papal worldliness.

The attack on the extravagance of the papacy came from a brotherhood of monks who claimed their order reflected Joachim's Age of the Spirit—which some among their ranks believed would arrive in 1260. These monks produced and circulated a compilation of prophecies falsely attributed to Joachim that, among other things, associated the Antichrist with the Jews. (This later contributed to the anti-Semitic sentiment that arose in Europe during the late Middle Ages.)

A number of groups laid claim to be Joachim's foretold order. One order in Italy, the Apostolic Brethren, gained public attention in the late thirteenth century when it openly challenged the authority of the pope—only to have its leader put to death by 1300, thus putting a swift end to the venture.

During the same period, the German territories were gripped by the belief that Frederic II, who seized control of Jerusalem in 1229, would bring in the millennium. The pseudo-Joachian writings fixing the date of the millennium at 1260 seemed to lend further credence to the heightened expectation. But then, ten years before the anticipated date, Frederic died. His passing, however, only served to inspire a new scenario in which he would return from the dead to establish a new order of righteousness. That hope lasted well beyond the fourteenth century. And even as late as the sixteenth century, the Frederic myth served as a vehicle to criticize the corruption associated with the clergy and the rich.

Rousing Radicals and Rebels

European history is replete with groups and individuals who challenged the existing order, justifying their actions by way of apocalyptic prophecy. The Taborites, for example, rocked Bohemia in the early fifteenth century when they resorted to bloodshed in their urgent bid to usher in the millennium. Believing that Jesus would soon return, many Taborites sold their possessions and moved to special towns they thought would escape divine judgment. After resisting an army of German and Magyar Catholics for a brief period, the Taborites were finally subdued and scattered in 1434.

During the Protestant Reformation of the sixteenth century, theologian and pastor Thomas Müntzer, formerly a member of Martin Luther's movement, became a leading figure of Germany's Peasant War in the 1520s. Müntzer's preaching on the apocalypse fanned the flames of the peasants' economic discontent and mobilized the masses, who eagerly awaited Christ's coming soon to join them in their battle against the German princes. The uprising was eventually squashed in 1526 with about five thousand rebels killed and Müntzer beheaded.

Of all the apocalypse-based movements of the time, few have received as much notoriety as those linked with the Anabaptists who strongly advocated a separation of the church from all worldly governments. The Anabaptists found their greatest measure of success among the poor and downtrodden in Switzerland and the Netherlands, where their emphasis on adult baptism and piety took a firm hold.

The Anabaptists taught the second advent was soon at hand and that even now Christ was engaged in the final battle against Antichrist. Because of their direct efforts to overturn existing establishments—heavily tied to their beliefs about the millennium—the Anabaptists developed a reputation as subversives who posed a serious threat to society.

In early 1534 Dutchman Jan Matthys gained control over the city of Münster in Westphalia and declared it to be the New Jerusalem. Nonconformists were forced out and their belongings taken over as the common property of the community. It wasn't long before Matthys and his followers found themselves locked in combat with the neighboring Catholic forces. Matthys and his band of men were killed in a skirmish on Easter Sunday, the day Matthys predicted the world would end.

A twenty-five-year-old tailor named Jan Brockelson quickly picked up the torch and assumed leadership over the Anabaptists in Münster. Claiming to have received instructions directly from God while in a trance, Brockelson quickly imposed a heavy-handed rule over the population. Claiming that God told him to, Brockelson took a number of teenaged girls to be his wives, along with Matthys's widow. Brockelson's pronouncements were met by vocal opposition. But in the end, the protesters and detractors were swiftly executed.

In the fall of 1534 Brockelson accepted the title of Messiah and began issuing minted coins bearing apocalyptic messages. Jesus Christ, proclaimed Brockelson, would soon return. A blockade was formed in 1535 by the cooperating armies of the local bishop and nearby German states, thus preventing the flow of goods into the city. However, the dwindling quantity of food and supplies didn't stop Brockelson and his close group of associates from their daily indulgence and extravagant lifestyle.

On the other hand, the mass population was nearing starvation. Soon they had to resort to eating grass, then shoes, rats, and dead bodies. Because of such harsh conditions, the invading forces met little resistance when they made their move in June, slaughtering those whom they promised safety. As for Brockelson, after being chained and exhibited around Münster, he and his two closest associates were tortured to death in public and their bodies subsequently displayed in cages hung from the tower of the town's church.

Millennialism on the March

Incidents such as those involving the Münster Anabaptists generated a strong backlash against those calling special attention to the millennium. Along with other radical millennialists, Anabaptists suffered persecution and even death.

Yet the practice of prophetic name calling persisted. A number of leading Protestant reformers invoked the imagery of the apocalypse in their denunciation of the Roman church, going so far as to connect the pope with the Antichrist. The Turks' expanding Ottoman Empire was also seen to have prophetic significance. Luther, for example, associated them with the description of Gog in Ezekiel 38.

The sixteenth and seventeenth centuries witnessed a flurry of calculations and explanations pointing to one figure or another as the Antichrist, the Beast, or the Man of Sin bearing the dreaded mark 666. Millennialism remained very much alive, and its themes commonly found their way into the popular literature and plays of the times.

Labeling someone as Antichrist proved to be a common means to launch an attack against any number of leaders, groups, and institutions. It seemed anyone and everyone qualified as a candidate—from the pope to the Turks to the Muslim prophet Mohammed to Charles I of England to Archbishop of Canterbury William Laud to Oliver Cromwell.

Theologians, activists, and politicians weren't the only ones caught up in the study of biblical prophecy. Some of the leading scientists of the seventeenth and eighteenth centuries, including Sir Isaac Newton, shared their views on prophetic cataclysms—supported with the latest theories and findings in the fields of mathematics and the natural sciences.

The American Mindset

"A City Set on a Hill"

America inherited a religious mandate from the time the Pilgrims landed at Plymouth Rock. The first Christian settlers came to the American continent to escape from the oppression of the religious mainstream in England. The Puritans did not intend to initiate a pluralistic society, but wanted to establish a purely Christian community based on their ideals and interpretation of the Bible. To be part of the Puritan community an individual had to be part of the church. Boston minister Increase Mather (1639–1723) believed that no people had ever so perfectly shaken off their worldly encumbrances as the Puritans. Those who opposed the group's ideas were banished, not just from the church but from the community. Rhode Island became the first haven of religious pluralism and tolerance.

John Winthrop (1588–1649), the first governor of the Massachusetts Bay colony and one of the original Pilgrims, coined a biblical phrase that Americans have since used to illicit religious or political zeal: "for wee must Consider that *wee shall be as a Citty vpon a Hill, the eies of all people are vppon vs.*" These sentiments were echoed by Boston politician Samuel Sewell, who believed America would be at the center of the "Divine Metropolis" during the millennium.

This Puritan ideal of being a city on a hill for all the world to see how genuine Christianity was to be practiced is taken from two sections of the Bible: from Christ's words in Matthew 5:14–16 ("You are the light of the world. A city set on a hill cannot be hidden. Nor do men light a lamp, and put it under the peck-measure, but on the lampstand; and it gives light to all who are in the house. Let your light shine before men in such a way that they may see your good works, and glorify your Father who is in heaven" [NASB]) and also from Deuteronomy 28:37 ("And you shall become a horror, a proverb, and a taunt among all the people where the LORD will drive you"). The second passage is spoken by God through Moses about the consequences of his people not abiding by the commandments Moses was setting forth.

The Puritans used much biblical imagery to portray their holy experiment. The New World was likened to the new Eden, the Promised Land, the New Israel, and the New Jerusalem. Furthermore, the Puritans saw themselves as the New Man who would demonstrate Christ on earth. The remnant idea prominent in many religious groups was evident in Puritanism also.

It was the son of Increase Mather, Cotton Mather (1663–1728), who created such a powerful zeal for the coming millennium that its effect lasted well past the American Revolution. Convinced that every prophecy set to take place before the second advent had been fulfilled, Cotton marked 1697 as the time of the end—only to see it come and go by uneventfully. He then changed his prediction to 1716 and, finally, targeted 1736 as the year that would witness the end. Two years before his death, a disappointed Cotton had all but abandoned his high hopes for New England.

"Manifest Destiny"

A natural outgrowth of the Puritan "city on a hill" metaphor is the idea of America having a special destiny from God. America was seen as the New Israel, as God's chosen people with whom he had covenanted. While America was never to be a theocracy the elected leaders of the nation were considered to be ordained by God to fulfill his purposes. During the nineteenth century this religious idea of a manifest destiny from God was exploited and secularized as the nation expanded westward and sublimated other peoples. It became the unfortunate rationale for many atrocities—from harsh treatment of Native Americans to the annexation of foreign peoples.

This concept of manifest destiny is so instilled in the American psyche that to think anything different seems foreign. The marriage of religious ideology with political ambition has birthed our American civil religion. It also inspired a home-made American religion, Mormonism. Mormonism has, at its core, a further revelation of Jesus Christ as he appeared on the American continent. America is the New Israel.

Millennialism and Revivalism

Pre-Civil War America came to be known as the Benevolent Society. During the years prior to the Civil War Americans were making great strides in the improvement of societal ills. Theologically, the dominant view on eschatology (the second coming of Jesus Christ) was postmillennialism. The church felt as though she would usher in the second coming of Christ. The betterment and redemption of society were sure signs of his coming. Temperance groups arose; the American Sunday School Union, the American Bible Society, and the American Tract Society were founded; the insane were given specialized help at asylums; improvements in medicine and education were on the rise; and the women's suffrage movement began. Of course, the most well known movement was the antislavery movement.

America was introduced to revivalism during the colonial period by such men as George Whitefield, John Wesley, and Jonathan Edwards. Nineteenth-century Americans had memories of the Great Awakening during the colonial period and the more recent Second Great Awakening, as the eighteenth century turned into the nineteenth century.

Charles Grandison Finney, the father of American revivalism, came on the scene during this period. Finney emphasized the importance of the individual's making a moral decision to turn to Christ. Christ was the example God provided to show us how deplorable sin was in his eyes. Finney introduced "new measures" that made many people uncomfortable. These included the practice of praying for people by name, females praying in public meetings, the invasion of towns without an invitation from the local pastor, overfamiliarity with God in public prayer, protracted meetings, inquiry meetings, and the immediate admission of converts into the church. Many of these new measures would be adopted not only by evangelicals, but also by groups that evangelicals would eventually classify as "cults."

Finney was from an area of New York State that was nicknamed "the burned-over district." It had earned this name because the fires of revival had swept the area so often that revival became commonplace. This is especially important to properly understand the beginnings of some of the nineteenth-century cults.

Some of the sects that arose from this area include the Shakers, Spiritualism, and the Oneida community.

Yes, it seemed as though the church would indeed usher in Christ's second coming. Revivals, expectation for Christ's return, social improvements—and then came the Civil War.

The Millerite movement was the first major resurgence of premillennialism in the United States. Until this time in American history, the millennial view was postmillennialism. The Millerites embraced the same ideals that were outlined above. However, William Miller's claim that the return of the Lord would be on October 22, 1844, had brought much ridicule to premillennialism. After the Civil War period premillennialism became the dominant eschatological view. Later, the influence of Charles Darby and the prophecy conferences brought a certain respectability back to charting endtime events.

The millennial aspect of Christ's return was an important thread in American Christianity as well as being influential in the thinking of many modern-day cults.

Perfectionism, Extremism, and Utopian Societies

The desire for perfection in the individual's life was a natural result of American pragmatism and the belief that people could pull themselves up by their own bootstraps. There have always been perfectionist groups in Christian history. Perfectionist doctrine made its way into America through the teachings of John Wesley and the Methodist Church. It was also an important aspect of Charles Finney's teachings. Through the influence of Methodism and its expansion into the prairies, perfectionism became a mainstay of rural America.

A further result of perfectionism was the question, How can I be perfect if I am living with people who do not have the same ambition as I do? This question led to many social experiments, including the formation of many communal societies. The nineteenth century saw the flourishing of many of these new communities. Communal groups separated from society in order to prepare themselves for Christ's return.

There was plenty of land on which people could establish their own religious experiments. Remember that during this time in America's history, the United States' westernmost border extended to the Mississippi River! California became a state in 1850 and at the same time, the territories of Utah and New Mexico were established. There was plenty of land out west where people could set up their own utopian community. There was also plenty of space in the hills in the eastern states. Joseph Smith, Jr., began a trek out west with his followers in order to find a land where they could practice their form of Christianity without interference from communities or governments.

Religious communal groups of the nineteenth century more often than not had some unusual, even extreme doctrines. Joseph Smith, Jr., taught the plurality of gods, the perfection of the individual, and new revelation from God. Ann Lee of the Shaker Community believed she was the reincarnation of Jesus.

There were also excesses in practice. Joseph Smith, Jr., received a revelation that authorized the practice of polygamy, while the Shaker community under the leadership of Sister Ann Lee received a revelation that sex was the original sin and that it should be avoided at all costs! The Oneida community believed in the practice of "complex marriage" or free sex (which was picked up by many 1960s communal groups).

Why the History Lesson?

Why is it important for us to take the time to understand what took place in America's past? Simply stated, the social and religious context of this nation has an important part to play in the makeup of modern-day sects. While the Puritans have provided the United States with a great religious heritage, some of the negative results of their aspirations are being reaped today.

American "Messiahs"

It is no wonder that America has given birth to so many charismatic leaders who have used American/biblical ideals to their own ends. This can be observed on the political scene as well as on the religious scene. Politically, each presidential election brings promises of a utopian future for America—"if you will only embrace the platform of God's candidate." Religiously, charismatic leaders arise who tolerate no other interpretation of Scripture except their own.

American messiahs appear in all shapes and sizes and can be generally classified into three categories. For purposes of this study we can distinguish three types of messiahs: the Prophet, the Eastern Guru, and the New Age Teacher.

The Prophet uses biblical terminology and Christian figures of speech. When at all possible, the Prophet tries to base his or her teachings and practices on the Bible. Prophets like these have been on the American landscape since the mid-nineteenth century. They avoid using the term "messiah," since there is only one Messiah, Jesus Christ. The Prophet sees himself (or herself) as the restorer of apostolic or New Testament Christianity. The argument goes something like this: The Christian church left the true teachings of Jesus sometime soon after the death of the twelve apostles and went into a period of apostasy, characterized by the domination of the Roman Catholic Church over Christendom. Martin Luther attempted to bring the church back to the Bible and made some headway. However, it was not until Prophet *(fill in the blank)* came along that True Christianity was restored. There is new revelation in the form of written material characterized as "new light" from the Bible. Traditional groups that fall in this category include Mormonism, Jehovah's Witnesses, and the Children of God. Many of the older groups within this category are seen today by some denominations as sects within Christianity and as "cults" by more conservative evangelicals.

The Eastern Guru arrived on the American scene much later than the Prophet. The teachings and practices of the guru are imported versions of religious teachings foreign to the Judeo-Christian tradition. The most prominent of the early gurus was Maharishi Mahesh Yogi. His transformation of Hindu meditation into transcendental meditation took root in American culture during the 1960s. Since that time others have come to America, including Bagwan Sri Rajneesh. These gurus either say that their teachings are compatible with other religions or consider their teachings as philosophies, not religious in nature.

The New Age Teacher is a combination of the first two and sometimes uses the title of guru. The New Age Teacher usually bases his or her teachings on Eastern philosophy or thought and also borrows moral teachings and the messianic idea from Christianity.

There are many New Age Teachers in America today, and they influence a large number of people. One of the most prominent is Elizabeth Clare Prophet of the Church Universal and Triumphant (CUT).

All messianic groups espouse the belief in continuing revelation from God—at least through the time of their leader. This new light manifests itself through the leader or leaders and authenticates their position of authority.

Many of these sects that have origins within Christianity at first appear to be biblically based or at least try to be, quite often citing Scripture to back up their peculiar interpretations. They are usually labeled by outsiders as a *fundamentalist* or a *legalistic* group. They usually deviate significantly from the major doctrines of the historic Christian faith: the Trinity, the deity of Christ, salvation by grace through faith, the substitutionary atonement of Christ, and the physical resurrection of Christ from the dead. Gradually the leader of the group receives more and more bizarre teachings. By this time, however, the group, having total confidence in their leader's anointing and calling from God, largely accepts the doctrine without question.

How dangerous are these groups? Quite often we don't find out how dangerous they are until after an event like Jonestown or Waco draws our attention to the seriousness of extremist groups. It is difficult to determine how dangerous an extremist group is until former members make it known. A key to finding out is to examine the doctrines, practices, and how the group views its leader. Countercult groups such as the Christian Research Institute (CRI) can be helpful in determining the threat of a particular group.

Many modern-day sects have their genesis in the nineteenth century or have been heavily influenced by groups from that era. If we can understand something about these groups perhaps we will be better prepared to deal with their extremism. How much better off would the federal agents in Waco have been if they had possessed a keener understanding of our nation's religious past, Branch Davidian history, and extremist sects in general?

In chapter nine we will look at various groups and the atrocities committed by their adherents *on the basis of the teachings or revelations of the prophet.* We will look at particular events, teachings, and practices.

There are some basic commonalties among these various groups:

1. Total commitment to the leader's interpretation of the Bible or other writings.
2. Belief that the leader can do no wrong.
3. Belief in continued revelation that can contradict previous revelations.
4. Strong belief that we are in the times prior to the end of the world (except for Christian Science).
5. A "we-they" mentality.
6. Pressure to conform to the dictates of the group (both minor and major issues), usually threatening disfellowshipping or excommunication for those who do not submit.

It is impossible to predict another Waco or Jonestown nor do we presume to do so in this book. What we do want to do is to point out some danger signs. One of the best ways to prevent another Waco is to be informed and educated. Most Americans today do not have a basic understanding of religion or the impact of religious beliefs on the devout follower.

Going Against the Grain

I'm at a place right now, if I turn my back on this message, I'm a gonner. I'm doomed.

—Steve Schneider, deceased Branch Davidian

Our individuality is appealed to every day. Television commercials unrelentingly push products made just for the real "you." High-priced cars are made to order for those who know what "they" want and can afford it. And, of course, fashion magazines feature and promote some of the most unusual outfits that, for those secure enough about their own unique identity, serve as the perfect expression of "self." Indeed, modern-day American society greatly rewards those who dare to "be themselves."

But society is not always so accepting when individuality translates into extreme devotion to religious beliefs and practices that "go against the grain" of societal norm. Such intolerance is often well justified.

The deeds of yester-year's extreme sects, coupled with actions taken by present-day fringe groups, amply prove that we must be ever watchful of those whose beliefs and zeal produce a cry of religious self-assertion at all costs. There has never been a shortage of such groups, nor does it seem that there will ever be (at least for the time being), as can be seen by the past and present actions of the following "Bible-based" religions.

The Church of Jesus Christ of Latter-day Saints

The Church of Jesus Christ of Latter-day Saints, also known as the Mormons, best portrays the nineteenth-century social and religious scene. Joseph Smith, Jr., the founder of the sect, lived in upstate New York. One event from history that involved Smith's group is especially significant for our study in this book.

The year was 1857. The place was the Utah territory. The Fancher party, a combined company of emigrants from Arkansas and Missouri, formed a group of about 125 to 140 men, women, and children. These emigrants were headed to California using the same passageway as many settlers before them. They passed through Utah only to be murdered in cold blood by the Mormon inhabitants. The entire company was killed except for 17 or 18 small children. The official report was that Indians had massacred the emigrants. However, the diaries of the settlers in the area and the confession of Mormon John D. Lee reveal that it was a Mormon-instigated crime. What is also revealed is a massive cover-up from local church leadership to the top of the Mormon hierarchy, Brigham Young, the successor to Joseph Smith, Jr.

The Mormon settlers had left the U.S. borders from Missouri to begin a trek westward under the leadership of Brigham Young on February 4, 1847 (about two-and-a-half years after the shooting death of Joseph Smith, Jr.). The Mormon emigrants arrived in the Valley of the Great Salt Lake on July 24 and established the State of Deseret on March 10, 1849. Young and the Mormons were now free to establish their own kingdom of God on earth independent of the U.S. government and its control. However, by mid–1850 California was granted statehood and the rest of Mormon country was divided up and named the Utah and New Mexico territories.

Young was allowed to remain as the governor of the Utah territory alongside federally appointed "gentile" (non-Mormon) officers. Some of these federal agents did not possess high moral standards and caused problems for the Mormon inhabitants. This was not at all pleasing to Brigham Young and the Mormon settlers. It was during this time that strong anti-American rhetoric came from Mormon leaders. In the May 4, 1855 edition of the *New York Herald* Brigham was quoted as saying, "It is reported that I have said that whoever the President appoints, I am still Governor. I repeat it, all hell cannot remove me. (Cries of 'Amen.') I am still your Governor. (Cries of 'Glory to God.') I will still rule this people until God himself permits another to take my place. I wish I could say as much for the other officers of the government. The greater part of them are a gambling, drinking, whoring set. . . . Do you think I'll obey or respect them? No! I'll say as I did the other day, when the flag was hauled down from before the military quarters—"Let them take down the American flag; we can do without it.'"

Heber C. Kimball, a member of the First Presidency, expressed the same anti-American sentiment. "Thank God, I say, that we are delivered from that Christian nation. Deliver me from their Christianity and from them. . . . I will tell you the day of our separation has come, and we are a free and an independent people, isolated a thousand miles from the Christian nation; and thanks be to our God for ever."

The U.S. government viewed these Mormon people as being in rebellion and seriously considered calling federal troops to bring them back in line. In anticipation of this, on September 15, 1857, Brigham Young issued the following proclamation:

Citizens of Utah:

We are invaded by a hostile force who are evidently assailing us to accomplish our overthrow and destruction. . . .

Our opponents have availed themselves of prejudice existing against us because of our religious faith, to send out a formidable host to accomplish our destruction. We have had no privilege, no opportunity of defending ourselves from the false, foul, and unjust aspersions against us before the nation. The government has not condescended to cause an investigating committee or other persons to be sent to inquire into and ascertain the truth, as is customary in such cases. . . .

Our duty to ourselves, to our families, requires us not to tamely submit to be driven and slain, without an attempt to preserve ourselves. Our duty to our country, our holy religion, our God, to freedom and liberty requires that we should not quietly stand still and see those fetters forging around, which are calculated to enslave and bring us in subjection to an unlawful military despotism such as can only emanate . . . from usurpation, tyranny and oppression.

Therefore, I, Brigham Young, governor, and superintendent of Indian affairs for the territory of Utah, in the name of the people of the United States in the territory of Utah,

1st—Forbid all armed forces, of every description, from coming into this territory under any pretense whatever.

2d—That all the forces in said territory hold themselves in readiness to march, at a moment's notice, to repel any and all such invasion.

3d—Martial law is hereby declared to exist in this territory, from and after the publication of this proclamation; and no person shall be allowed to pass or repass into, or through, or from this territory, without a permit from the proper officer.

In keeping with Young's proclamation the Mormon settlers in Utah refused to sell food and supplies to the "gentiles" passing through their land. This helped fuel the animosity toward the Mormons. The emigrants from Missouri, who called themselves "hell cats," caused most of the problems with the Mormons as they passed through. Further they threatened to report to the U.S. government the poor treatment they received while in Utah. This would most certainly bring federal troops into the territory.

And then came the Fancher party. According to Mormon testimony, members of the this party (presumably those from Missouri) taunted the Mormon settlers by saying that they had participated in a slaughter of some Mormon settlers in Missouri. One individual even stated that he had the gun that shot Joseph

Smith, Jr., and that he wouldn't mind taking a shot at Brigham Young either. These comments exacerbated the hostile feelings among the Mormons. All sincere Mormon men who upheld the Mormon priesthood were sworn to "avenge the blood of the prophets." Perhaps God was delivering his enemies into their hands for vengeance!

One further important element that added to the seriousness of the situation was the doctrine of *blood atonement* that was preached by Brigham Young and other Mormon authorities. According to the Encyclopedia of Mormonism, Mormons believe that "the shedding of the blood of Jesus Christ . . . is efficacious for the sins of all who believe, repent, are baptized by one having authority, and receive the Holy Ghost by the laying on of hands. However, if a person thereafter commits a grievous sin such as the shedding of innocent blood, the Savior's sacrifice alone will not absolve the person of the consequences of the sin. Only by voluntary submitting to whatever penalty the Lord may require can that person benefit from the atonement of Christ." In practice, this works out to the shedding of one's own blood. This doctrine of blood atonement was taught by the leaders whom the people believed were inspired and could not give a wrong order. Thus it was believed that the only way that the guilty members of the Fancher party could be saved was for their blood to be shed.

After the regular Sunday meeting, the local Mormon leaders of Cedar City held a priesthood meeting (a meeting designated for all males who hold the Melchizedek priesthood in the Mormon church). On the agenda was the question of what to do with the Fancher party. There was much discussion. The consensus was that they must be stopped. But how? A plan was concocted that involved the local Indian tribes. But before the local Mormons decided to act they wanted to get the advice of the Prophet. A messenger was commissioned to travel to Salt Lake City to explain the situation to Brigham Young and get advice. They also decided to send for John D. Lee who was the Farmer for the Indians. He was a devout Mormon who lived in nearby Harmony. Lee was a close friend and admirer of Young. Brigham had often called him "son," and Lee returned the endearing term by addressing Young as "father."

On Tuesday the Indians attacked before the Mormons wanted them to. The Fancher party dug in to protect themselves in the Mountain Meadows. This was a strategic place for them to be. It was a broad enough area to encamp and to be able to defend themselves.

The emigrants decided to send three representatives back to Cedar City for help from the Mormon inhabitants they had been ridiculing. They sent William Aiden, who had lived among the Mormons in the past and had a good relationship with them. It was assumed that the Mormons would help them hold off the Indian attack even though they had taunted them. The Aiden party never reached Cedar City. They were ambushed by some Mormon men. Aiden was killed immediately. The two other men took off and were shot down. The Mormons feared that the Fancher party would identify these assailants as white men and that word would get out that the crimes were not done by the hands of the Indians. This would certainly draw American troops in to subdue the Mormons.

A plan was devised to take care of the rest of the Fancher party. Lee and Charles Hopkins would approach the entrenched settlers to offer help. They would then convince the wagon train to lay their weapons and ammunition aside and march out of the camp to Cedar City—a whole thirty-five miles away! The wounded and children would be loaded in wagons; the women would march out followed by the men, who would each be accompanied by an armed Mormon man for protection.

No one knows why the Fancher party agreed to such a strange arrangement. Perhaps they were running short of supplies and needed food for their families. Whatever the reasoning, they did as they were told. Lee and two other men were with the wagon of children and wounded men followed by the women and men. At the signal "Men, do your duty!" the Mormon men murdered the men walking next to them. The women were ambushed by the Indians, and Lee and his companions killed the wounded. Everyone was murdered accept for seventeen or eighteen children who were too young to talk about what they had just witnessed.

The Mormon men buried the dead in shallow graves and took the children to Cedar City to be cared for by Mormon families until they could be transported back to relatives. It was reported that weeks after the horrible affair wolves had dug up the shallow resting places and then scattered the remains throughout the area.

What followed was a series of steps to cover up the crime. Blame was shifted from one person to the next. The man sent to get advice from Brigham Young returned to Cedar City the day after the massacre. When the residents of Cedar City got the message from Brigham they became worried. Young had counseled them not to meddle with the emigrants. He advised the Mormons to let them go in peace.

The men were in a predicament. John D. Lee was surprised. He thought that he was under the orders of Young from the beginning. It was decided that Lee should immediately go to Salt Lake City and give a full account to Young. Young's reaction was one of horror. The next day Young told Lee that he had spent time in prayer and God had told him that what they did was all right. There would be no repercussions upon the men. He told Lee to write a report blaming the massacre on the Indians. Lee did just that. The booty from the massacre was put in the church relief fund to be distributed among the people in need.

John D. Lee was the scapegoat for this incident. He was excommunicated from the Mormon church. Almost twenty years after the event, Lee was executed at the same spot as the actual massacre. But before he was killed, Lee wrote out his last confession. Lee wanted to make sure that he would meet God with a clear conscience. So he wrote out a detailed account of the event. Much of our knowledge concerning the massacre comes from the last statements of a condemned man. Lee does not indict Brigham Young in the massacre. However, he is critical of Young's handling of it after he was apprised of the event.

Was this, finally, just a case of "wild west justice"? No, this tragic event cannot be written off that easily. There were certain actions that brought the Mormon people to this crime. We should not indict the Mormon people. Rather, we need to blame a religious system that took normal people and brought them to a point where they were willing to kill for their prophet. As we have seen with Koresh, the process takes place over a period of time; there is isolation from outside thoughts or influence; and there is religious justification.

There are at least five aspects of Mormonism that provided the rationalization for the Mountain Meadows massacre:

1. Authority of the leadership. The leaders of the people deceived their followers. They claimed that federal troops were going to rape and plunder the land. The people believed, unquestioningly, that the priesthood could not give an order that was wrong.

2. The doctrine of blood atonement. The Mormon people were under the assumption that at least some of the Fancher party were responsible for the death of Joseph Smith, Jr., and some of the saints in Missouri. The only way salvation could be possible for these people would be for them to have their own blood shed.

3. Revered literature. One of the four sacred writings of the Mormons, "Doctrine & Covenants," gives justification for taking revenge. Section 98:23–32 states that "thine enemy is in thine hands; and if thou rewardest him according to his works thou art justified; if he has sought thy life, and thy life is endangered by him, thine enemy is in thine hands and thou art justified."

4. The patriarchal blessing given to William H. Dame by Patriarch Elisha H. Groves on February 20, 1854: "Thou shalt be called to act at the head of a portion of thy brethren and of the Lamanites in the redemption of Zion and the avenging of the blood of the Prophets upon them that dwell in the earth. The Angel of Vengeance shall be with thee, shall nerve and strengthen thee. Like unto Moroni, no power shall be able to stand before thee until thou hast accomplished thy work." Dame, having been thus encouraged to avenge the death of Smith, viewed this as his divine appointment.

5. Vows to avenge the death of the prophets. Each man in the priesthood had vowed to avenge the death of Joseph Smith, Jr., and his brother.

6. Mormon Eschatology. Mormonism's goal was (and is) to establish a theocracy in the United States. According to John Heinerman and Anson Shupe, Mormons see themselves as the "true Israel" and do not wish to simply coexist with other religions but to supersede them. Joseph Smith, Jr., prophesied in May 1843 that "You must continue to petition Congress all the time, but they will treat you like strangers and commissioners, you will see the constitution of the United States almost destroyed; it will hang by a thread, as it were as fine as the finest silk fiber . . . and it will be preserved and saved by the efforts of the White Horse and the Red Horse, who will combine in its defense." Brigham Young affirmed Smith's prophecy and added that "they will have to call for the 'Mormon' Elders to save it from utter destruction; and they will step forth and do it."

The Watch Tower Bible and Tract Society

The Watch Tower Bible and Tract Society (WTBTS), also known as Jehovah's Witnesses (JWs), is best known for its adherents' refusal to salute the flag, join the armed services, or celebrate holidays and birthdays, proselytizing door to door, and prophecies regarding the second coming of Christ. The WTBTS has a dangerous religious system that is thinly veiled with biblical terminology.

The Watch Tower Bible and Tract Society is based on the teachings of Charles Taze Russell, "Judge" Rutherford, and the current governing body of the organization located in Brooklyn, New York. The Jehovah's Witness would claim that Jesus Christ is the head of the organization and is ruling invisibly through God's faithful slave—the Watch Tower Bible and Tract Society. The job of the WTBTS is to portion out "truth" to the rest of Jehovah's followers. The light (or clarity of "truth") grows brighter and brighter through the revelations that come from the Watch Tower organization. Hence, the justification for past false prophecies.

Reports from former members reveal an organization that effectively rules the lives of its members through fear and intimidation. The Governing Body of the Watch Tower Bible and Tract

Society is the final authority on matters of faith and practice. Members are not allowed to read any material from "anti-Witness" sources; they cannot associate with anyone who has been disfellowshipped (or excommunicated)—even if this includes immediate family members. A person can be disfellowshipped for any number of things—from gross immorality, smoking, drinking, to having a blood transfusion, to reading unapproved materials, to associating with (or even talking to) a disfellowshipped Witness. Members are to go door to door to proclaim the "gospel of the kingdom." But in reality, members go door to door because they are, in essence, doing works that will save them from the wrath of God at Armageddon.

The WTBTS historically has a propensity for setting dates for Armageddon. Expectations within the organization are kept high for the day of destruction for Christendom and the world. Some have called the WTBTS "Armageddon Incorporated" because of the number of false alarms. Below is a list of some of these prophecies:

1897	"Our Lord, the appointed King, is now present, since October 1874."—*Studies in the Scriptures*, Vol. 4, page 621
1899	" The 'battle of the great day of God Almighty' (Rev. 16:14), which will end in A.D. 1914 with the complete overthrow of earth's present rulership, is already commenced."—*The Time Is at Hand*, page 101 (1908 edition)
1916	"The Bible chronology herein presented shows that the six great 1000 year days beginning with Adam are ended, and that the great 7th Day, the 1000 years of Christ's Reign, began in 1873."—*The Time Is at Hand*, page ii
1917	"In the year 1918, when God destroys the churches wholesale and the church members by the millions, it shall be that any escape shall come through the works of Russell ."—*Finished Mystery*, page 485

1918	"Therefore we may confidently expect that 1925 will mark the return of Abraham, Isaac, and Jacob and the faithful prophets of old, particularly those named by the Apostle in Hebrews 11, to the condition of human perfection."—*Millions Now Living Will Never Die*, page 89
1922	"The date 1925 is even more distinctly indicated by the Scriptures than 1914."—*The Watchtower*, 9/1/22, page 262
1923	"Our thought is, that 1925 is definitely settled in Scriptures. As to Noah, the Christian now has much more upon which to base his faith than Noah had upon which to base his faith in a coming deluge."—*The Watchtower*, 4/1/23, page 106
1925	"The year 1925 is here. With great expectation Christians have looked forward to this year. Many have confidently expected that all members of the body of Christ will be changed to heavenly glory during this year. This may be accomplished. It may not be. In his own due time God will accomplish his purposes concerning his people. Christians should not be so deeply concerned about what may transpire this year."—*The Watchtower*, 1/1/25, page 3
Sept. 1925	"It is going to be expected that Satan will try to inject into the minds of the consecrated, the thought that 1925 should see an end to the work."—*The Watchtower*, page 262
1926	"Some anticipated that the work would end in 1925, but the Lord did not state so. The difficulty was that the friends inflated their imaginations beyond reason; and that when their imaginations burst asunder, they were inclined to throw away everything."—*The Watchtower*, page 232
1929	"The Scriptural proof is that the second presence of Jesus began in 1874."—*Prophecy*, page 65
1931	"There was a measure of disappointment on the part of Jehovah's faithful ones on earth concern-

	ing the years 1914, 1918, & 1925, which disappointment lasted for a time . . . and they also learned to quit fixing dates."—*Vindication*, page 338
1941	"Receiving the gift, the marching children clasped it to them, not a toy or plaything for idle pleasure, but the Lord's instrument for most effective work in the remaining months before Armageddon."—*The Watchtower*, 9/15/41, page 288
1966	"1975 (in early autumn) will be the end of the 6th 1,000-year day of man's existence. It would not be by mere chance or accident but would be according to the loving purpose of Jehovah God for the reign of Jesus Christ to run parallel with the seventh millennium of man's existence."—*Everlasting Life in Freedom*, page 30
1968	"True, there have been those in times past who predicted an 'end to the world,' even announcing a specific date. Yet nothing happened. The 'end' did not come. They were guilty of false prophesying. Why? What was missing? . . . Missing from such people were God's truths and the evidence that he was using and guiding them."—*Awake*, 10/8/68. (see Luke 21:8)
1968	"The Battle of Armageddon will be over by the autumn of 1975. It may involve only a difference of weeks or months, not years."—"WHY ARE YOU LOOKING FORWARD TO 1975?'" *The Watchtower*, 8/15/68, page 494

The latest such prophecy was for the year 1975. Former members report that because of the anticipation of the Battle of Armageddon in 1975 they put off marriage, having children, and business decisions; some even sold their property to give to the society. Shattered and disillusioned, many JWs left the organization.

What was the response of the WTBTS? In the July 15, 1976 *Watchtower*, the WTBTS stated that there were time factors that

God had not revealed, such as the time lapse between the creation of Adam and Eve. In the March 15, 1980 *Watchtower*, the WTBTS decided to address the problem further:

> In modern times such eagerness . . . has led to attempts at setting dates. . . . With the appearance of the book *Life Everlasting—in Freedom of the Sons of God*, and its comments as to how appropriate it would be for the millennial reign of Christ to parallel the seventh millennium of man's existence, *considerable expectation was aroused regarding the year 1975.* There were statements made then, and thereafter, stressing that this was only a possibility. Unfortunately, however, along with such cautionary information, there were other statements published that implied that such realization of hopes by that year was more of a probability than a mere possibility. . . . Nevertheless, there is not reason for us to be shaken in faith in God's promises. . . . Likewise, Jesus said to his apostles about the time for establishing God's kingdom: "It does not belong to you to bet knowledge of the times or seasons which the Father has placed in his own jurisdiction." . . . It is impossible for us to figure out the world's end in advance.

While the WTBTS acknowledged a mistake it accepted no responsibility for the lives that were put on hold or the faith that was wrecked because of the wrong prophecies.

One of the most tragic and physically harmful doctrines among the Jehovah's Witnesses is their teaching regarding blood transfusions. The newspapers routinely announce headlines similar to these:

"Pregnant Woman Refuses Blood, Dies"
"Teen Dies Rejecting Blood"
"Refusal of Blood Transfusion Brings Death, Murder Charge"
"Boy Gets Court-ordered Blood"
"Witness Wins In Court, Dies In Hospital"
"Anemia Kills Woman After She Refuses Transfusion"
"12-Year-Old Kidnapped From Illinois Hospital Bed"
"J.W. Woman Dies Refusing Transfusion"
"Father Takes Child From Hospital, Flees State"

Countless numbers of Jehovah's Witnesses are dying from surgical procedures and medical problems that could easily have been avoided. This, is due to a ruling by the Governing Body made in 1945, loosely based on some passages from the Bible (Gen. 9:4; Lev. 3:17; Acts 15:28,29). The original ruling was a ban on all forms of blood use. It has been modified somewhat today.

According to the American Red Cross 10 percent of all Americans need some type of blood product annually. Jehovah's Witnesses claim that 1,910,194 people nationwide attended their annual Memorial of Christ's Death in 1991. If this is the case, that means that *191,019 Americans are potentially at risk of physical harm due to refusal of blood products!*

In some cases hospital officials obtain court orders to provide the needed treatment for children. The June 15, 1991 issue of the *Watchtower* magazine states that "Christians today must also be steadfast, firmly resolved not to violate divine law, *even if that puts them in some jeopardy with secular governments.* The highest law of the universe—God's law—requires that Christians abstain from blood. . . . If a court-authorized transfusion seemed likely, a Christian *might choose to avoid being accessible* for such a violation of God's law" (italics added).

In *How Can Blood Save Your Life?* (1990) the Watch Tower Bible and Tract Society explains their view in the following way:

> God told all mankind that they must not eat blood. Why? Because blood represents life. (Genesis 9:3–6) He explained this further in the Law code given to Israel At the time the Law code was ratified, the blood of sacrificed animals was used on an altar. . . . God himself explained the principle underlying those sacrifices: "The soul (or, life) of the flesh is in the blood, and I myself have put it upon the altar for you to make atonement for your souls, because it is the blood that makes atonement by the soul in it. That is why I have said to the sons of Israel: 'No soul of you must eat blood.'"— Leviticus 17:11,12 . . . It thus becomes plain why we need to have God's view of blood. In accord with his right as Creator, he has determined its exclusive usefulness. . . . They [Israelites] had to avoid sustaining their lives with blood, not primarily because doing otherwise was unhealthy, but because it was unholy to God. They were to abstain from blood, not because it was polluted, but

because it was precious in obtaining forgiveness. . . . How wise, then for us to take to heart all of God's requirements! That includes obeying his commands about blood, not misusing it even in medical situations. We thus will not live just for the moment. Rather, we will manifest our high regard for life, including our future prospect of everlasting life in human perfection.

Since the original ruling in 1945, the WTBTS has modified its view somewhat, allowing for certain types of blood use, such as albumin, immunoglobulins, hemophiliac preparations (Factor VIII and IX), and the diversion of a patient's blood through a heart-lung machine or other diversion in which extracorporeal circulation is uninterrupted.

In evaluating the WTBTS position, we have to look at what the Bible actually says about blood. Our purpose here is not to belittle someone's sincerely held belief. But any belief that is based on a faulty interpretation of the Bible must be reconsidered. We will briefly show that the Bible does not support this view of blood transfusions.

The biblical passages quoted by Jehovah's Witnesses do not deal with blood transfusions at all but rather the *eating of blood:*

"Only you shall not eat flesh with its life, that is, its blood." Genesis 9:4

"It is a perpetual statute throughout your generations in all your dwellings: you shall not eat any fat or any blood." Leviticus 3:17

"And you are not to eat any blood, either of bird or animal, in any of your dwellings. Any person who eats any blood, even that person shall be cut off from his people." Leviticus 7:26–27

"For it seemed good to the Holy Spirit and to us to lay upon you no greater burden than these essentials: that you abstain from things sacrificed to idols and from blood and from things strangled and from fornication; if you keep yourselves free from such things, you will do well. Farewell." Acts 15:29

The punishment for eating blood was being cut off from one's people. "Cutting off" does not mean to kill. It means to be excommunicated (see Lev. 17:10, 14). Numbers 15:35 states that the punishment for breaking the Sabbath was death. If Moses had meant to say death when someone ate blood, he certainly could have. Also, we see that Jesus broke the Sabbath in Luke 6. The Pharisees were condemning Jesus for doing so. What is Christ's response? "I ask you, is it lawful on the Sabbath to do good, or to do harm, to save a life, or to destroy it?" The answer was "To save it!" Christ broke the Sabbath and was therefore subject to death; yet because he was doing good, he was not condemned.

Furthermore, there is no law in the Bible prohibiting blood transfusions. Eating blood and transfusions are two separate and distinct processes. This is shown to be true by orthodox Jews who have no prohibition against blood transfusions yet keep the strict dietary laws.

Thus, just as the WTBTS has wrongly prophesied the end of the world by taking the Bible out of context, so has the WTBTS wrongly concluded that God prohibits the transfusion of blood. Because of their faulty interpretation countless Jehovah's Witnesses have suffered needlessly and some have even given their life for their organization.

Children of God

Most people have not heard anything about the Children of God (COG) for a number of years. The name may bring back memories of the 1970s Jesus Movement. Founder and leader Moses David Berg has led his group around the world. The group is best known for its sexual practices; from "flirty fishing" to sharing partners among adults, and even sex with and between children. In the late 1970s Berg left the country along with many of the COG members.

The COG (also known as "The Family of Love" and "Heavenly Elite") are still active throughout the world and reports indicate that they are returning to the United States. While their popularity has decreased in recent years they are still receiving funds from evangelicals who are unaware of their activities. Funds are solicited in the United States under the auspices of the Christian Children's Mission and similarly named organizations.

Moses David was God's End-Time Prophet and spoke to his followers through his writings (called *Mo Letters* or Moses Letters). Through the Mo Letters Berg defended "flirty fishing" (the practice of women seducing a prospective follower and having sexual relations with him in order to get him into the group) and various other sexual practices. It is in these writings that we see the real Moses David and how he manipulates the members of the group. His letters attempt to use Scripture to justify his practices.

Berg teaches that the COG are God's faithful remnant, the 144,000 mentioned in Revelation 7:4 and 14:3. Everyone else is part of "the Devil's System." As with many of the cultic groups mentioned, there is heavy emphasis placed on eschatology. This provides the leverage to keep the follower busy doing the Lord's work. If the Lord is coming back very soon, then you don't want to be caught idle and be embarrassed when he comes! But David Berg has also made a number of false prophetic utterances: that California would fall into the sea due to an earthquake and that the comet Kahoutek would destroy America.

In the summer of 1990 the *Christian Research Journal* gave an update on the Children of God. Dalva Lynch was a COG member for fifteen years and is very concerned about the group because she still has family members inside. According to Lynch, COG is reaping the results of their legacy of sexual promiscuity. She relates how widespread sexual promiscuity is. From earliest infancy, the cult's children are taught sexual freedom. Dalva says that COG has set up Teen Ranches that are essentially centers for psychological indoctrination.

Church Universal and Triumphant

One group that has been compared to the Branch Davidians is the Church Universal and Triumphant (CUT). CUT is a New Age group with headquarters on a 63,000-acre ranch near Livingston, Montana. Elizabeth Clare Prophet, known as "Guru Ma," is the self-proclaimed leader.

CUT has been tagged as the "Doomsday cult" because of its fortress-like ranch in Montana. There are lookouts on property lines that neighbors and critics have called gun turrets. Elizabeth Clare Prophet believes that on April 23, 1990 the world entered a 12-year era of negative karma that has been accumulating over the past 25,800 years. March and April 1990 were supposed to be an especially high period of danger. As a result of this impending threat 46 shelters were built and underground bunkers were dug for the protection of the membership. One shelter was large enough to house 756 people.

There have also been charges made against CUT that allege the stockpiling of weapons. The official stand of the group is that they are not stockpiling these weapons. Prophet says that the guns are owned by private individuals, not by the church itself. However, in 1989 Edward Francis, Prophet's husband, was charged with illegally purchasing weapons which included .50 caliber semiautomatics. He was convicted and imprisoned.

Prophet is one of the best-known figures in the New Age movement and lectures throughout the English-speaking world. She claims to be the spokesperson for the "Ascended Masters," who include Jesus, Gautama Buddha, Saint Germaine, and El Moyra. She receives dictations from these masters. Prophet's promotional material indicates that she is fully conscious and in possession of her faculties, yet in an exalted state, while delivering the words of the heavenly host.

CUT originated in Virginia under the name Summit Lighthouse. It was founded by her first husband, Mark Prophet. Elizabeth Clare took over in 1972 after he died. The group moved to Malibu and changed the name to Church Universal and Triumphant. In 1987 Prophet moved the group to Montana.

CUT has 120 chapters in the United States and teaching centers in 40 other countries. The teachings of Elizabeth Clare Prophet are an eclectic mix of Christian mystical ideas as well as Eastern thought. She authored, among other books, *The*

Astrology of the Four Horsemen and co-authored with her husband Mark *The Lost Teachings of Jesus* (3 vols.).

The question has been raised by cult watchers, "Is this another Waco?" Can we expect the same results in Montana as we saw in Texas—or even worse?

It is difficult to predict the outcome of any particular group. Perhaps with the amount of attention that has been focused on CUT any possible danger has been thwarted. Prophet sees herself as the founder of an established religion. In fact, a recent press release in the wake of the Branch Davidians quotes Clark Morphew, a religion writer for the *St. Paul Pioneer Press,* as saying,"Elizabeth Clare Prophet is a part of our religious history, and someday the Church Universal and Triumphant will be as honored as Mormonism is today."

But what of the potential threat? CUT does display some disconcerting features:

1. A strong, charismatic leader who claims to receive special revelations ("dictations") from God (or the spiritual realm).
2. Communal living isolated from the rest of the world.
3. Siege mentality with predictions of and a strong belief in a coming holocaust.
4. Unquestioned authority. For example, without any extraordinary provocation, CUT members built bomb shelters on the basis of messages that Prophet had received.

To conclude, no one can predict that there is imminent danger in Montana. But one should keep a careful eye on what could be a volatile situation.

The Christian Identity Movement

Christian Identity is a militant, extremely right wing, white supremacist movement that holds that one is saved by race, not by grace. According to Church and Society, there are as many as 30,000 Americans who are somehow associated with the white supremacist movement. Identity churches believe that the Jew-

ish race is the seed of Satan and that the white race is the seed
of Adam. Abraham, David, and Jesus were white, not Jewish.
Jesus was from the pure tribe of Judah. White Americans are the
Ten Lost Tribes of Israel (Anglo-Israelism) and the U.S. government is called the Zionist Occupation Government (or ZOG).
Believers will go through the Great Tribulation mentioned in the
Book of Revelation and need to prepare for these events. The
pretribulational rapture is a deceptive doctrine from Satan in
order to lull whites to sleep. All whites must prepare for war by
stockpiling weapons, learning to use them, and being trained in
survival tactics.

The Order, a white supremacist group with some ties to the
Identity groups, was reportedly involved in the shooting of a Jewish talk show host in Denver, Colorado, and some bank robberies
in the Seattle area. It was stated that they also had developed a
plan to poison the water supply of Los Angeles, disrupt phone
service for the entire region, and wreck all the electrical power
transmission lines coming into the region.

Sound farfetched? There is a large minority of white suprema-
cists who are promoting these teachings, creating fear and
hatred. Christian Identity is on the rise. Its message is getting
out into mainstream Christianity by means of radio, cable television, contacts in prisons, and computer bulletin boards.

All Christian Identity teachers do not necessarily subscribe to
all the same teachings. However, most hold to the Anglo-
Israel/Lost Tribes of Israel teaching. Among the names associ-
ated with Christian Identity are Richard Butler, Pete Peters of
Laporte, Colorado, and Ben Williams of the American Covenant
Church.

It is difficult to determine whether the religious nature of the
movement is the justification for the white supremacy or if it
simply legitimizes the racial hate. In any event, the theological
framework has provided the rationalization for other white
supremacist groups. The Jewish race is the target of these hate
groups but blacks also have been singled out. Some forms of
Christian Identity say that blacks are the result of the angels
rebelling against God in heaven. The goal for these groups is to

have a white nation. When asked what the solution to the "Jew-ish problem" is, one individual said, "Six million more."

Unlike denominations strongly tied to the Christian church, groups such as those we have studied in this chapter have been singled out as cults—not because of their attraction to biblical prophecy but because they have either subverted crucial doc-trines of Christian belief or have engaged in socially. deviant practices.

Yet today there remains a great deal of confusion about what it means to classify a group as a cult, as has been done in the case of the Branch Davidians. Because the term is used so often, it is important for us to know what qualifies a group as a cult.

10

A Cult Recipe?

And I say to you, that every careless word that men shall speak, they shall render account for it in the day of judgment.

—Matthew 12:36

After stepping past the entry, I was asked to give the "guardian of the gate" the secret handshake along with the accompanying password. I then donned my robe, draping the hood over my newly shaven head, before slowly making my way down the corridor to the darkened chamber where the rest of the group had already gathered.

No sooner had I stepped into the room when I was greeted by a gush of icy cold breeze. Candles, numbering about two hundred, provided the only source of illumination within the sanctuary. Swirling smokes emanating from the incense burners filled the dimly lit chamber as fifty shadowy-garbed figures, still and silent as statues, faced the marble altar.

There was no need to ask anyone how they felt. The swell of excitement brewing couldn't be contained—not by the seeming austerity of the scene nor by the dark and heavy robes that masked our individual identities.

Tonight was special; someone was to be initiated into our ranks.

*****

All too often images like this come to mind when we hear the term "cult." Secret meetings, bizarre teachings and doctrines, strange rituals and practices, deviant and sometimes illegal activities, weird characters—this is what people typically associate with cults.

Is this an accurate picture?

So far, we've traced the rise and fall of the Branch Davidian cult headed by David Koresh. We've also looked at other religious groups who focus their time and energy specifically on doomsday prophecies and the coming endtimes—groups that have been labeled as cults. And, of course, the media occasionally provides a story of some dangerous cult.

With so much discussion about cults, it would seem that everyone knows what a cult is. Yet classifying a group as a cult is not as simple as it sounds. In fact, it can get very confusing.

The Social Factor

Sociologists have, for a long time, used the terms "sect" and "church or denomination" to classify various religious groups. Churches make up the largest individual bodies of organized religion (in terms of membership) and express the spiritual beliefs of the majority of society. They are part of the religious mainstream. The Roman Catholic Church, the American Baptist Church, the Christian Reformed Church, and the United Methodist Church are among the more recognizable churches or denominations today.

Sects, on the other hand, refer to groups that have come from one of the many established churches. While continuing to acknowledge and draw from the teachings and traditions of their respective denominations, sects have distanced themselves from churches, and to some degree the predominant culture they represent, in order to emphasize one or more beliefs or practices they feel have been lost to "worldliness."

The Quakers and Mennonites, who protested against acts of warfare, were classified as sects. So were the various "holiness" congregations that took part in the movement stressing the importance of personal piety along with a strict code of morality (including dressing properly).

In the early part of this century sociologists tried to figure out how they could classify groups that didn't fit neatly into the prevailing categories. Where, for example, could Christian Science or the Self-Realization Fellowship or the Theosophical Society be placed? It was then that the term "cult" was developed. Any religious group that didn't qualify as a church or sect was labeled a cult. It was, in a sense, used as a "leftover" category.

Social scientists have since set out to refine their definition of "cult" into something more descriptive and precise. Yet no matter what they came up with, they invariably saw cults as religious groups that *stood over against* the prevailing belief systems of the culture—which, of course, were reflected by and identified with the Judeo-Christian religious institutions.

Sects were recognized as offshoots that, for the most part, still held to the religious and cultural traditions from which they emerged. Cults, meanwhile, had a religious structure wholly alien to the prevalent religious communities. In a 1978 article written for the *Annual Review of the Social Sciences of Religion*, sociologist James T. Richardson explained that

> a cult is usually defined as a small informal group lacking a definite authority structure, somewhat spontaneous in its development (although often possessing a somewhat charismatic leader or group of leaders), transitory, somewhat mystical and individualistically oriented, and deriving its inspiration and ideology from outside the predominant religious culture.

The exotic beliefs and practices of a group may be due to its originating from a foreign land and culture, as in the case of various Hindu-based and Buddhist-based groups. In other cases, the personal innovation of the founder (or founders) of the group whose ideas derive from a variety of sources could be credited. It's also possible that elements of both factors combined to give rise to the group's peculiarities.

In their handling of the issue, social scientists have tried to maintain a relatively value-free definition of the term "cult." Cults are groups that stand out against the mainstream; they're organized differently from the more common churches and sects; and they have practices and beliefs that run counter to the prevailing majority. They're not necessarily good or bad, just different.

Because the term "cults" has acquired a negative connotation sociologists have adopted others, such as "new religions," "new religious movements," "alternative religions," "alternative groups," "alternative faiths," and "emergent religions."

The Canon of Orthodoxy

All disciplines have a fixed point, a foundation with guidelines that allow for the study of a given subject. Sociologists describe and assess religious movements in terms of the prevailing social circumstance, using the predominant religious groups as their point of reference. Christian theologians, on the other hand, use the Bible as their anchor.

While social scientists in the early twentieth century were busy formulating their definition of a "cult," theologians and apologists from conservative Protestant denominations (evangelicals) also set their sights on the growing number of non-Christian religious groups.

For the most part, the works they produced focused on showing how divergent groups differed from historical Protestantism and its attendant views concerning key doctrines in the Bible—including the divine inspiration and supreme authority of the Bible, the Trinity, humanity in relation to God, the identity and work of Jesus Christ, and the way to salvation.

One of the earliest books to come out on the subject was William C. Irvine's *Timely Warnings*, released in 1917 and later retitled *Heresies Exposed*. In the book, Irvine and others discussed groups that promoted heresy, which he defined as "Some theory tenaciously held, but not in subjection to the authority of Scripture." Included in the wide-ranging list were Mormonism, Spiritism, Atheism, Unitarianism, and Christian Science.

Another significant book titled, *The Chaos of Cults*, was released in 1938. In it, Jan Karel Van Baalen classified all religions into one of two categories: those that teach only God can save, and those that claim humans are capable of saving themselves. Groups belonging to the first category are Christians, Van Baalen argued, while those belonging to the latter are not (whether or not they claimed to be Christian) .

Seventeen years later Walter Martin's book, *The Rise of the Cults*, was introduced to the public. A leading evangelical authority on the subject and a staunch defender of orthodoxy, Martin laid out his definition of cultism as follows:

> *By cultism we mean the adherence to doctrines which are pointedly contradictory to orthodox Christianity* and which claim the distinction of either tracing their origin to orthodox sources or of being in essential harmony with those sources. Cultism, in short, is any major deviation from orthodox Christianity relative to the cardinal doctrines of the Christian faith.
>
> The most prominent among the cults are those that have been termed "the big five." These are *Jehovah's Witnesses, Christian Science, Mormonism, Unity*, and *Spiritualism*. All the aforementioned *deny* both the doctrines of the Trinity and the deity of Jesus Christ.

Evangelical countercult ministries or organizations, which specialize in the study and analysis of contemporary religions, generally classify as cults those modern-day groups that claim to be Christian while denying the fundamental tenets of historic Christianity. Martin's procedure, as outlined in his book, *The Kingdom of the Cults*, exemplifies the approach taken by most evangelical countercult organizations today:

> My approach to the subject then is threefold: (1) historical analysis of the salient facts connected with the rise of the cult systems; (2) the theological evaluation of the major teachings of those systems; and (3) an apologetic contrast from the viewpoint of Bibli-

cal theology, with an emphasis upon exegesis [interpretation of Bible passages] and doctrine.

Not all Christian cult specialists take such a strongly theological approach, however. Some tackle the issue from sociological, anthropological, and psychological angles—relating and commenting on individuals who are or were formerly involved in groups labeled as cults.

Moreover, evangelical Protestants aren't the only religious group actively addressing the issues. Roman Catholics and Jews have also become involved in the matter, though for the most part they've done so within the secular anticult community.

Family Affair

The 1960s witnessed the dawning of the "Age of Aquarius" in what seemed to be a sudden and unexpected boom in Asian religion—most notably Hindu-based and Buddhist-based groups. Many of the new members, usually in their late teens and early twenties, came from middle-class urban families.

Their parents' puzzlement quickly turned to concern and then fear. They had lost their children to alien religious groups. Strange new people had broken apart their families and taken from them their beloved offspring. What could be worse?

Why, they asked, would their son or daughter do something so drastic as to leave school, abandon work, and move away from home? It seemed extremely odd and unnatural that their children should undergo such a quick change in outlook, attitude, behavior, and attire. They weren't acting like their normal selves. What could have possibly made them that way?

The answer they arrived at was plain and simple: their rational faculties had been subverted; they were brainwashed. The Moonies, the Hare Krishnas, the Children of God, the Scientologists—these and other "destructive cults" manipulated and tricked the youth into giving up their lives and surrendering themselves wholly to the groups and their leaders.

Something had to be done. Outraged and stricken with grief, the parents consoled one another and organized themselves to counter the cause of their pain. These "destructive cults" posed a serious threat to society and had to be stopped.

Thus was born in the 1970s what has come to be known as the secular anticult movement (though its ranks include ministers, rabbis, and lay members of various Jewish and Christian denominations).

At first, members of the movement drew from the works of evangelicals to familiarize themselves with the "field of battle." They were determined to learn everything they could about their adversaries. But some adjustments had to be made. Religion scholar J. Gordon Melton explains in his *Encyclopedic Handbook of Cults in America* that

> [w]hile drawing upon Christian counter-cult literature in the beginning, the secular anti-cultists gradually discarded any overtly religious language as a means of designating cults in order to appeal to government authorities and avoid any seeming attack upon religious liberties. Thus, "cults" have come to be seen as groups that share a variety of generally destructive characteristics.

Several violent incidents involving relatively small and obscure groups only served to heighten the perceived threat: the Tate-La Bianca murders committed by the Manson family; the Symbionese Lebanese Army's abduction and transformation of heiress Patricia Hearst into a terrorist; the tragedy at Jim Jones' People's Temple commune in Jonestown, Guyana, involving the mass suicide of over nine hundred adults and children and the shooting of Congressman Leo J. Ryan and members of his party.

The parents were joined in their cause by mental health professionals, lawyers, and former members who had dedicated themselves to combatting the further growth of groups they once joined. Many respected psychologists and psychiatrists helped give the movement credibility in the eyes of the media and the larger public. One such individual, Michael Langone of the American Family Foundation, set forth the movement's understanding of destructive cults in a 1982 booklet titled *Destructive Cultism: Questions and Answers*:

> A destructive cult is a highly manipulative group which exploits and sometimes physically and/or psychologically damages members and recruits.
>
> A destructive cult: a) dictates—sometimes in great detail—how members should think, feel, and act; b) claims a special, exalted status (e.g., occult powers; a mission to save humanity)—for itself and/or its leader(s)—that usually sets it in opposition to the mainline society and/or the family; c) exploits its members, psychologically, financially, and/or physically; d) utilizes manipulative, or "mind control," techniques, especially the denigration of independent critical thinking, to recruit prospects and make members loyal, obedient, and subservient; and e) causes considerable psychological harm to many of its members and to members' families.
>
> Although some people deem a group destructive merely because it is deviant or "heretical," the point of view advanced here reserves the label for groups that tend to be exploitative, manipulative, psychologically damaging, exclusive, and totalist. According to this perspective, a group may be deviant and "heretical" without being destructive.

In 1988 Langone co-wrote a book titled *Cults: What Every Parent Should Know*, defining destructive cults as "those which tend to use extreme and unethical techniques of manipulation to recruit and assimilate members and to control members' thoughts, feelings, and behavior as a means of furthering the leader's goals."

What's particularly significant is the final sentence of that paragraph, which reads, "Although most cults have aroused concern are religious, they can also be political, commercial, or pseudotherapeutic." Thus, it seems that within the secular anticult community a group doesn't necessarily have to be religiously oriented to qualify as a cult.

Clearing the Confusion

So far we've seen the various definitions that the term "cult" has been given. In the first instance, sociologists apply the classification in a purely descriptive sense without indicating whether particular cults are good or bad. Then, there are evangelical countercult organizations who label as cults groups that deviate from the fundamental doctrines revealed in the Bible and embraced by historic Protestantism; the negative slant they give the term "cult" is in reference to theology.

Whereas the two definitions above employ the term "cult" in a religious context, the final definition, coming from secular anticultists, does not view the term as necessarily having a religious character. Rather, the distinguishing feature of a cult is its unethical and manipulative treatment of unwary members. The negative connotation of this last definition is far more reaching than the second definition, whose negative pronouncement may only be regarded as such by evangelicals.

By and large, whenever the media reports on a "cult," chances are that it usually concerns a group that is a combination of definitions two and three above—that is, some unorthodox group (by evangelical standards) that has or continues to engage in unethical and/or manipulative practices. The complication isn't helped by the fact that the terms "denominations," "sects," and "cults" are sometimes used interchangeably.

Richardson, along with a number of other sociologists, laments that the term "cult" has been used "as a 'rug' under which were swept the troublesome and idiosyncratic religious experiences of mystics and other religious deviants."

So far, at least one attempt has been made by sociologists to redefine the term "cult" to accommodate the more popular usage while at the same time retaining it as a relatively value-free description that's still useful in the area of social science. But as we've noted above, there seems to be a growing consensus among sociologists to discard the term altogether in place of something else that's not so negatively loaded.

Yet even those terms referring to "new religious movements" or "alternative religions" have been met with stiff opposition by the secular anticult groups. "Although 'new religions' lends more (sometimes deserved) respectability to many groups," comments Langone, "it may, on the other hand, lend a false respectability to dubious groups."

How strongly do secular anticultists feel about their stance? In one instance they wrote that "[a]lthough we have placed the adjective 'destructive' in front of 'cult' in order to emphasize that some cults are benign, we, like most writers in this field, will use the word 'cult' with the pejorative connotations of 'destructive' implied."

In some cases secular anticultists label a particular group as a cult that sociologists and evangelical countercult specialists will not such as a group galvanized around a particular political persuasion. In other cases, evangelicals may classify a group as a cult that the other two may not, such as the Church of Jesus Christ of Latter-day Saints, better known as the Mormons.

Given the fact that there's currently no universal definition of a cult, it seems best to ask one simple question whenever someone begins talking about cults: "Just what do you mean by the term 'cult'?" You may not agree with the way the person uses the term, but at least you'll know where he or she is coming from.

You may also want to ask yourself the same question before referring to any group as a cult. It may not be such a bad idea to begin by explaining what you mean by the term "cult" in order to avoid any potential misunderstanding. You never know. All the while you're talking about cults, the person listening may have a different concept altogether.

Epilogue

And this is my prayer: that you abound more and more in knowledge and depth of insight, so that you may be able to discern what is best and may be pure and blameless.

—Philippians 1:9–10

Difficult questions remain regarding the tragedy at Waco. Why did it happen? What would make people so blindly follow a misguided leader, even to death? How should society respond? How should we as individuals react? The above passage from the Bible gives some rather sound and straightforward advice.

First, we need to be *informed and fully aware,* or knowledgeable, of the "darker side of religious devotion." Zeal and devotion to religious beliefs do not always yield positive results. Unchecked religious fervor can lead to excesses, perversions, and deceptions.

Second, believers and nonbelievers alike need to be *insightful.* One must look beyond the superficial, examining the history, doctrines, and practices of a group before deciding to become a part of it or recommending it to others. *Anyone* can be led astray.

Third, we need to be *discerning.* Jesus said that his followers would love God with all of their heart, soul, *mind,* and strength. Consequently, we all must use our minds; we must think, reason, and analyze—especially before committing ourselves to any group or cause. All too often, an "ounce" of discernment could have prevented what turned out to be a disappointing, damaging, or deadly consequence.

In another part of the Bible, those who called themselves Christians are instructed to be "in the world, but not *of* the world." Being "not of the world," however, does not mean being blind to facts, no matter how terrible and troubling they may be. Being "in," but not "of" the world means living in the realm of the here-and-now while looking forward to the future. It is *seeing* and *reacting* with the world as it is, while attempting to change things for the better. It is understanding at all times what is temporal while keeping an eye on, and waiting for, that which is eternal.

The Waco tragedy—and others like it—have shown the results of having one's heart, soul, mind, and strength focused narrowly on a false messiah. Such "messiahs" can only mislead and destroy the faith and lives of sincerely devoted followers. To Christians, there is but one Messiah who can provide truth, give light, and offer hope—Jesus of Nazareth. It is to him, and him alone, that true Christians should always turn.

A Chronological History of the Branch Davidians

1782
William Miller is born.

1827
Ellen G. Harmon (later White) is born.

1843
The Midnight Cry begins publication. On January 1, Miller commits himself to dates: "I am fully convinced that somewhere between March 21st, 1843 and March 21st, 1844, according to the Jewish mode of time computation, Christ will come."

1844
In March, Miller states, "If this chronology is not correct, I shall despair of getting from the Bible and history a true account of the age of the world." In May, Miller writes "I confess my error and acknowledge my disappointment." Most followers, however, do not leave the "Millerite" movement. One of Miller's adventist followers, Samuel S. Snow, revises Miller's timetable and places Jesus' second coming at October 22, 1844. Miller eventually accepts and promotes the revised date. When the October 22 prophecy fails, the date becomes known as "The Great Disappointment." Miller retires from active leadership; the movement falls into confusion; and numerous adventist factions break off from the movement. One faction also begins holding to the additional belief that the seventh-day Sabbath should be observed. Members of this group come to be known as "seventh-day" adventists.

1849
William Miller dies.

1860
The name "Seventh-day Adventist" is officially adopted by the denomination.

1915
Ellen G. White dies.

1918
Victor Houteff, a Bulgarian immigrant, joins the Seventh-day Adventist church.

c. 1929–1930
Houteff begins teaching doctrines that eventually get him expelled from the Los Angeles Seventh-day Adventist church of which he is a member. Despite his ousting from the church, Houteff continues to preach his message and gain additional followers.

c. 1930–1932

Houteff publishes his views in *The Shepherd's Rod Vol. 1* and *The Shepherd's Rod Vol. 2*. He and his followers come to be known as the "Shepherd's Rod Seventh-day Adventists."

1935

Houteff and some of his followers set up headquarters at Mt. Carmel, Texas, on the outskirts of Waco.

1942

Houteff's group changes its name to the "Davidian Seventh-day Adventists."

1942–1954

The Davidians target their evangelistic efforts at the Seventh-day Adventist denomination.

1955

Victor Houteff dies, leaving his wife, Florence, in charge. Almost immediately she gives a three-and-a-half-year prophecy: God's earthly kingdom will be established on April 22, 1959. She also issues a call for all faithful Davidians to gather during the week prior to the endtime occurrence. One follower, Benjamin Roden, disagrees with Florence and asserts that the establishment of God's kingdom will occur in 1960 rather than 1959.

1955–1959

Roden claims that he is the one who should fill Victor Houteff's shoes as leader of the Davidians. Consequently, he launches a letter-writing campaign to convince Seventh-day Adventists and Davidians of his views.

1959

Florence Houteff's prophecy fails. Numerous factions break off from the once unified body of Davidians. The largest faction is led by Benjamin Roden, who has made himself rather well-known to Davidians through his letters. He names his following the "Branch Davidians."

August 17, 1959

Vernon Wayne Howell is born.

1960

Ben Roden starts back-pedaling on his belief that the end will come in 1960. He changes his previously published chronological timelines, editing out what he had predicted.

1962

Ben Roden and his followers legally obtain Houteff's Mt. Carmel property.

1962–1977

Roden adds various doctrines to Houteff's teachings.

1977

Ben's wife, Lois Roden, has a vision in which she claims to have seen the Holy Spirit. Lois reveals she learned from the vision that the Holy Spirit is female.

1978

Ben Roden dies and Lois takes over as the head of the Branch Davidians.

1979

Howell is baptized into the Tyler Seventh-day Adventist church.

1981

Howell joins the Branch Davidians.

1983

Howell gets his "message" and begins his live-in relationship with Lois Roden. His authority and influence start to grow.

1984

Twenty-four-year-old Howell weds fourteen-year-old Rachel Jones. After a heated conflict with Lois Roden's son, George, Howell is forced out of Mt. Carmel with his wife. They move to Waco.

1985–1986

"Branches" (members of the group) begin to forsake Lois Roden and move away from Mt. Carmel to live under Howell's leadership. Howell eventually acquires some property in Palestine, Texas, where he and his followers settle. Conflict between the Rodens and Howell continue.

January 1986

Australian Marc Breault joins the Branch Davidians.

March 1986

Howell takes thirteen-year-old Karen Doyle as his second "wife."

August 1986

Howell secretly takes twelve-year-old Michelle Jones (Rachel's little sister) as his third "wife."

Late 1986

Howell teaches that he is entitled to have at least 140 wives.

Early 1987

Seventeen-year-old Robyn Bunds becomes Howell's fourth "wife."

August 1987

Diana Ishikawa (pseudonym) becomes Howell's sixth "wife."

November 1987

Howell and eight of his male followers are arrested for attempted murder after being involved in a shoot-out with George Roden at Mt. Carmel.

December 1987

Ishikawa (pseudonym) becomes the first of Howell's Song of Solomon "wives" to become pregnant.

April 1988

Howell and the eight others tried for attempted murder are set free. Within a few months, all the Branch Davidians move back to Mt. Carmel with Howell as their leader.

1988–1989

Howell continues to take more "wives."

August 5, 1989

Howell teaches the "new light" doctrine of 1989 while staying in the Pomona, California home of Donald and Jeanine Bunds. The "new light" makes Howell the rightful husband of all women in the group, including those who are married. Husbands and wives are separated and the wives become part of Howell's harem.

August–September 1989

Marc Breault and his wife, Elizabeth, leave the group and begin a letter-writing campaign to alert their friends to the fact that Howell is a false teacher.

1989–1990

Most of the Australian and New Zealand members break away from Howell.

Spring 1990

Vernon Howell changes his name to David Koresh.

c. June–August 1990

Robyn Bunds leaves Koresh.

September–December 1990

Koresh's temperament increasingly becomes more volatile and his behavior irrational. He begins requiring members to watch violent war movies on a regular basis.

1990–1991

Several local law enforcement authorities from Texas, California, and Michigan start to take serious note of Koresh and the Davidians due to reports by ex-members and numerous investigations.

1991

Diana Ishikawa (pseudonym) breaks away from Koresh.

February 1992

David Jewell obtains custody of his eleven-year-old daughter, Kiri, who is removed from the group.

May 1992

The *Waco Tribune-Herald* begins an in-depth investigation into Koresh and his followers.

May–June 1992

The Bureau of Alcohol, Tobacco, and Firearms (ATF) launches its investigation of Koresh and the Davidians.

February 27, 1993

The *Waco-Tribune Herald* begins its seven-part investigative news story on Koresh and his group.

February 28, 1993

The ATF launches a massive raid on the Davidian compound. Six Davidians die and four ATF agents are killed. Numerous individuals on both sides are injured.

March 1–April 18, 1993

Of the approximately one hundred Branch Davidians present in the compound on February 28, approximately fourteen adults and twenty one children leave.

April 19, 1993

FBI agents attempt to end the siege by using tear gas, but the compound erupts into flames. Between seventy-five and eighty-five Davidians die in the flames, including approximately twenty-five children. Nine members survive.

April 22, 1993

The possible remains of David Koresh are pulled from the ashes of the Davidian compound.

May 2, 1993

Koresh's charred body—lying next to his top lieutenant, Steve Schneider—is officially identified using dental records. Medical examiners cite a gunshot wound to the forehead as the likely cause of Koresh's death.

May 27, 1993

Koresh is laid to rest during a small ceremony held by his mother, Bonnie. His remains are buried in an unmarked grave. Only his mother, step-father, brother, and maternal grandmother are in attendance.

July 1993–present

A handful of Koreshians remain alive. Eleven of them will face trial on a variety of charges. They are like sheep without a shepherd and view the current situation as a time when they are to be scattered. They do not expect a new leader to take over Koresh's place. Instead, they continue to wait for the day when Koresh and the rest of the Davidians will return in glory to execute judgment on the earth for what has taken place. As one faithful follower put it, "They'll be back. They'll all be back."

Our Lives Were Forever Changed:
Interviews with Those Who Personally Knew David Koresh

During the Waco siege (February 28–April 19, 1993) and in the weeks following the Davidians' fiery end, Richard Abanes conducted a series of interviews with individuals acquainted with Koresh. The following are transcripts of some of those interviews.

Bonnie Haldeman is the mother of David Koresh. She spoke with Richard Abanes on March 28, 1993, and April 6, 1993. The following is a condensed and edited version of those interviews.

Richard　I only have a few questions, Bonnie.

Bonnie　I am not supposed to be talkin' to anybody. This is from the attorney's recommendation.

Richard　I don't really want to get too much involved in what's happening now because I understand your position.

Bonnie　Okay.

Richard　What do you think of all the wives that Vernon supposedly has? What do you think of all the young girls as young as eleven and twelve years old that he is allegedly having sex with, and producing children with?

Bonnie　I would say it is allegedly. I do know that there are several wives, other ones that he has.

Richard　Do you believe that he is having sex with young girls and also the married women of the commune?

Bonnie　Well, the only women that I have seen that have children by him are not young girls, they're of age. But I have not, other than a few times in the last few months, visited there in two years. Having sex, I think with ten-, eleven-, twelve-year-old girls is just totally obnoxious. I think, I think it's lies.

Richard　How do you feel about him even having more than one wife? Do you believe it coincides with being inspired of God?

Bonnie　It bothered me at first. But the Mormons, a lot of Mormons [pause]. Isn't it the Mormons that have more than one wife?

Richard Those are the fundamentalist Mormons.

Bonnie Yeah. I'm not sayin' it's the ideal situation, but [pauses and laughs] you know, I, I, I, I, [laughs]. Ah, [silence]

Richard You've seen it before?

Bonnie I've seen it all over. So, hey, who am I to say well it's, it's you know, it's not ah, [extremely long pause] I, I, I don't know, I have mixed feelings on it.

Richard Let me ask you this: What do you think Vernon is trying to say to the world by staying in the compound and refusing to come out to the law enforcement authorities?

Bonnie To get his message out I think is the main thing he wants to do. And they're not gonna let him do it. I see a lot of things that are totally wrong and I don't think the tactics they're using are right. My husband has offered to go in, and several people have offered to go in that might be able to do some good and the FBI won't even consider it. Whether that's right, or whether that's wrong, I don't know. I'm no expert. But my own personal feelings is, why don't they let someone else go in and talk to him? Let somebody that's completely neutral go in?

Richard Do you think Vernon and his followers are dangerous because of all of the guns that they have?

Bonnie No, I don't. I don't think [long pause], I don't think there should have been any blood shed at all to start with if the situation would have been handled right.

Richard Do you feel that perhaps some of the charges of child abuse—like beating children until their their bottoms are bloody—are not true?

Bonnie I have never seen that. I have seen him discipline these children.

Richard How so?

Bonnie I've seen him and his wives discipline them in different ways, discipline their children in what I feel like is a very, very

correct manner because I did everything wrong.

Richard Can you give me some examples of the correct ways that you've seen him and his wives discipline their children?

Bonnie Well, when a child did somethin' wrong they didn't get beatings, they didn't necessarily get spanked all the time. But they did spank their children. They'd put 'em across their knees, with a little wooden paddle and spank 'em on their bottom, and say, "Okay, this is what you're being spanked for."

Richard Would you consider Vernon to have been a spoiled child?

Bonnie No, I spanked Vernon, but I did everything wrong. I didn't do it right. I let my emotions, you know, get away with me. I hollered all the time, and a lot of times I spanked out of anger, and that's wrong. You should never spank out of anger.

Richard Why did he drop out of the ninth grade?

Bonnie Well, he, he ah, I thought, I thought he started in the tenth, but I may be wrong.

Richard Why didn't he finish ?

Bonnie [pause] I really don't remember. [long pause] I don't remember. I remember him goin' to school and runnin' track, and I guess he wanted to get out and go to, ah [pause] I, I really don't remember why he quit. I remember he got a job with my husband in construction, and he worked with my dad some, but ah, I, I really honestly don't remember. Isn't that terrible?

Richard Well, it was a long time ago. Bonnie, do you have any pictures we could use for our book?

Bonnie I don't know if I'll give you any pictures or not. . . . I might wanna write a book myself. I don't want this to sound commercial or anything—I'm a nurse, my husband's retired, we don't have any money. I hope this comes out to a good situation, but if there's some way I could make some money to help my grandkids. Cause I know he's gonna be locked up for a long time if he come out of this alive. And that's positive, the way I'm hopin' to think. It could go the other way, but why should I give everything away if them kids are gonna need some means of being raised?

Richard   Sure, I understand.

Bonnie   I hope and pray that they just all, every one of 'em come out of there alive, but still the main thing that goes through my head is God is in control of everything. I hope and pray that he is guiding whatever's happenin' and that everything will come out okay.

Richard   Did you always believe Vernon's message, or was there a time when you wouldn't accept it, and you kind of were at odds with him?

Bonnie   [extremely long pause] Well, uhm [pause], that's a hard question. There are some things that, you know, I had trouble accepting. Just little things, but just a combination of things too you know.

Richard   Can give me an example?

Bonnie   [extremely long pause] Not really, not right now. Like I say, I don't want to say too much because ah, I just wanna wait 'til all this is over with. I may talk to ya after that.

Richard   Do you believe that your son is a prophet of God?

Bonnie   I did. I really did, for several years. But like I said the last couple years I've had, you know, I've had, uhm, my doubts, misgivings, and confusion. I would like to see it turn out the way he says it is for all their sakes. I sure don't want to see 'em wrong. You know, I've got a lot invested in this. Got my son, my grandkids, my daughter-in-law, plus I have a lot of friends there. A lot of people I don't know too well, but I do have some really good friends in there. And I'm very close to 'em you know. And his father-in-law was killed, and I found out about it on TV and it just, it crushed me. So I mean, hope for all their sakes

that God's with 'em and takin' care of 'em.

Richard   Bonnie, I thank you so very much.

Bonnie   Mmm hmm.

Richard   Take care now.

Bonnie   Okay, bye-bye.

Bobby Howell is the father of David Koresh. He was interviewed by Richard Abanes on April 25, 1993, via telephone. Like Haldeman, Howell was advised by his attorney to not speak with anyone. But he, too, eventually consented to grant an interview. Some very interesting details surfaced about Vernon and gun-running activities.

Richard   Hi, Bobby. My name is Richard Abanes. I just want to talk to you for a few moments if you have the time, to ask you some questions?

Bobby.   Okay.

Richard   Do you have any thoughts at all about, you know, what's been going on recently? Something you want to share with the world basically, any kind of words of expressing your feelings or anything like that?

Bobby   Well, all I can say is fear the government.

Richard   Fear the government?

Bobby   Yes. I mean that was a botched situation in the beginning and a lot of innocent people died. But they're claimin' it's [pause] they're puttin' out a lot of lies about it.

Richard   Do you know personally any of those "lies" that have been put out? Or, do you just feel that maybe that's the case?

Bobby   I just feel like that's not the case. I wasn't up there. Last year when last I talked to him we had a long discussion about what he was doing up there.

Richard   I'm sure you probably saw the [Waco] *Tribune-Herald* article on Vernon that talked about his underage wives and things. Do you believe all of that?

Bobby Well, I thought some of it was true. I don't know about underage, but I know that he had a lot of wives. There's been too many confirmed stories. If that's his belief, I guess if they're not underage, I don't know. Like the Mormons, they have several wives. Violatin' the laws of the country, you know. Maybe they thought he was livin' under, livin' under a different law I guess. This last year he came down and I told him I says, "I want to talk about you and I don't want to talk religion." So we had a discussion about what he was doin' up there and he was restorin' some classic cars and things like that.

Richard Did he mention anything about the guns or anything that he had bought?

Bobby Well, he told me he bought three AK-47s. That's what he was down for. The gun show, him and Steve Schneider. They stopped by my mother's. We all went out to eat and he was tellin' us about the guns he was buyin'.

Richard He got three AK-47s that day?

Bobby At the gun show.

Richard Did he mention any other stuff he had acquired?

Bobby No, he told me he was buyin' guns and takin' 'em to California and doublin' his money on 'em.

Richard I'm sorry?

Bobby He told me he was buyin' the guns and takin' 'em out to California and doublin' his money.

Richard He used to do the same thing with sound equipment.

Bobby Yeah.

Richard Do you know about how many times he came out to California to sell those guns?

Bobby Oh, we didn't discuss it, but that's just what he told me.

Richard Was that the plans he had for these particular AK-47s?

Bobby That's what he said.

Richard Okay. Thank you for your time Bobby, I really appreciate it.

Bobby All right. Bye.

Lynn Ray is a Tyler Seventh-day Adventist church elder. He was present when Koresh was baptized into the church in 1979. Elder Ray was interviewed by Richard Abanes on March 28, 1993, and May 2, 1993.

Richard When did you personally meet Vernon Howell for the first time?

Lynn In 1979.

Richard What was his personality like?

Lynn He liked to be the center of things.

Richard I spoke with another member of the church, a Bob Jinks, and he mentioned to me that Vernon was somewhat disruptive. Can you comment on that?

Lynn Yes, he was. He was disruptive in the organized meetings and he would encourage the young people to stay out of church and talk to him, and he would try to indoctrinate them in doctrines different than the mainline Seventh-day Adventist church.

Richard Do you feel that the Seventh-day Adventists' view of Ellen G. White as a prophet influenced Vernon into believing that there needed to be a succession of living prophets following Ellen G. White leading up to today?

Lynn I'm sure that it did because it wasn't long after he left Tyler that he started telling people that he was a prophet.

Richard How does his view of a line of succession of prophets following E. G. White differ from that of the mainline Seventh-day Adventist denomination?

Lynn We as Seventh-day Adventists are open to prophecy, but we have a test of prophecy and prophets. If they don't meet certain qualifications, we don't accept them as prophets.

Richard What would those qualifications be?

Lynn Well, we take our understanding of a prophet from the tests that were made on Daniel when he was in a trance. And being inspired by the Lord and also John the Revelator. They had no strength of their own, they didn't breath

Richard at all during the time that they were in a vision.

Richard Is there any room in the Seventh-day Adventist denomination for some kind of a successor to E. G. White? To become, in other words, the prophet of the Seventh-day Adventists?

Lynn We don't expect that to happen.

Richard Do you believe that the tendency of Seventh-day Adventists to concentrate a great deal on the prophetic somehow influenced Vernon Howell to be consumed with a lot of prophetic passages of Scripture?

Lynn Probably so. We do delve a great deal into prophecies as they relate to the time in which we live and of the end of the world. Now Vernon decided that he was going to put time to prophetic utterances including his own and he has caused himself and a lot of other people a lot of trouble.

Richard From what I understand, the Adventist church usually tries to keep a pretty tight rein on the doctrinal beliefs of its members. I was told by Bonnie [Koresh's mother] that it was a Harriet Phelps who introduced Vernon to the Branch Davidians because Harriet subscribed to many Davidian beliefs such as the Holy Spirit being a female.

Lynn Yes.

Richard Given those types of beliefs that are held by Harriet Phelps, would she be considered an Adventist in good standing? I mean, having gone so far away from what I understand to be Adventist doctrine?

Lynn Well, she attends church every week. I personally don't consider her a member in good standing of the church, but of course, she says I'm critical and don't know what I'm talking about.

Richard Bonnie told me that there was, for lack of a better expression, "an underground group" within the Tyler church that holds to Branch Davidian-like doctrines.

Lynn Yes.

Richard Would it not be prudent for the leadership to weed out these members as possible instigators of false doctrine? Isn't that how the Adventist church works?

Lynn The Adventist church doesn't work that way. Anyone that basically subscribes to the beliefs of the church are given a certain amount of freedom to disagree without any action from the church body.

Richard You said anyone who "basically subscribes to the beliefs of the church." What would be those beliefs be if they don't include, for example, a correct view of the Godhead or a correct view of the personality of the Holy Spirit? What doctrines would be more important than those doctrines?

Lynn Well, first of all, we would disfellowship someone who used alcohol, or tobacco, or drugs. We would disfellowship those people. If someone took a job to work on Saturday, which is our Sabbath, we would disfellowship someone for that.

Richard So what you're saying is that, to the Adventist it would be more important for an individual—who is a member of their church—to not work a secular job on the Sabbath, than it would be for that individual to have a correct view of the very Godhead that they are supposedly worshiping?

Lynn Well, you know, ah [pause]

Richard I'm confused. I, for example, could hold to not working on the Sabbath and be right on the money there, and yet feel that the Godhead is a foursome that has four heads and two horns. You see what I'm saying?

Lynn Yes.

Richard So where does the doctrinal aspect of whom you're worshiping come into play?

Lynn Well, of course, when you become a member of the Adventist church there are twenty-seven basic beliefs that we ask the people, "Do you agree with this, do you agree with this, and so forth."

And they have to answer affirmative to be taken into the church. After they become a member of the church, if they want to vary a little bit on their assent to these beliefs, we're not looking to disfellowship anybody. When we disfellowshipped Vernon, he had broken too many rules to be kept in the church.

Richard   All right Mr. Ray, I think that should be it.

Lynn   Okay, I wish you success.

Richard   Thank you very much for your time.

Lynn   Thank you for calling.

Sue Johnson is the sister of Steve Schneider, Koresh's right hand-man who handled most of the negotiations between Koresh and the FBI during the Waco siege. Schneider's charred body was found next to Koresh in the ruins of the Davidian compound. Schneider died from a bullet to the head. Conflicting autopsy reports put the bullet's point of entry at either the back of the neck, the back of the head, or under the chin. The final answer to *exactly* how, or who, shot Schneider may never be known. Richard Abanes interviewed Steve's sister on April 21, 1993, and May 20, 1993. What follows are edited and condensed highlights of those two interviews.

Richard   Sue, do you think the Davidians committed suicide?

Sue   No, I don't. David [Thibodeau, a survivor] told me the last thing he heard Vernon say was "We're gonna try to get this thing worked out and we're gonna try to get the communications going again." And he said, "Don't worry, we're gonna get it worked out." Does that sound like somebody who was planning on committing suicide?

Richard   David [Thibodeau] said he actually heard Vernon saying this?

Sue   Yes. That's the last thing he heard Vernon say.

Richard   So, David [Thibodeau] maintains that it was just an accident?

Sue   Yeah. In fact, Belinda [Thibodeau's mother] told me that no way would they ever commit suicide because Vernon taught that it was a sin to commit suicide. My brother told me on the phone, "Do not worry about us committing suicide, we'd never do that." They would never have gone through six, seven years of hell, gave up everything to end up committing suicide. It was never part of the prophecies. David Thibodeau told me they were all planning on coming out. And they were very excited about coming out.

Richard   When were they planning on coming out?

Sue   I don't know, he said they were very close to having the manuscript done. He said it was really close to being done. Steve talked to Zimmerman [Steve's lawyer] on the phone a few days before [the end]. He said to Zimmerman on the phone, "Should I have someone cut my hair before I come out, or should I wait and let them do it in the jail?" My brother was the type that always worried about how he looked. If he wasn't planning on coming out, he wouldn't have asked that question.

Richard   Why did some of the cult members leave and others not leave?

Sue   According to Dave [Thibodeau] there was a bunch of them that was going to leave, and they [the FBI] started using those tactics and everybody got scared and chickened out and changed their minds.

Richard   So, a big group of them were going to leave in a few days?

Sue   Yeah. Dave Thibideau said that the day before the fire there were about twenty that started talking about wanting to leave. And another thing I was told was that they all had planned if things got really bad they were gonna let the kids go out. They were gonna send the rest of the kids out if things looked bad.

Richard   You were pretty tight with Steve?

Sue   Yeah.

Richard   Why did Steve give Judy over to Koresh?

Sue   I don't think he did that very easily. Everybody tells me that Vernon was especially hard on Steve and Judy because a lot of people looked up to them. A lot of people stayed in because of them. Everybody made Steve out to be this intelligent theologian who knew a lot about the Bible and could make sense out of it. Koresh never left Steve alone, or out of his sight. He never let Steve and Judy go anywhere by themselves. People constantly had to be with them. They never had an opportunity to leave or anything.

Richard   Did you talk to Steve about it?

Sue   Steve denied it.

Richard   Steve denied that he had given Judy to Koresh?

Sue   Yeah. When I asked him about it a year ago. But then, in some ways he admitted it, but he still didn't come right out and admit it. He would just talk about what was in the Bible. He would say it was in the Bible.

Richard   He gave you Bible verses he felt supported it, but without admitting it?

Sue   Yeah. He never would come right out and say he and Judy were like that.

Richard   Both you and your brother were raised Seventh-day Adventists?

Sue   Right. We were all into that strong type of Ellen White stuff.

Richard   Prophecy?

Sue   Yeah. Steve was so into prophecy and Ellen White. And when he met Marc Breault, Marc was into all that prophecy too.

Richard   Why was Steve so into prophecy? What was the great emotional attraction to prophecy? Why did the whole prophecy subject appeal to Steve emotionally?

Sue   Vernon brought this all out by saying the end was just right around the corner. When we met him, he was claiming "this is it." It was all going to be over in six months to a year. There are so many people that just constantly go on and on. Everything that happens in the world means the world is about ready to come to an end because every little thing is related to "the end" somehow or another. Some people are almost paranoid because of it. I was told as a kid by Adventists that I'd probably never grow up cause the world's gonna come to the end before that.

Richard   And Steve wanted to be right with God before the end happened?

Sue   Right. He wanted to be a part of all that. He thought this was it. And see, they worked extra hard on Steve. He was an intelligent guy that had a lot of training and liked to study the Bible. And also, our background is in selling. So, Steve knew how to not only present himself, but how to sell anything.

Richard   He was a good salesman?

Sue   Yeah. So, you combine his selling abilities with his knowledge of the Bible, and his interest in prophecy. He had a real dynamic personality, real easy to talk to, outgoing, and just enjoyed studying with people—the whole thing all fit together.

Richard   If he knew so much about the Bible, how did he become so deceived by Vernon?

Sue   I think it was just because Vernon was a very good manipulator. One of Steve's good friends—who studied with Vernon and almost got caught up in it—claimed that Vernon would kind of study a person and find out where your weaknesses were, and what you liked, and what you were interested in, and then he would use that. Like for instance, Steve's friend was a pilot, and so Vernon used that. Vernon said, "Well, if you join the group. I'll buy a plane and you can be my personal pilot." And like he'd fly him all over. Vernon found something for everybody that they liked and he used it. Steve wanted to be an evangelist and Vernon talked like Steve was going to be an evangelist for him. Vernon kind of used all these different things on different people.

Richard He found your weak spot and then he capitalized on it?

Sue Yeah. Plus he really knew how to manipulate people. Steve was a person who would sit up hour after hour and study the Bible. And Vernon had Steve go for days and days without any sleep studying the Bible with him.

Richard So you think Steve really believed everything?

Sue Yeah, I do. I asked him a couple of times and he said, "If anybody could prove to me that this isn't in the Bible, I'd leave." And we didn't know how to disprove it. And Ruth Mosher said her daughter [Sherri Jewell] would say that to her all the time, and she looked all over for scholars trying to find somebody who could disprove it and no one could. Does anybody else know how Steve got into this thing under Vernon?

Richard Just what you said about how he was interested in prophecy, met Marc, and went down to Texas. David Bunds was the one who went and picked Steve up from the airport.

Sue Yeah, Steve was so excited about meeting a prophet. Oh, I'm telling you it just makes me [pauses]. My brother was such a different person before he got into this. I've been thinking about this, and thinking about this, and his biggest weakness was just believing in a prophet. I mean, [pause] I mean he was not the kind of person that got totally hung up on one thing like this either. He enjoyed so many things in life. He just loved backpacking, and mountain climbing, and he loved nature, and he was into photography, and he loved snorkeling. He had so many interests.

He was never just caught up in one thing like how he got into this.

Richard Just because he wanted a prophet?

Sue Yeah. Marc convinced him about all these visions, and then through listening to all these hours of studies he got convinced that this stupid Vernon was a prophet. It's just so terrible, he was so close to the family. And to give up the family was such a torturous thing for him. Because he just loved the family.

Richard When you say he had to give up the family, what do you mean?

Sue Well, Vernon forced everybody to give up their families because he didn't want them to have any emotional attachments. He was worried they'd leave. Vernon made us out to be enemies because we wouldn't accept his message.

Richard Did Steve cut ties with you?

Sue Yeah, pretty much. But he always did somehow stay in touch. Now and then we'd hear from him. And if we didn't call him on Christmas, he was almost devastated.

Richard He wanted to be with you, but couldn't?

Sue Yeah, that's how it was. In fact, when I talked to him at Christmas just this last year he told me it was like torture being away from the family. He said, as much as he knew he had to give it up, it was the hardest thing for him being away from the family, especially on the holidays. He was really depressed. It was terrible. Before he got into this he was the type of person who would call me up all the time, and say, "Hey, what are you doing." When he was in town he'd just pop in and say let's go here, let's go there. He was always [pause] doing stuff and [pause]. This was just not like him at all.

Richard Why did it happen to him?

Sue I don't know [long pause]. I think the big thing was fear. He was convinced that Vernon had all the knowledge and could interpret the Bible. Vernon had given these people so much fear through the Bible, and if they didn't stick with his message they were lost. He'd say they were going to burn forever if they left. And that's what kept him in it—fear. They had so much fear, it was just incredible. Everybody that I've talked to said that was the main reason why they stayed in it. They hated it. And the only reason they stayed was the fear of being lost. That was the main thing. Everyone just hated it. That lifestyle and living like that. Steve told us he was tormented [pause]. He felt tormented. He was afraid to leave. In fact, he said to my parents—just before this happened—he said to my parents, "If only this wasn't true, I'd take Judy and go back to Hawaii." He said, "There's nothing I'd rather do than have Judy and be living back in Hawaii."

Richard Did they think God wanted them to suffer like that?

Sue That's what I even said to Steve, "What kind of God would that be if he wanted you to be so miserable?" And he said, "Well, you know, we are looking forward to something better. We're going to have our reward later." So they thought they were going to get quite a reward for giving up everything. I think, too, that these people who claim to be these messiahs create paranoia. They make them afraid of all kinds of things. They make it seem like, how are members ever going to live on their own. They give up everything, so if they leave, they have nothing. So, they can hardly just walk out the door.

Richard When was the last time you spoke with Steve?

Sue During the siege.

Richard When they used their cellular phone without the FBI's knowledge?

Sue Right. And then, before that I spoke to him out in California around the 1st of February or the end of January, about a month before the shoot-out.

Richard Did he mention anything significant?

Sue The only thing he said was when I asked him if he had any doubts. And he said he did. I asked him, "Why don't you leave for a while and think about it?" He said to me that he and Judy had discussed it and decided to stick with it and that they were just going to take it one day at a time, and that they were going to stick with it for now.

Richard What did he say during the siege?

Sue That was hard because their batteries were going dead. He said we didn't have much time and he was trying to talk really fast. He basically told me that [pause]. See, I'm not supposed to even be telling any of this. The lawyer we hired for Steve doesn't want us to give this information out yet.

Richard What would be significant about that?

Sue I don't know. The best conversation was two calls in one night. The first one was the one where he told me he didn't trust the FBI. That they were lying and that they wanted to get them killed and stuff like that. He also told me, "Don't worry, we are not planning on committing suicide." And I asked him if they were coming out. He said only Vernon knew the answer because only he knew the seven seals. He also told me he believed now more than ever in Vernon because every single thing that Vernon had predicted was coming true.

Richard What happens now, Sue?

Sue I don't know. My parents are in so much pain over this. My dad is just taking it terrible. He's just devastated, so is my mother. They just [pause]. It's just terrible, I don't think they'll ever get over it. And then, today they came out in the news claiming that Steve shot Vernon and himself.

Richard They're saying Steve shot Vernon?

Sue Yeah, but I can't imagine Steve shooting. Steve always hated guns. He never liked anything to do with guns. Even during the shoot-out, he told Zimmerman that he wasn't one of them shooting. And Marc Breault even told me before this happened that if there was ever a shoot-out, Steve would not be one of them involved in it. He never cared for guns or shooting.

Richard If you could say one thing to help people, what would it be?

Sue Don't follow people. Don't put all your faith in one person interpreting the Bible and just believing that somebody's a prophet. Always check them out. Never just follow somebody and let them use fear because they say "the end is coming." You have to check them out. Check out what their life has been like.

Richard I appreciate all your help, Sue.

Sue Okay. Good luck with your book.

Richard Thank you, Sue. Take care now.

Sue Okay, bye.

Diana Ishikawa (pseudonym), an ex-Branch Davidian, agreed to be interviewed on May 30, 1993, by Richard Abanes. She was Koresh's sixth "wife" and requested the use of a pseudonym in order to protect the identity of her two children who were fathered by Koresh. She was the first of Koresh's multiple "wives" to become pregnant.

Richard When did you first get involved with Koresh and how old were you?

Diana I was twenty years old. It was in early August of 1986.

Richard How did you hook up with the Branch Davidians?

Diana Steve Schneider was a good friend of mine, and he was a good friend of Marc Breault's.

Richard Marc got Steve involved, and then Steve got you involved?

Diana Right. First, there was this controversy in the church which peaked my curiosity. I couldn't get straight answers from anybody. I would just hear stuff like, "Oh, they're saying weird things." And I'd say, "Well, what kind of weird things?" And they'd say, "I don't know, but they're wrong."

Richard So, you got interested in who this Koresh was?

Diana I wanted to find out for myself what this man was saying that caused so much controversy and anger in people.

Richard Did you hook up with a Bible study they were having in Hawaii?

Diana Yes. That was how I got started. First, through Marc Breault. I only went to a couple of the ones Marc had, and then Vernon came to Hawaii and I attended some of his studies.

Richard And you believed what he was saying?

Diana Yes.

Richard Why?

Diana It was straight from the Bible. It made sense.

Richard Did being a Seventh-day Adventist prepare you in any way for his teachings?

Diana Oh yes. Definitely.

Richard How?

Diana Adventists believe heavily in prophecy. Adventists continually study prophecy.

Richard Did he mention Ellen G. White at all?

Diana Yes. He was very, very heavily into many quotes that Ellen made: she said there would be an Elijah who would come to prepare the church for the second coming of Christ; that the church would need to be cleansed; that it was as Babylon. It matched up with what was happening at the time. The Adventists had just had some scandal with stocks or something, some kind of investment. He would point to the corruption in the church at all levels, and you could look around and see it in all the churches.

Richard When you first met Vernon, what about him made you think that he—out of all the people in the world—was the one who had the truth?

Diana He was really intense. When he spoke there was kind of a spirit in the room. It was kind of like having a religious conversion experience all over again. He inspired these feelings in people very easily, especially by going through the Scriptures the way he did. He went through it so rapidly you would catch certain key phrases and ideas in your head and those were the ones that would stick. And then, he'd take that idea and go off onto another thing and keep bringing you back like an ever winding spiral.

Richard In a way, then, it was not exactly *what* he was saying, but *how* he was saying it?

Diana Yeah.

Richard Was it the emotional feelings and excitement that you felt while listening to him that caused you to think, "This has got to be a prophet"?

Diana The timing was right for me, too. I was kind of in a transition because I had decided that I did not want to be a doctor anymore and I was left wondering, "What am I going to do with my life now?" He came just at the right time.

Richard So, you were kind of lost and looking for somewhere to go in life?

Diana Right. And here was a man with answers that were deeper than the ones that I was looking at. We're talking spirituality here.

Richard When you moved to Texas what year was that?

Diana I went down to Palestine in January of '87.

Richard He already had more than one wife at that point.

Diana Right.

Richard How did you view his polygamy?

Diana When I first went over there I did not know. Someone came up to me the first night I was there and said, "Hey, guess what, Vernon's got two wives and he's gonna have a whole lot more," which freaked me out completely. But I had already gone through so much. My family had been ripped apart. I'd gone through so much just to get that far. I decided, "Wait, I'll just listen and see what happens. Hear what the man has to say"—because it might not have been right what this other guy was telling me. So, I stayed [pause]. I

wanted to leave the first night I got there when I heard that, but I decided I'll hear him out. And so, he went into this doctrine with the Song of Solomon which said that he would have basically 140 wives. And I was still kind of in shock, but I thought, "Well, if it has some kind of biblical basis I'll listen to what he has to say." That's basically why I stayed. The whole time that I stayed, whenever a doubt came into my mind I'd tell myself, "Wait, and listen to what he has to say."

Richard Through his Bible teaching, then, he convinced you that it was legitimate that he had more than one wife?

Diana Right.

Richard When he started building up the House of David, how did that make you feel?

Diana Since it didn't directly concern me, for a while it didn't bother me. It wasn't public knowledge exactly who these women were—or girls, I should say. I didn't really find out who all was involved until I became involved myself.

Richard Did you want to become part of the House of David before he actually took you?

Diana In theory yes. In actuality, to me it wasn't the most thrilling thing in the world to have to do what I knew I'd have to do and to then share someone with a bunch of other women.

Richard When you say "in theory" you wanted to be part of the House of David, was that because of its spiritual significance?

Diana Right.

Richard What was the spiritual significance of being part of the House of David?

Diana He had a doctrine known as the Bride of Christ in which Christ would be on earth to marry a human woman and have a family with her and they would be together forever because he wasn't able to do that the first time he was here.

Richard And how did that fit in with marrying Koresh?

Diana It would be one of the women he had.

Richard How would she be chosen?

Diana She would be the one from whom he gained the most comfort. The one who would be spiritual. Someone who could see what he was trying to do and understand it, who wouldn't get caught up in all the petty jealousies of daily living, someone who he could depend on.

Richard This was before he taught that he was Christ so basically he taught that he would give that woman over to Christ?

Diana Right. In other words, she had her training ground with Koresh. When you were with him you were learning the sorrows of life and you would eventually become the woman in Proverbs 31.

Richard And you really believed this?

Diana I had a lot of trouble making connections, but because this Bride of Christ doctrine was so tied up in a lot of his other doctrines it was really easy to see yourself in those prophecies.

Richard And that brought you what? I mean, emotionally.

Diana It brought a lot of satisfaction. It was a very spiritual high.

Richard How did you become involved yourself? When, and how did that happen?

Diana In August of '87. See, he had a thing where races did not intermarry with each other. I'm Japanese. And so, I would constantly ask him, "Well, what does this mean for other women of other races?" He kept saying, "I don't know, I don't know." Then, he came up with a prophecy in Isaiah where the Lamb goes to Moab and the daughters of Moab meet him. He took that to mean that they would become the Lamb's wives too. That was his justification for interracial marriages. I was the first one of an outside race that he took.

Richard Before you joined the House of David, were you in love with Koresh? Or, was it just this whole spirituality that drove you to want to be with him sexually?

Diana I was not in love with him. And I don't think he was very attracted to me either. But the spiritual part of it, the ideology behind it was beautiful to me. I accepted that part. I really didn't concentrate on what I was doing here and now, it was more on the hereafter.

Richard This is difficult for me to understand.

Diana Well, it was difficult for *me*. It wasn't a firm decision in my mind—ever. When the time came where he actually did "call me," I was very nervous. I didn't know if this is what I wanted to do. I kept thinking, "This is only a test. This is not real."

Richard How did he call you?

Diana I use to rub his back for him because I was into massage therapy and I'd walk on his back for him. And basically during those times he had Novelette there.

Diana Novelette Sinclair?

Richard Right, he had her there. We'd do the massages in her bus. She was the chaperone. The impact of what he was teaching [about the daughters of Moab] came up one night, and it was implied very heavily that I was being issued an invitation to become part of the House of David. Of course, this was while Novelette was still there. I remember one night he was doing my neck and all of a sudden he started to touch my face in a very intimate way which made me very uncomfortable. Even Novelette saw that. And that was the night it became clear to me what he was saying. I remember asking him, "Do you mean that the House of David is also open to other women?" He would bring me back to that study on the daughters of Moab which meant "yes." So I went home that night feeling very much in the state of shock and knowing that pretty much my turn was about to come if I wanted that. And I had to decide really soon.

Richard	What made you finally decide, "I want to be in the House of David"?
Diana	I thought that's what God wanted me to do.
Richard	How did you come to think that's what God wanted? Did you pray and feel God telling you this?
Diana	I never felt any direction from God. I felt like I'd been left out in the rain and had to decide for myself. In the end, I just decided, "Well, if this is supposed to be such a great thing and I'm being offered it—even though I don't really see exactly how this is all supposed to work—I assume that I will in time." And I decided if the opportunity came up, I would just go ahead and do it.
Richard	When did that opportunity arise?
Diana	Within a couple days. He called me. He was talking to Novelette and some other people from Australia in Novelette's bus. And that was really special. You wanted to be in on his little private discussions with people. He gave information then that just didn't get out to the general public. Afterwards he said that he wanted to talk to me, so we went and sat in his car for a while and talked. And I remember asking him, "If I don't, will I be lost?" He said no. He even told me that I could marry Jeff Little if I wanted to. He was a friend of mine from Hawaii who I was very close to. That kind of struck me as funny too, because Jeff was Caucasian. So, I guess little bells went off in my head, but again, the spirituality of it was what drew me in. Whereas, I know some of the other girls fell in love with him, I mean, really in love. I did love him later on.
Richard	So, that night is when you joined the House of David?
Diana	Right. And he was the first man I was ever with. I considered it a marriage.
Richard	How old were you?
Diana	I was twenty. I was the old lady of the bunch [laughs].
Richard	Yes. That would seem to be so. When

	did you become pregnant with your first child?
Diana	I got pregnant in December of that year. I was the first person to become pregnant under his Song of Solomon doctrine—the Bride of Christ. See, part of this thing about the Bride of Christ is that you would bear babies for the Lord.
Richard	How many wives did he have at that time?
Diana	I was number six. At the time I became pregnant with my first child he had just taken a couple more so there may have been eight or nine of us.
Richard	How did he choose who to "be with"?
Diana	I don't really know. Sometimes he told you that God told him to do this. He once apologized for lusting after me.
Richard	Even after you were his?
Diana	Yes.
Richard	Why?
Diana	I don't know, but I do remember early on, right around the time I became pregnant he actually apologized to me. He said, "I lusted after you. Just the sheer feeling of a man wanting a woman." He had sex with me that night and apologized afterwards.
Richard	So he actually felt that each time he had sex with one of his wives it was something that was God-directed, and not something out of his own desires?
Diana	Right. That was the feeling I got a lot of the times that he spent with me. It was that God made him do this.
Richard	It was something that he didn't want to do, but it was something he was directed to do?
Diana	Right. He did it because God made him do it—which made me feel really great.
Richard	You told me that when you first had sex with Vernon, you didn't love him. What did that do to you psychologically, especially because you were a virgin? I mean, having your first sexual encounter with that kind of a man, in that kind of a situation?
Diana	I loved him as a person, as my teacher.

I loved what he was teaching, the *idea* of what he was teaching. For me, that was enough at the time. And it didn't take long for me to have feelings of love for him after that just because of the nature of our relationship. Eventually, I think that's what kept me in, too. I did love [pause], I loved what he [pause], I loved [long pause], the idea.

Richard How did you feel knowing that one night he was with you and the next night he would be someone else? How did you justify that in your mind? Did you think this was what God wanted, and so regardless of your feelings your spirit had to override that?

Diana Yeah, something like that. Basically, what he did with someone else wasn't my business. That's how I thought of it. The time I had with him was my own time, and the time someone else had with him was their time. I chose not to think about it too much.

Richard Do you regret having had your first sexual experience in a situation like that?

Diana Yes I do. Because if it weren't for that experience I'd still be a virgin until I'd have gotten married. That was what I wanted [pause]. It's not something I dwell on continually. I can't change it.

Richard Were you there when he started taking all the married women?

Diana Yes.

Richard How did that make you feel?

Diana I used to wonder about that before the doctrine came out. If it was supposed to be such a prized position to have, I used to feel sorry for the married women. Yet, at the same time, I felt sorry for them because they had to choose between their husbands and God. By the time this happened the choice that I had they didn't have. I asked, "Will I be lost if I don't do this?" And the answer was no. Whereas this time around, they would be lost if they didn't do it.

Richard Did you not see an inconsistency there?

Diana I did [pause]. I did. I really felt for the

couples, but again, it didn't directly concern me. It wasn't my controversy.

Richard If you heard Vernon tell you that you would not be lost if you didn't sleep with him, and yet all of a sudden in '89 he was telling the married women that they *would* be lost if they didn't sleep with him, how did you justify him switching truth like that?

Diana Well, by that time his word was law. By then, the message had changed a lot too. And by then, I had learned to stay out of it. It was not my problem to deal with. I was already a part of the House of David. I didn't have a controversy. I mean, I felt for these people around me, but at the time it wasn't my battle to fight.

Richard How did you ever come to the place where you left?

Diana I was separated from my oldest son in July of 1990. Many of us were at the California house and David sent back everyone who didn't need to be there which was all the children and some other people. My son was being taken care of in Texas by someone who really didn't like him. But she had to take care of him because that's what David told her to do.

Richard Who was that?

Diana Rachel.

Richard I can see why she wouldn't like your son.

Diana I guess she learned to love him in her own way. I was allowed to go visit him when I could, but it wasn't often. And people would tell me stories about how he was being neglected and needed love. It was a difficult situation, but I felt this was what I had to do. Then, I became pregnant.

Richard When was your second child born?

Diana Not until 1990.

Richard Then you started having doubts about Vernon?

Diana It was a lot of things: his language was getting bad; he was a vegetarian, but then he started saying that we would be eating meat in the kingdom; then he started watching movies, having people watch these movies.

Richard   Like *Platoon* and other violent movies.

Diana   Yes. The violent movies. He also started putting the girls through military drills to get in shape. He said Israel would be a very demanding place to be and it seemed that's where we were going to go. All during this time he was getting more and more radical. He started to lose his temper more, he started to yell at people more.

Richard   What about the child abuse?

Diana   He would have them spanked if they were afraid of him or if they cried when he told them not to cry. When they started crying more, he would have them spanked harder to get them to stop crying. That was rough on the mothers. That was really rough because they had to do what he told them to do or he'd make life miserable for you.

Richard   Was he violent with the women sexually?

Diana   No, but the circumstances around it were kind of strange. Like sometimes he'd just call you into the room and you'd [pause] "do it" and then you'd leave.

Richard   Like a duty?

Diana   Not always. It was just kind of funny. You know, you'd disappear for a few minutes, for a little while, and everybody knows what you've been doing. Then, after a while he also started getting very graphic talking about his experiences.

Richard   Who would he talk to about his experiences with the women?

Diana   Everybody. In his studies he would talk about it.

Richard   What would he say?

Diana   Well, one night I remember he went around the room asking every woman what it was like to have an orgasm. He would talk about various parts of people's anatomy. He would get very graphic. He embarrassed me com-

pletely all the time, but eventually I just got used to it because he had this thing about oriental women. He said that they were made for sex. Since I was the only one who was fully oriental, everyone knew who he was talking about.

Richard   How did he justify such statements?

Diana   It would just be his experience.

Richard   How did you end up actually leaving the group? When did you start really doubting him?

Diana   Vernon started implying that he was Jesus Christ. I had a really hard time with that. That was one of my personal fears that he would start saying that. That's when I started having serious doubts. But I stayed. I thought I'd wait it out. He'd always lay it back to rest. And then, the cycle would come along and it would always get plugged back in. I had a really rough time with that. I could accept him as a messenger from God, but I could not accept him as God no matter how hard I tried. And I reached a point where [pause], he would tell people how to think and he would tell people to follow a certain way even though they disagreed with him. It was rough on me being told what I could, and could not, think.

Richard   Sue Johnson told me you started studying cultic behavior in some college course and that helped you leave.

Diana   In nursing I had to take psychiatric medicine. The thing that struck me the most—and this was right before I left—was not so much seeing David's behavior, but seeing my own in a textbook. I saw myself. And I had already admitted to myself almost a year before I left that I really didn't believe this anymore. I would catch myself. He would make a comment in a study and I'd think to myself, "Oh yeah, right buddy." And I knew I was in trouble then. I kept that to myself though because he didn't like people complaining openly.

Richard   When you made your final break you were living in California?

Diana   Yes. My oldest son was allowed to come visit me and during that course of time he broke his arm. I took him to a hospital, had it X-rayed, and put in a cast. I then called Texas to let them know what had happened. After that I got a call in the middle of the night, and David chewed me out for doing this without his permission. Even if I'd been able to reach him, he probably would have told me to take him to the doctor. I thought I'd just save him the trouble, but he really let into me for that. He just kept going on and on and it wasn't making any sense to me. When he hung up he said, "I love you." And I said, "Yeah." That night I didn't go to sleep for a long, long time. I walked around the house and I knew I was on the verge of leaving. But still, something in me said wait. Someone was about to have a baby and I decided to wait until she had her baby.

Richard   Who was that?

Diana   Nicole Gent.

Richard   And after she had her baby?

Diana   Before she was even home from the hospital I was gone. I left the house and stayed with my uncle. The night I left was a big shock to everybody because I didn't tell them. I had withdrawn from school, I called my parents and told them I wanted to come home, I called my uncle and asked him if he would like to help me get out of there. And he said, "I've been waiting for years for this call!" And he lived just down the street so he could be there in two minutes. So, I went home that night and I called my uncle to come get me. Once I started throwing everything downstairs and getting ready to leave, people started realizing something's up. Someone said, "Do you want to talk to David?" I said, "No." They called him anyway, but I refused to talk to him. I didn't want to have anything to do with him. At that point I wanted to get out. The people in California also had my uncle's number so they called me a lot during that

time to try and get me to come back, but I wasn't going to. A week later I went back to Hawaii. Eventually I did call David in Texas to say goodbye to him because I felt I owed him that much. It was a very difficult phone call.

Richard   And that was the end?

Diana   That's the last time I ever spoke to him. One of the last things he ever said was, "Well, you know you're still my wife and I'll always just tell people my wife left me." It was really hard.

Richard   Are you psychologically completely away from him now?

Diana   Yes. Yes I am. I think because of the fact that I left because I no longer believed and finally admitted it to myself. I didn't go through the hell those people went through in fear of God's punishment. I don't have that.

Richard   Where do you stand now in your beliefs?

Diana   I'm still sorting through that. I still believe there's a God. I still believe the Bible is true. I'm just not sure who that God is. It's very, very difficult. I believe that there is a God who got me out of that situation, but it's very difficult to understand why he let me get into it. I believe he still has some kind of a hand in what goes on in the world, but it's very difficult to understand why.

Richard   Any plans for the future?

Diana   I'm going to finish up my degree and get on with my life.

Richard   How do you feel about those years you spent as one of David's wives in the cult? Are you angry or bitter?

Diana   So far no. I have not been angry at David, which surprised me. He never treated me personally very badly. When I left it wasn't because I hated him. I just did not feel it was right for me anymore. Also, I'm able to take something away from it. I have two children that are the joy of my life. I appreciate them a lot more than if I hadn't gone through what I went through. I am much more accepting of people where they are. The world is not a black and white place, it's pretty much gray. I learned that because of my experience with David. In many ways he helped put me on the track that I am now.

Richard   If there's one thing you could say to the world, to people involved in cults, or to those who have family members involved in a cult, what would it be?

Diana   I would be very wary of any group that separates you from your family. I would also like people to try and understand that the power the leaders have over their followers is astronomical. You cannot comprehend that kind of control. And you cannot just forcibly remove people from that kind of situation and expect them to get better any time soon. You may take the person out of that situation, but they'll still believe.

Richard   I really appreciate the time you've spent and the honesty with which you've spoken. Thank you so much.

Diana   Okay.

Richard   If there's anything I can do for you, please call me.

Diana   Okay, I will.

Richard   Thank you, Diana.

Diana   Thank you very much.

Angela Koaha (pseudonym) granted an interview with Richard Abanes on May 11, 1993, with the condition that *all* the names mentioned during the interview (except Koresh's) be changed. This was due in part to the condition of her sister whose story appears in Chapter 4. Given the sensitive nature of the information obtained during the interview, we agreed to honor the request.

Richard   Thank you for allowing me to interview you. I know it's a difficult thing to do.

Angela   Yes.

Richard   When did you first get involved with the Branch Davidians?

Angela   In mid-1986.

Richard   How did you get involved with the group?

Angela   My husband had a brother who resided in Hawaii. And he contacted us early in 1986 and started sharing what he termed inspired messages.

Richard   And how old were you?

Angela   About twenty-six.

Richard   When did you first move to Mt. Carmel?

Angela   We visited in 1986. They were in Palestine, Texas.

Richard   What was Koresh like when you first met him? Was he charismatic?

Angela   He was impressionable. He was charming. He met people at their need. He seemed to know exactly what you were like and met your need directly and spontaneously. I suppose that's what drew us to him, as well as his awesome skill at quoting Scripture without even opening up the Bible.

Richard   Did you ever live at the Mt. Carmel complex?

Angela   Yes. When we went back later to check out some so-called new light in 1990.

Richard   Did you continue to live down there at that time?

Angela   No. We returned to New Zealand.

Richard   Is that when you had the break from the Branch Davidians?

Angela   That's right.

Richard   What was your reason for leaving?

Angela   It wasn't an immediate or sudden break away. It was something we had to psychologically release ourselves from. We had the advantage over the majority of people in the group to come away and to assess the two main teachings that were being taught since 1989. So we came back after hearing the new teachings, and we were able to assess them from the Scriptures.

Richard   Did Vernon try to pressure you to stay there?

Angela   Very much so.

Richard   How did he do that? What did he say or do?

Angela   Well, he verbally and directly threatened my husband because he wasn't

	adhering or responding to a lot of questions Vernon was putting to him.
Richard	Did he threaten to beat up your husband or kill you?
Angela	Yes. His words were, "I can get one of these big guys on you." That's what Vernon was saying to him. "I can get one of these big guys on you." And then another statement was, "I can hunt you down in New Zealand. You can't run away from me."
Richard	Did Vernon at that time try to pressure you to become part of the House of David?
Angela	Not directly, but through the meetings he was constantly referring to all the women.
Richard	When you were down there, the men and the women had already been separated by 1990, correct?
Angela	That's right.
Richard	What was your impression of the overall mood of the commune?
Angela	It was very, very different from the first time we'd been in 1986. Different in the sense that people weren't as friendly or as warm. They were distant. They weren't as happy or relaxed. There was a lot of hostility among individuals.
Richard	Did you speak to any of the women there who were part of the House of David?
Angela	Yes I did.
Richard	How did they feel about being part of his harem?
Angela	They encouraged me to be a part of it. They said, "It's wonderful. It's the only thing that will save you and your family. It's the only thing that will bring about salvation for the rest of the world," and "It's a great privilege to be one of his wives."
Richard	And they really believed this?
Angela	They really believed it, yes.
Richard	Did they not experience any kind of emotional difficulties leaving their husbands and being sexually intimate with another man? Did they ever express any kind of remorse?
Angela	I believe there was remorse. There was evidence that the couples who had already been married were missing each other. And there were times when they would sit at the tables automatically and start sharing, and in meetings.
Richard	The husbands and wives would sit down together almost out of habit and start talking?
Angela	Yes.
Richard	How could the men justify letting Koresh have sex with their wives? How did they rationalize that in their minds?
Angela	All they would say was that this was the only way God could give them, and their wives, and their children, perfect salvation. They were acknowledging that Vernon was God. And that whatever God wanted, that was the best for them.
Richard	How many years in total were you involved in the cult?
Angela	About five years.
Richard	How do you feel about those years?
Angela	Initially I was bitter. Once I realized what we'd been through I asked, "God, why did you let us go through all that?" But I look back now and see God allowed us the choice, and he would always allow us a choice, and when we make the wrong choices, he is still there to help us through. There is so much that I've learned from it in terms of the spiritual. I've just become more aware of the spiritual powers of darkness.
Richard	Regarding the people in the group, what were they like, and what do you think drew them to Vernon Howell's message?
Angela	I know that there were a lot of sincere people there searching for truth. A lot of people that were disillusioned by the system, or the teachings, or not being able to advance in truth in their own church affiliation. And I believe they went out sincerely and honestly to find the truth, and to grow in the truth.
Richard	Did you personally witness anything

	that you would consider to be child abuse?
Angela	Yes I did.
Richard	What did you see?
Angela	I saw children being beaten until their bottoms would bleed.
Richard	Was this a one time thing, or more than once?
Angela	More than once.
Richard	Did you have any other family members involved in the group besides yourself?
Angela	Eight of us.
Richard	Did all of the eight leave eventually?
Angela	No.
Richard	Did you have any relatives who perished in the fire at Waco?
Angela	Yes I did.
Richard	[pause] I didn't know. I'm very sorry.
Angela	Yes, I'm sorry about that too.
Richard	Can you tell me who they were?
Angela	My husband's brother, his name was Danny, and his wife Cassandra. And I had a sister who perished in it as well—Miriam.
Richard	You mentioned earlier in our conversation "the powers of darkness." I read an account from Marc Breault about something that occurred to your sister Eileen while she was a Branch Davidian. It seems to be what many would categorize as demon possession. Can you tell me about that?
Angela	[long pause], I [pause], I would like you to mention her experience, but not to name her. She is actually still going through a recovery process and [pause], I'm not quite sure at this stage whether to identify her. I think it's important, but on the other hand, I don't want her to lose her confidence in me. I realize the importance of getting her experience out, knowing exactly what happened to her. I would not like anyone to go through what she went through and I believe that revealing her experience is the only way that perhaps we can deter that in the future.
Richard	Whatever you can tell me.

Angela	Most of her experience we would like to reveal ourselves when we believe it's time, but I will try and share with you generally some of the things she had to go through.
Richard	Marc mentioned that at one point when you were trying to explain to her from the Bible why Vernon was wrong, she manifested certain signs like low voices coming out of her mouth. Can you talk to me about that?
Angela	We had a desire for her to know what was truth. I felt very uncomfortable, and very ill-at-ease, and ill-equipped to know how to deal with the condition she was in. I realized there was a power beyond my control that was controlling her. I asked certain pastors if they could advise me what to do. I didn't really get much assistance on that so I turned to the Scriptures and my husband and I prayed. Eventually, we were led to a couple of Scriptures in the New Testament where Christ had dealt with the demonic man, and another incident. I read it to her, and there's a part where Christ asked, "What is your name?" I turned to her and I said, "What is your name?" directly to her and the whole room just went cold, and a great gush of wind came through and she just cocked her head back and laughed. It wasn't her laugh. It was another voice coming through. A low guttural sort of voice.
Richard	Were there any doors or windows open for the gust of wind?
Angela	No, no. It was just cold all of a sudden. And after it cocked her head back and laughed, it just began, "Who do you think you are?" It was just so frightening to me not having dealt with this sort of thing before.
Richard	And did you respond?
Angela	I did. I repeated the question.
Richard	And was there an identification given?
Angela	There was no identification given. It kept mentioning David [Koresh], this voice inside her.

Richard   What did the voice say about David [Koresh]?

Angela   That he was going to come and kill us. Kill my husband and I.

Richard   Did it talk about any other things?

Angela   It talked about prophecy coming to fulfillment. I vaguely remember a text or two that it quoted.

Richard   So this voice would quote the Bible?

Angela   Yes.

Richard   Now you're telling me that it was a significantly different voice? I mean, I can change my voice and talk low or talk high. But you're telling me that this was a totally different voice that came out of her.

Angela   Yes, it was. *Very* different. And the expression, her glazed look. Her eyes were protruding out of their sockets.

Richard   So there was an actual facial change as well?

Angela   Yes. I [pause], I'd rather not talk about this anymore.

Richard   I understand. What is the one thing you want to say to the world about your involvement with the Davidian cult?

Angela   I would say that every one of those people in the group, those that perished, and those that are still alive, and believe in Vernon's teachings are really beautiful people. The ones that died didn't die because they, they were [extremely long pause]. I'm sorry.

Richard   That's all right.

Angela   [almost ten seconds of silence]

Richard   Would you rather not continue?

Angela   Ah, no, they died because ah, they were [pause], they believed with their whole hearts that they were following the truth and [breaks down and cries—cannot continue].

Richard   I'm sorry. [pause] Please take your time.

Angela   [extremely long silence] I believe we should, we should know how to [pause], we should be taught how to read the Scriptures. Two main things are to read Scripture for what it says and in context, and certainly to balance that Scripture out with the rest of the Bible and we will not go wrong. Going back to the very reason why we got into the group was because of the Scriptures. We felt this man was imparting truth.

Richard   Thank you, Angela.

Angela   Please, don't hesitate to call back if anything was unclear.

Richard   I won't.

Angela   Okay, bye-bye.

David and Debbie (Kendrick) Bunds, former Branch Davidians, agreed to be interviewed on more than ten separate occasions. The following is a condensed and edited compilation of those interviews conducted via telephone by Richard Abanes between March 3, 1993, and June 10, 1993. Erwin de Castro also participated in one of the interviews that took place at the Bunds' residence in late May. David's father is still a staunch follower of Koresh. Debbie's parents also remain faithful to Koresh. Debbie's father, Woodrow Kendrick, is currently in FBI custody for direct involvement in the February 28, 1993, gun battle with the ATF. He shot it out with federal authorities in order to escape, but was apprehended several days later. Woodrow faces a variety of serious criminal charges.

Richard   David, how long were you a Branch Davidian?

David   I became a Branch Davidian when I was five years old. I was involved with David Koresh from ages eighteen to twenty-four.

Richard   When did you leave the Branch Davidians?

David   May 4, 1989.

Richard   How about you, Debbie?

Debbie   Under Koresh about five years. I was born at Mt. Carmel, grew up there. I was fifteen when Koresh started his message and I was twenty when I left.

Richard   So you met Vernon before David met him?

Debbie   Yes.

Richard   When you first met Vernon what was he like?

Debbie   He use to be nice, very witty, very funny. But the longer he went, the harder he got. He got harder and harder, and got greedier and greedier. The Vernon that died in that fire was not the Vernon that started his message. The Vernon that started his message and that married Rachel [Jones] died a long long time ago. I'll put it like this. Sometimes he felt bad that Rachel and I didn't get anything special ever, and so he'd have David go down and get ice cream and special stuff for her and me. He paid for it all and basically gave Rachel and I something that everybody else didn't get. But within a couple years he just really changed.

Richard   Like after he took his second wife?

Debbie   Yes, once he got that message, he got much meaner much faster. Very quickly. It totally screwed him up. That's when he started really getting into his vices. And once he got into his vices he flipped. He just went ballistic. He couldn't handle it. He just got real, real nasty after that.

Richard   What else was interesting about him when you first met him?

Debbie   He would try to fix things around the property. He blew up cars [snickers]. He blew up motors [laughs].

Richard   He blew up motors?

Debbie   Yeah. He would try to fix 'em. He was a very bad mechanic—at that time anyway—he'd try fix things and then they wouldn't run. But Lois Roden didn't want this to make him feel bad so she would make my father, who was an excellent mechanic, go in and fix everything at night behind his back so that he wouldn't know he messed things up. It was never told to Vernon that things had to be fixed because Lois didn't want to hurt his feelings. So you see, she helped build him. It was like the worst thing she could possibly have done.

Richard   What about Rachel and Vernon?

Debbie   It was a really strange relationship. It was like a crush. She also knew she had some kind of power over Vernon. He would keep goin' back to her and she just tormented him to death because he would go down there to go see her. He got permission one time by Lois Roden to go down and visit Rachel and court her, and he would go down to see her [laughs] and she would be called out and she'd go out there and wouldn't say a word to him, or she'd get up and go back in the house and leave him with her brothers. I mean she was so cold to him, it would just make him crazy and she knew it. And she played him because he was the kind of person. The colder she was, the more he wanted her. It was like a game to her. She was the kind of person that liked to have power over people. She just had a crush on him. If he'd have left she'd have gotten over him and no problem. It was ultimately a game. When they got married she was told it was gonna be a brother-sister thing. She told me that herself. In the van, right after they got married, my mother and Vernon were sitting in the front seat of the van talking and Rachel and I were in the back where the bed was. In fact she was in bed cause it was night. We were just goin' over the story and everything and she said "Yeah, Vernon tricked me," she was kind of laughin,' and I said, "Oh, how?" She said, "Well, Vernon told me that we were gonna be brother and sister." And she was whispering this cause he was right up in the front. And I said, "Oh and that's not the way it was?' And she says, "No, the night we got married, I went to sleep and he said he was gonna sleep in the chair. And I woke up and he was takin' off my clothes and I just let him." That's how he went to bed with her younger sister as well. He started talking off her clothes—Michelle Jones.

Richard How did you end up accepting Vernon?

Debbie How I ended up accepting Vernon was after he basically took over, he made me come to the studies. And that's why my mother spanked me, because I was mouthin' off to him. But he made me. I used to go to meetings and sleep. And he made me start staying awake for them. And then, he started acting very nice to me.

Richard Did Vernon already see food as evil?

Debbie From the very beginning he came, he was very against the food that we ate like: store bought mayonnaise; anything with sugar in it; anything with vinegar (white vinegar because it had no nutritional value); nothing with corn syrup. He didn't believe in drinking milk either. He said that it was just for babies and he taught that it was actually a sin to drink milk. I mean you were selling your soul if you drank milk. And chocolate, do you know what he told me about chocolate?

Richard What?

Debbie He said that chocolate is completely indigestible. All the chocolate you've ever eaten in your life just gets into a big huge ball in your body and stays there because it's absolutely impossible to digest. He honestly believed it. In fact, about a year after he moved onto the property he left for like six months and his major sin when he was gone was eating carrot cake. And he believed this to be a sin even though everybody at Mt. Carmel ate it. He believed it was a sin because there was artificial coloring, artificial flavoring there was sugar, and just horrible stuff in it. He actually went to Lois Roden and said, "Oh I'm sorry I did this when I was gone."

Richard Why?

Debbie Why did he say it was a sin?

Richard Yes.

Debbie Because it just was.

Richard I've read a lot about how Vernon would eat meat, is that true?

David Mmm hmm.

Richard But he says on a tape, "No meat eater will enter the kingdom of heaven."

David What tape are you talking about?

Richard "Judge What I Say."

David "No meat eater is going to receive the kingdom of God." Yeah. Okay. He's saying that in order to possess the land of Israel you had to be a vegetarian. He's saying in order to go there and be in the kingdom you had to be a vegetarian.

Richard But that would mean he excluded himself.

David Well, you gotta understand. You gotta tack this up under progressive truth. In other words, he teaches a certain thing at this point in time. But then as we learn, and go through, and study, we learn more. And we find out, well we can eat meat. I know it's confusing. It's confusing to me, too, but I'm saying this is the way these people think. As far as they're concerned, this tape and this study. If you were to take it to a Branch Davidian now, that proves this is what he said, they don't care. This was a long time ago, that's old light, it's basically worthless.

Richard That's exactly like the Jehovah's Witnesses.

David Oh sure. Yeah. All cults have to develop those kind of things, but it's totally irrational. It's completely crazy. And they've been doing that for decades.

Richard Now David, you met Vernon a few years after Debbie met him. What were your first impressions of him?

David He was very humble. He was very sincere. He seemed to have a very good knowledge of the Bible and seemed to be very sure of what he was teaching so he came across to me as being a very likely candidate for a prophet of God. As I was with him for the following few months after I first met him he impressed me as being a true prophet who wanted to help the people of the Branch to move on to the kingdom of God and to try to get back on track with the Branch message. I just thought of him very positively.

Richard Were you happy as a Branch Davidian?

David Well, yeah. I don't think that being a Branch Davidian really affected my life too much up until the time I was involved with Koresh. We lived out here in Los Angeles and went to school and did the things anyone else would do. I don't think it really affected my life much until I came in contact with Koresh.

Richard How did that change your life?

David All of a sudden everything became very intense. Everything all of a sudden was hell or heaven. It was life or death, an all or nothing type thing where I had to totally devote myself to Koresh and his message or else not have anything to do with it at all. I had to not go to college. I had to go where he wanted me to go, do what he wanted me to do, live where he wanted me to live. Get married when he decided that we could get married. And then, once we were married be together when he decided. He just totally controlled our lives.

Richard Did you live down in Texas?

David Yeah. When I joined Koresh, I went down to Texas that summer of '84.

Richard That means you lived in Palestine?

David We lived in Palestine starting in May of '85.

Richard Then you went to Mt. Carmel?

David When we were in Houston for four months they moved onto Mt. Carmel in April of 1988. When we came back after the death of our son in June of 1988, we stayed there for ten months.

Richard At Mt. Carmel?

David At Mt. Carmel—the compound.

Richard What was life like at Palestine and Mt. Carmel?

David Well, life at Palestine was very rustic. We didn't have any running water. We didn't have any electricity. We had lights through Coleman lanterns. We had buckets that we used for toilets and buried our waste. It was pretty primitive. We had little cabins, plywood cabins that we built. Basically it was just plywood slabs laid on a foundation with a plywood roof on the top.

Richard How big was it?

David Ours was about 8 x 16 feet, so we had about 120 square feet to live in. But that was better than what we had before which was tents. Other people lived in school buses. And we had a central kitchen area.

Richard What was life like at Mt. Carmel? Any better?

David Life was a little better because we had some plumbing for toilets. We didn't have any running water. Well, at first we did, but then the well dried up. We had better houses, but in the end it was worse because of the abuse by Koresh.

Richard What kind of abuses?

David At first it was a lot of mental abuse, a lot of emotional abuse, playing with your mind. He was very strict and required a lot from you. Always threatening us with impending ejection from the camp for just, in his words, "doing our own thing and not wanting to be with the program." In a sense, he was correct. We lived there, but we really didn't want to be there. We were there because we thought, "Well, this is what we have to do to go to heaven." It was very works-oriented. We thought, "Well, okay we're here, and as long as we're here and we go to the meetings and put up with this guy, then maybe God will let us into heaven." But for Koresh that wasn't enough. He wanted us to totally give ourselves up to him unquestioningly. He just got worse and worse the year we were there. He was tightening his grip on the group. People who didn't want to come under the line and under his reign. He was trying to purge the camp. We were kicked off because we broke dietary laws. But we were probably kicked off just in general because of our bad attitude. And I think that he was trying to kick us off to teach us a lesson. I think he was going to let us come back eventually. He never did that with anybody else because I think he realized that when he kicked us off he lost control of us. So I think that from that point on instead of doing that, I think he took other measures with people to try and get them under control.

Richard   What about the physical abuse?

David   My father was beaten up personally by Koresh. There was a disagreement between Steve Schneider and my father over some clothes that had to be brought from California. Steve was mad at my father and they were yelling and fighting and then my father went down to where he was staying, and Steve went to Koresh and said, "Look, Don Bunds is doing this and that." So David Koresh went down there and grabbed my father and beat him up. He hit him in the stomach and punched him out a little bit and taught him a lesson—humbled him.

Richard   Debbie, did you ever witness any kind of child abuse?

Debbie   Yes. One incident specifically I think was the worse incident I ever saw. It was with Tarah Tom. She was a little eight-month-old girl. He took the baby away from the mother and pulled down her diaper and started beating her with a wooden spoon. He beat that baby for forty minutes. He kept saying. "I'm not going to stop 'til you stop cryin.' " And of course, an eight-month-old is not gonna stop cryin.' I mean he put his hand way up in the air and he came down as hard as you could. I mean it resounded the slap was so hard. By the time he was done, that baby was just [pause], its butt was just swollen and flaming red. I mean, forty minutes is a long time. You try to imagine enduring that for forty minutes.

Richard   Was it constant?

Debbie   Yes. He didn't stop. He'd stop for like a second and go, "Well?" Then look at the baby. He'd go like this, he'd pick it up off his lap, look at it in the face and say, "Are you gonna stop crying?" It'd keep cryin' so he'd lay it down and start it again. He'd stop for maybe five seconds. The mother was so upset she ran out of the house. The father said that he felt like beating Vernon.

David   But he couldn't?

Debbie   He couldn't because he knew that if he did, he would be beaten. There was nothing he could do to stop it.

Richard   How many people witnessed this?

Debbie   Oh, I would say at least twenty people did.

Richard   What was everybody's reaction?

Debbie   Silence. Complete and total silence, tried to just blend into the woodwork. I mean, a lot of us were, I think, were very upset about it. I know it upset me, but those of us that were upset about it couldn't do anything. And the ones that weren't were like, "Well, see it's your fault" (the parents' fault), "because you didn't discipline your child correctly. So this is your fault." It was either blame the parents for what Vernon had to do, or there was either nothing wrong with it at all.

Richard   And he justified this?

Debbie   Yeah. He spanked children like that quite a lot. Not for forty minutes, but he would just decide that he was upset with the child, even if it wasn't his own. In the worship meetings, if the parent didn't do something as fast as he wanted it to get done, he would reach over, snatch the child, take it in the other room, or sit right there in front of everybody and just start spankin.'

Erwin   Now you said some of the parents did not react because they feared him. Did they fear him because they were going to get trounced on, or did they fear him because they were going to go against a prophet, or both?

Debbie I would say both. First of all, there's always a real fear that he is the prophet and he's doing something that you just don't know about. He knows more than you. And also you're afraid of being trounced on, especially in that last year. He was very violent. I mean, if he got mad at you, he was having people hit and slapped and spanked left and right all over the place.

Richard How could people watch him do something like that and still consider him a prophet?

David It was considered to be completely normal. It was part of his authority for him to be able to do things like that and he was always seen as God will direct all his ways. That was one of the things I had a problem with. He taught that God directed all his ways. Everything that he did was directed by God—everything. Everything he did was supposed to be directed by God. So if he did something that would normally be very strange and weird, if he did it then, "No, that's God. That's the Spirit working." We were always thinking—every time it got weirder and weirder and more intense—"Well, that's the way it's supposed to be. God works in strange ways."

Erwin With regard to some of the manipulation going on, did he always appeal back to his authority as a prophet?

David Oh yeah, always. That was his ultimate authority. He always appealed to his authority as a prophet. His authority as his position given to him by God, being Cyrus, this anointed messiah who God is directing and using to shape and mold his people (his followers) into a group that is going to be the elect. He's always molding them and cultivating them. The ones who don't want to go along (like us) we're pruned out. His authority never was questioned. If his authority was questioned, he dealt with it hard and fast right there and took care of it one way or the other. Whether

kicking people out, or disciplining them, or withholding food, or getting a paddle and beating them on the behind as he did to Joel Jones, Perry Jones' son, Michelle and Rachel Jones' brother who was there for a time.

Debbie He had Joel beat up?

David Yeah, he had Joel beat up by some of the other young men in the group because he was constantly sleeping and being late for studies.

Debbie He was asleep and some people came and started beating him up while he was still asleep.

Erwin Now David, you said earlier that you basically endured a lot of the things that were going on because you thought this was the way to go to heaven. That seems to be another type of fear element. How much of a factor do think fear played as far as individuals staying in the group? Fear of Vernon, or fear of losing their salvation? Would you say it's more of a fear factor that's holding the people together as opposed to a devotion to someone they believe is a man of God?

David Some people I think were more devoted to him, but even those people had a lot of fear motivating them because they were just scared to death of going to hell.

Debbie Yeah. Fear of hell was, I would say, was top on the list of fears.

David Even those who were devoted to him had a fear, but they also might of had a devotion to him because they were treated better.

Debbie David's mother is a good example of someone that was never really treated bad. Vernon never yelled at David's mother.

David You know who a better example for this is? Floracita Sonobe. She had sort of an immunity. She was one of those people who, for some reason, Vernon just did not really bother. And always we were hearing where she would do something that somebody else in the group maybe couldn't do, we would hear this "Well, she's new in the group and she hasn't accepted it yet." I mean, two years of this excuse. Others came in the group and they [snaps fingers] had to accept it like that.

Richard How do you explain that?

David I don't know, it was just up to Koresh. He mostly did things on a whim. He was very motivated by emotions and feelings. The people that he didn't try to control were people who didn't really need as much control.

Debbie Right.

David In other words, somebody like Floracita Sonobe, she just stayed there, minded her own business, kept her mouth shut, and didn't really cause any trouble.

Debbie So he left her alone.

David He didn't really see any reason to bother her.

Debbie There were also people (Perry Jones is a perfect example of this), when a wrong was done against him he didn't see it as a wrong—not if it was done by the prophet. He decided it was a test by God.

David Perry Jones, when he first joined Ben Roden in the 1950s or 60s, had a car that he owned, and he had it by his house. Ben Roden came down and took it one day, just drove it from Perry's house up to in front of his big house, and left it there and just let it sit there, and just basically let it fall apart and rot. And Ben Roden just said, "Well, it's mine now." And Perry said, "Okay, Well, that's God."

Debbie And he had eleven kids and no car.

David This is the mentality of these people. See, once you can convince a group of people that you are a prophet and that God is calling the shots through you, then you can get away with almost anything, just about anything, given enough time.

Erwin What would you say were the top five things he did to convince them that he was the real thing?

David He would use the Bible. He would show his ability to use the Scriptures.

Debbie He would also use the fact that he found out, or pointed out things that nobody had seen before.

David Right, yeah.

Debbie In life and in the Bible.

David He would try to impress people with his ability to read people.

Debbie Oh, yeah, definitely. He thought he could read you after just basically saying hello to you.

David He thought of himself as having very deep insight. He could see the situation and just understand the spiritual significance. He thought he could see things that nobody else could see. For example, I had some money that my mother had sent me. We were living at the Waco house in '84 and I was being sent money. She sent me some money one time and I went down and bought me some food at the store.

Debbie Cause he was always hungry.

David We were not getting enough to eat, as far as I was concerned. Well, the next time I got a check, he was there and the check came and it was just a routine thing. All of sudden Vernon goes, "No, David can't have his money, let Perry control the money for him. Let Perry dish out the money and decide what David can buy and what he can't buy." I was very upset because that meant that I couldn't buy the food. But later on I confessed to Vernon. You know, you'd have these moments of guilt where you'd go to Vernon, and confess to him your sins. I said, "Oh Vernon, you remember that time when you took my money, well you know I was buyin' food, Vernon." Vernon said, "Oh, see Dave that was God. I didn't know why I took your money away, but see, God showed me you were doing bad things."

Erwin Okay. In other words, he took every circumstance and he sort of developed it and showed that there were things behind the situation?

David   Right.

Erwin   It seems to me that both you and David saw little faults here and there. Would you say that there was a process of self-rationalization to legitimize you staying there?

Debbie   I'll put it like this. When we got kicked out for the food, I got sick of the rules. The rules for the food were always changing. One day you could eat something with corn syrup in it, and the other day you couldn't. Or, you could have tomato sauce with corn syrup in it, but you couldn't have juice with corn syrup in it. After we were kicked out, I finally came to the realization that it wasn't what was in the food, it was what he gave permission for. Like, we could eat chicken hot dogs, but we couldn't eat chicken bologna. You know, stupid things like that. That got on my nerves, I thought it was stupid. But then I decided, Well, he's just trying to teach us that we need to do only what he tells us to do. So, I finally realized that my sin was not in eating the same kind of thing, it was in not getting his direct permission. So, we worked it out in our minds to where we knew that ultimately we had to get direct permission for everything we thought, did, or said.

Richard   So it wasn't necessarily what he told you to do, but rather that he told you to do it?

Debbie   And when he told us to do it.

Erwin   Did you go through a process of rationalizing, saying, "This doesn't make sense, but I know he's a prophet of God"?

David   Oh, yeah. You have to.

Debbie   Constantly.

David   You had to try and figure out a way that he was still right. I mean, the things that I would see him wrong in were tiny, were little things.

Erwin   But they added up?

David   Yeah. The way I looked at it, if he was

so inspired, then he wouldn't make stupid mistakes with grammar and spelling, or meanings of words. I thought, "Gee, that's basic stuff."

Richard   But why would someone continue making rationalizations in order to make Koresh out to be right, rather than going the other way, to the conclusion that maybe he wasn't a prophet?

Debbie   It just never occurred to us. I mean it really didn't because we grew up with this.

Erwin   There was a conditioning?

David   This is were the programming comes in. His members were programmed in that sense. It's like a program that may analyze data and collect information but that one conclusion is completely off limits. Any time that your mind would start to approach any type of conclusion like that, all the alarms would start to go off. That was totally and completely impossible. That is one thing that was absolutely impossible—for him to be actually false and wrong.

Debbie   You see, no matter what he did he had to be right. Whatever he did had to be right somehow.

David   You had to figure something out. Usually what you ended up doing was thinking it was some kind of test of God. God is punishing me because of my sin.

Debbie   Oh, yeah.

David   God is teaching me a lesson. God is testing my faith. This may seem strange, but you would almost come to the conclusion: Well, Vernon doesn't really understand everything about what's going on here himself, but God knows what's going on, and God knows what he's doing through Vernon.

Debbie   Right, and Vernon will find out later why he did that. We were always taught daily that we had to be tested. I grew up with that it in my mind. Even though I didn't really realize it, that we were taught that God tested you all the time.

I mean, continually. And so, whenever something happened we couldn't explain—"Well, God's testing us to accept this even though we don't understand it."

David   There seemed to be a lot of negative reinforcement in the sense of, "God must be putting me through something. This is why I'm experiencing confusion." Is there any instance where he would reward somebody for being good and towing the line? I mean, as one way to make sure that the person continues following the line?

Debbie   Every now and then.

David   In meetings he would single out a person and say, "Oh, so and so has done so good, everyone let's give him a hand." And everybody would clap.

Debbie   For the person it's great, but for the other people it was like, "Oh, why can't I be like that?" The thing is though, that kind of environment doesn't really make you work to do better, not consistently. It's like, "What's the use, it's too hard."

David   That was one of his biggest problems. His complimenting was more motivated by his own whims. For my sister, for example, no matter what she did, she could never do anything right.

Richard   That was Robyn?

David   That was Robyn. No matter what she did it didn't make any difference. If he was ragging on her for her weight and she lost a lot of weight, he didn't care.

Debbie   And she tried a lot a harder in a lot of things than I ever did.

David   She put forth amazing effort.

Debbie   She would starve herself.

David   He never made any distinction between her performances, it was always the same. So, of course this totally depressed her and she left.

Debbie   And he decided before her child was even born that he didn't like Shaun because he was her child, and if Robyn was bad and disobedient, then her child was going to be horrible because of her.

David   See, he also believed that no matter what happened Robyn would stay cause he thought that Robyn was strong. When Robyn left it burst his bubble.

Debbie   He told Robyn's mother all the time, "I messed up."

David   It was such a blow to him that he had to rationalize it by saying God punished him by taking her away. He was so caught off guard by her leaving. And when she took the Laverne [California] Police to the Laverne house and said, "Give me my son back," he was just devastated, he could not believe it. He flipped. So, he had to develop an entire doctrine around it.

Debbie   He always did. If something went wrong that he did not expect, and it flipped him out, he was flipped out for a very short period of time and then BAM! There was this big huge explanation.

David   Long studies.

Debbie   By the time he was done you don't know what he explained, but you accepted it.

David   Same thing in Australia. He was there trying to get people to accept his "new light" regarding him having all the women, including the married women. An earthquake happened in Pomona [California] which damaged the house in Pomona, and he saw it as a sign that God had punished him because he had spoken to Marc Breault. He claimed God told him not to speak to Marc until he had received a written apology.

Debbie   Whereas when the Roden house on Mt. Carmel burned down shortly after that, that was seen as God telling him to just move on and go forth. See, that was seen as a good thing.

David   Yeah. There were things in the Roden house he wanted to go through, a bunch of stuff that belonged to Lois Roden, but the place burned down.

And so he said, "Oh, this is a sign from God that we need to just go forward and not mess with that stuff; not go back in the past." He always interpreted stuff according to what he wanted.

Erwin So, in other words, no matter what happened

Debbie [interrupting] It worked out for his best interest ultimately.

Erwin Now, you said that when he was caught off guard he would develop a teaching around it. Are you saying that was to make it seem like, Yes, he anticipated this, things are not out of hand?

David Yeah, but also he would sometimes say it was God punishing him. You may find it strange to hear that he wanted to maintain this sense of being perfect, and yet would say that God punished him. He always maintained that he was disobedient at times, but he always defined that disobedience.

Debbie He was the only one that could define that.

David Nobody went to him and told him that he was doing wrong.

Debbie Right. And nobody could punish him but God.

David He always said, "This is what I have done wrong. This is what I did, and this is what God did." He declared that completely.

Richard In other words, only he could declare his sin.

David Completely controlled it.

Debbie He declared his own sin and he declared his own punishment. Because he said that the only one who could punish him, or reprimand him, or even point it out would be God. So he had total control of it.

David He had nothing to lose. That impressed people. That sort of maintained the sense of, "Well, you know he's so humble. I mean, even God punishes him."

Richard He admitted his sins, but nobody could see that he was the one deciding what the sins were.

David Right.

Debbie Also, you can get full of yourself when you say, "God punished me."

David Yeah, exactly. God is so close to you that he'll actually personally mold you, punish you. "Wow, that means that God must really love him."

Debbie In fact, he taught that the more God punished you the more you were punished, reprimanded, and watched, the more God loved you. Koresh taught that if he was totally leaving somebody alone, then that's because God had basically given up on them. Which was ridiculous. You could tell by his actions he didn't mean it.

David Cause people he would leave alone, he thought were great.

Erwin It seems to me that there came a point where some individuals said enough is enough. This would completely go against the allegation by some people who study groups such as the Branch Davidians who say that when they have a totalitarian-type leader, he exercises total control over his followers to the point where they're not thinking anymore. It seems to me that they are thinking, but something is keeping them there—like another desire.

David Oh yeah, they do a lot of thinking.

Erwin Then, it's not like they're mindless robots all of a sudden?

David Let me explain in more theological terms. Nobody believes nothing. Everybody believes something. Everybody has a worldview. If you go to most people and talk to them about what they believe, they (even people who you would consider to be not particularly religious) really have very highly developed theological systems worked out in their mind to explain everything that they deal with in the world. Even a bum on the street has got some type of worldview system that he has formulated in his mind and everything that he deals with in his life he sees through this worldview. Christians have a worldview that is based on Scripture.

Branch Davidians have this same kind of thing. They have a presuppositional base, a worldview set in their minds through which they interpret everything. All the information they receive they put through this interpretational system. So, like I said, it's programming. When they start to get information that would normally indicate, or should indicate, "Well, wait a minute, this is wrong, this is false, something's funny here," instead they interpret it by running it through their processing system and figure a way out of the dilemma. They'd work it out to where they'd think, "No, this is okay. This is God's doing. God works in mysterious ways, and then blah, blah, blah." So, this idea that they were mindless, unthinking, people is not true. They thought a lot. They did a lot of thinking, a lot of analyzing, and a lot of data processing, but their entire base, their entire worldview, their presuppositional base was completely crazy. It was false.

Debbie It was crippled by their beliefs.

David Yeah, it was crippled. They had faulty programming, so to speak. They were not able to properly analyze the information they received.

Erwin It seems to me, because there were people who left, including you, they were not confined to that way of thinking.

Debbie There were different levels.

David Most people, except for the Australians, left because they just couldn't take it anymore. Just couldn't handle it anymore. The abuse and the environment. They just couldn't deal with it.

Debbie But they also could not accept the fact that it's wrong. At least not at first.

David Yeah, not at first. After they're out for a while and they're in another environment where they're able to maybe be deprogrammed a little bit by being in the real world for a little while, then they might be able to deal with some of the things.

Debbie But when you do it that way you always have baggage that you keep with you and it becomes a permanent part of your thinking, like David's mother.

David My mother left mostly for emotional reasons.

Debbie And that's basically the only reason. She believed for a long time, like the first Christmas she had out (she'd only been out for a few months) she still was so much into this protecting him [Koresh] that she even said he never slept with twelve-year-old girls and she delivered from a girl that he slept with at twelve. It takes a long time. She still has moments where she's just totally terrified that she's going to hell because she's not following him. She didn't have anything on which to base him being completely 100 percent wrong.

David Now other people left, like the Australians, because they came to the conclusion through the Bible that he was wrong. That happened to me, too. And when that happens to you, what happens is that all of a sudden the foundations of your thinking [pause], the very roots of my thinking were completely destroyed. I had to totally replace everything that I had believed my entire life with biblical truth.

Erwin It seems to me that you were helped by being kicked out.

Debbie Oh, we were. It was the most wonderful thing that ever happened to us.

David We were kicked out, and therefore, we had the freedom to be alone and when I did finally study the Bible for myself I could do it. I didn't have to be under any kind of pressure.

Debbie I'm sure it's possible to be around Vernon every day, to be a clear enough thinker to realize and come to the conclusion that this is wrong, but that is very rare to have a mind that is strong enough to do that. In most cases you have to get away from him and stop living that daily kind of thing and hearing

David   him all the time to be able to start clearing your mind up.

David   When people lived there day after day, there was a routine that you went through, a lot of indoctrination—constant. He was a master orator in that he always had something to say and he could talk for hours. He did it very well.

Debbie   And this became your world and universe.

David   He exuded confidence, supreme confidence about what he was saying.

Debbie   Oh, yes. Always.

David   And it wasn't so much what he was saying. If you understood something that he was saying, and accepted it, okay. If he was saying things that you didn't quite understand, you were just carried along by the momentum of his forceful delivery. You would just go along with it.

Debbie   When I found out he was taking other men's wives, I immediately thought well, it must be true because he said it.

David   Marc Breault is an example of someone who was in his group day after day, was in his studies, and yet was able to think and analyze critically what he was hearing and eventually just made a decision to leave because he knew that Vernon was wrong. Now when he left he did not 100 percent reject Koresh. He just had some problems with Koresh. He felt, "Well, I need to leave and then I will dialogue with Koresh and then we will come to an understanding about the problem, to get back on track." But as he tried to do that, he began to see that was impossible. Koresh was not going to give a millimeter. Never. And Marc started to see that this man was really very irrational. And he was not willing to even look at the remote possibility that he was wrong on just the smallest, little, tiny thing. I mean, he would not give on anything.

Debbie   He wouldn't give on anything, not even something that didn't matter. Like if he said we were fighting. If we said, "But we weren't fighting," you'd think he'd accept that because we were the ones who were saying it. But no.

David   He'd say, "No, you were fighting." He was always right—period. See, that's why in a sense, he was so deluded. In order to be a healthy person, you have to live in a world where you have to constantly come to terms with your own errancy. You've got to admit that you're wrong sometimes. He lived in a world where he was never wrong. After a person lives in that kind of an environment for years, they will eventually become deluded in their thinking. They never have to deal with the fact that they're wrong. I cannot imagine living like that. Never knowing that you're wrong about anything. That is just crazy. You'll go nuts. Vernon was not nuts in the sense that he was unable to function. He could function very well, but he functioned within his environment. Vernon wasn't a good listener. Whenever people tried to tell him something he wouldn't listen. That was a constant problem with Vernon. We'd try to tell him something and if he didn't want to listen to you he wouldn't even listen. He wouldn't even try to understand the other person's argument. That was the problem with this "new light" thing. We couldn't even get him to shut up long enough to listen to our arguments to why he was wrong. Vernon called me once in 1990 when he was trying to get me to go back to Mt. Carmel and in the conversation he ended up telling me point blank, "I have never been wrong." He told me that on the phone. So, when I talked to my father a few months later in 1990, I told him that. I said, "Vernon said he's never been wrong." And my father would not accept it. So what happened was, about a year ago I brought that up again and this time my father accepted it. I think he must have had some kind of encounter with Vernon where he had to come to terms with the fact that Vernon's never been wrong. So, basically what he told me was that he believed Vernon's never been wrong. Like, God will make Vernon right no matter what—just to show us wise guys a lesson. The whole Branch message is based on the idea that you're supposed to listen to anybody if they claim to have a message from God. No matter who they are, where they come from, or what their character is. See, I don't agree with that. But that's what they believe. They believe that if someone comes to you in the name of God, with a message from God, you're supposed to sit down and listen to them no matter what. It doesn't matter what you think they're doing, what rumors you've heard, or what you know they're doing, or where they've been. Theoretically, they're supposed to sit down and listen.

Richard   Paul Fatta in the *New York Times* stated, "Don't judge a man by what he does, judge what he says."

David   Right. And that is a long-standing Branch teaching. In fact, in a tape of June 26 of '85 Vernon says, "The Holy Spirit's message stands on its own regardless of the messenger. That's why we in present truth stand on present truth independent of the messenger, right?" In other words, just like any other Branch, he completely separated the truth that was taught from the conduct of the messenger. It's just a tactic the Branch uses to get you to listen to them. But see, when Marc Breault claimed to have a message, no one would listen to him. So, all that noble teaching about listening to people went out the window. It only works for them, otherwise they could care less. If you tried to get Paul Fatta right now—based on that same thing he said—if you tried to get him to listen to Marc Breault he wouldn't. To actually quote him, and

then say, "Now, why don't you listen to Marc Breault?" He won't. No matter what you try to do to show him his statement is false because he won't abide by it, it won't matter. These people are inconsistent. What they mean is, "You need to listen to Koresh and don't listen to anybody else." That's what they mean. But they won't say it that way, cause that sounds a little strong. See, this taunt that he gave the ATF, "We'll come out if you prove us wrong." It wasn't an actual offer to sit down and have a study, it was a taunt. It was just bragging. Those people never had any intention of listening to anybody.

Erwin   You've presented a position that basically says the reason people kept on believing him was because they were looking at things through a particular set of lenses. And that was reinforced because of the living conditions and the environment around them. What about the people that were not living with him, but were part of the sect?

David   The Australians would be a good example of that. It's interesting that they were all removed by thousands of miles away from Koresh by way of legalities. They had no choice but to come, stay for a while until their visas were up, and then go back. They were in a situation where they were able to be more independent. And so, when Marc Breault went out there and started teaching, he initially didn't have a lot of success because of fear, but eventually he was able to more or less convince most of the Australians that Koresh was false.

Debbie   If Vernon could have stopped that and kept those people with the others he would have. As soon as he took over he started making us all eat together everyday, we could not eat as a family, or at your house. You had to do everything together. He started incorporating the group so that they had to stay together all the time because the closer

	you get people into a group and you get them away from outside things the more you can control that. And he did that on purpose.
Erwin	How big was the fallout when he started instituting these very rigid conditions?
David	When he started taking other men's wives was the only time he had a big fallout.
Debbie	He lost maybe twenty people.
Richard	Why was he so popular? Why did so many people latch on to him and think he was wonderful and start following him?
David	It was just the doctrine. And he delivered it well. He's charismatic. He speaks with authority. He talks like he really knows what he's talkin' about. He can quote the Bible profusely. He will barrage you. He's probably ten times better than the most elite Jehovah's Witness. He will just barrage you with text. He can quote entire chapters, especially from the Old Testament prophecies. He'll quote entire chapters of Isaiah just right off the top of his head. He'll barrage you and just overwhelm you.
Richard	How did you two start seeing the truth?
David	In 1988 he started teaching that he was the Lamb of Revelation, but he did not teach he was Jesus Christ. I believed that Vernon, that David Koresh, was the Lamb personage of Revelation. I believed that, I really did. Now at this point, the personage of Jesus Christ was still in Koresh's theology a separate person. As the Lamb of Revelation he had a very special position because the Lamb gets to open the seals, and gets to do all these things through the Book of Revelation. In 1989 when he developed this doctrine further, he decided that he had the right to take other men's wives for himself. Not only that, later on in his theology he taught that he would have to die for the sins of the world. He taught that Jesus Christ's

atonement only atoned up to the cross, up to A.D. 31, and he would have to die for the sins of the New Testament people from that point up to modern times. This is where my friend Marc Breault comes in. Marc Breault was a theology major at Loma Linda University. He was in a position of where he was looking for some other group to identify with. Vernon came along and he hooked up with him. Marc rather quickly became Vernon's right-hand man theologically. He had the authority to give studies, to establish doctrine as long as Vernon agreed with him, to teach, to correct people who he thought were incorrect in their teaching in the group. He was right up there, right up next to Vernon. He had a lot of authority. Vernon used to take him up into his private sessions to discuss things with him. But when Vernon established this new "I'm gonna get the wives" teaching, that was the line that Marc could not cross. He could see clearly in the writings of Paul especially, that there's no way that you could justify taking wives away from their husbands. It's impossible. It's just physically impossible. So Marc left. Marc broke. Vernon told him to go to Texas to the compound there to get his punishment because he was disobeying. Instead, Marc went to Australia to be with his wife.

Richard	Why did Steve Schneider go along with Vernon?
David	Steve Schneider was initially very upset and rejected the teaching, but he was so scared of being lost. Steve just could not deny what he perceived to be such glorious truths coming out of Vernon's mouth before. It ultimately pressured him into following Vernon. He just simply could not free his mind up to see the glaring error there. So, he went the other way.
Richard	Now Koresh didn't start out in '81 claiming to be any of these grand titles.

How did he change from just wanting to be called a Bible teaching musician into identifying himself as the Son of God?

David   It was gradual. Evolution. See that's the thing about these groups. Again, they have this concept called "progressive truth." Truth is always in flux, progressing, advancing. "New light" is coming.

Richard   Like the Jehovah's Witnesses when they say the "light" is always getting brighter and brighter?

David   Right. The light's getting brighter and brighter. Changing. Even the Adventists, in a sense, have the concept of this. They have more of an idea though that new truth will not contradict past truth. Vernon, on the other hand, or David Koresh (whatever you wanna call him), he has a concept of new truth can supersede and replace old truth. Will not necessarily harmonize, but will obsolete it. It's a "that was true then, but now this is true" type of thing. By the way, Davidians are King James only people. In fact, Koresh is absolutely dependent on the King James translation of the Bible for his doctrines because if he departs from it a lot of his key phrases and things disappear. All of his doctrines are based not only upon the wording of the King James translation, but his understanding of the linguistics and the changes in meanings.

Richard   When you would question him, would he get angry?

David   Oh sure, totally. Yeah, he would not tolerate any disagreement with his doctrine at all.

Richard   How could the men be so motivated that they would give their wives over to Koresh like that?

David   My father wrote a letter to my mother one time, and this is what he said. You gotta understand their doctrine. He taught that God originally created twelve worlds, twelve Adams. One of them fell (that was our world). The other eleven Adams are out there in the universe unfallen. Okay? Those unfallen worlds are now fully developed. They're fully developed kingdoms. The original Adams are kings over their planets and have their children that they reign over. And they're perfectly righteous cause they didn't fall. But our world is the focus of attention cause we fell and God has a plan of salvation. Now, my father said that comparing the lowest, most lowest guy in the Branch Davidians to the richest, most powerful king of the eleven unfallen worlds, is like comparing a Rockefeller to a skid-row bum. Okay? So they believe that when they finally are exalted to their position, they will literally be the greatest, most powerful kings in the universe, second only to the Lamb and God himself. This is what's motivating these people, you gotta understand they really believe this. I'm not kidding. They believe this with all their heart. You see, they're not afraid of those FBI people out there. They don't care. They're happy. They're going home. It's almost over. This is something that I think the authorities seem to be getting a glimmer of. But they haven't really hit home with what's motivating these people.

Richard   Have you shared these doctrinal things with the FBI?

David   Yeah, I've tried. I've interviewed with the FBI. I've tried to convey to them the best I can in laymen's terms what gist of their beliefs are.

Richard   Do you think Koresh is planning on harming members of the community?

David   No, no. He's waiting to be glorified. He's gonna ride forth and he's gonna fulfill Revelation 19. He's gonna destroy Babylon. He's gonna fulfill Isaiah 13. He's gonna destroy Babylon on his horse. Psalm 45 is quoted by Paul in Hebrews. Koresh believes he's that personage in Psalm 45, he's gonna ride forth on a horse, destroy Babylon.

Richard	So he's waiting to be glorified right now?
David	Sure, yeah. That's what he's waiting for. See, "God told him to wait." That's a classic pattern. He's waiting for God to glorify him. I suspect that he was quite shocked when he played that message. I think that was supposed to be a farewell message to the world. I wouldn't be surprised if he told his followers, "Look, when they play this message, that's it, it's gonna be over." Then, it didn't happen. So now, he sort of goes back on his set stand-by plan, "Well, let's just wait." I'm almost positive that's when it was supposed to happen.
Richard	Have you also told federal agents this information?
David	Sure, I told the FBI agents all that today.
Richard	Okay. Let me ask you this: Did Koresh, like the Jehovah's Witnesses, also instruct his followers to not talk to apostates, or people who have left, or those who have been kicked out because they're evil or of Satan?
David	Yeah, especially apostates. Here's the problem. The only way you can really understand Koresh's message is to have been in the group. But the only time you'll want to fight against Koresh's message is if you're out of the group. If you're out of the group you're an apostate. If you're an apostate and you want to help people who are in the group, and they see you as an apostate, you can't help them. If you haven't been in the group, then you don't know what they believe and you don't know what you're talkin' about. That means if you try to deprogram one of them, they're just gonna look down on you because you don't know what you're talkin' about. You've got a catch-22 there.
Erwin	Was he ever very concerned with getting new people in the group, or just keeping the ones he had?
David	He always was recruiting.
Erwin	Tell us about how he recruited people?
David	He did most of the recruiting himself. If anybody else did recruiting, all they could say was, "We know this guy who really knows the Bible." They would just try to convince you that you had to come listen to this guy cause he was so amazing. It depended on who it was too. Let me qualify. I'm talking about just the average person. The average, nonteaching member. Some members, like Marc and Steve, could teach.
Debbie	But even then only very, very select things were taught because most of the stuff under Vernon had to be kept secret.
David	A teaching member could teach anything pertaining to the kingdom, the Bible, and the last days. But nothing having to do with the House of David, having wives, anything sexual, things like that were off limits. But anything else, they could use to try and bait people to come in.
Erwin	How did they get to the person? What did they say?
David	Most of the people were recruited through the Adventist church. So, in order to understand why Adventists would be susceptible to recruitment you have to understand the way an Adventist thinks. An Adventist is supposed to believe certain things which was a hook that Vernon could latch on to and pull on. A good Adventist would believe that Ellen G. White was the spirit of prophecy. She was a prophetess, inspired. God spoke to her. All her writings are inspired of God. So Koresh would pull those books out and he would use these tools to try to pull these people in. He'd say, "You see, she had light, but she didn't have it all brother. You gotta go on. You gotta progress. I have more to show you." And they would start to see, "Oh, yeah." And they'd get impressed and he would excite them with all this, "We're going to get to go to the kingdom. And we're going to have our own land and there'll be no crime or sinners, just righteous

people. And we're gonna have a King David up there."

Debbie   And he would use the fact that your prophet is dead and you need a living prophet. Then, they'd slowly attend whoever was recruiting them for a while. Some people got to meet Vernon before they came to Mt. Carmel. Some people went there to meet him.

David   Most of them, even the people who lived in Hawaii, made a decision pretty quickly just to follow him.

Erwin   Did they just pack up and leave?

Debbie   Yes.

David   They sold their stuff, got their stuff together, and came out. At that point they had made a decision to follow Vernon.

Debbie   By the time they came to Mt. Carmel, they had already given up their lives for it. When you recruited somebody, you just didn't give them an hour study. You talked to them whenever possible, for as long as possible.

Erwin   If they gave you only a few hours of study time, wouldn't that limit the number of people who could be recruited?

David   No.

Debbie   They would always try to get groups.

David   Yeah. They would find a church where there were a lot of potential recruits.

Erwin   Would they go into an SDA service and hand out something?

Debbie   They would go into SDA services, and some of them would stand up. Like Vernon would actually stand up sometimes and interrupt the service.

David   Yeah, he did that sometimes. Most of the time though he stood outside on the sidewalk legally and just handed out literature. But you know really, that never was very effective. The most effective way of recruiting was when they got a lead. For instance, when Marc Breault came in. He was a connection back to Hawaii to the church where he used to go in Hawaii. So he thought, "Hey, I know this church in Hawaii where I know all these younger people. They're newer Adventists. They're hungry. Let's go out there." So with that lead, Vernon was able to make an entrance in there and reap quite a large following.

Debbie   Marc went around and said, "Hey, come listen to this guy."

Richard   He called his friends?

Debbie   Right.

David   Now there were other times, South Carolina is a good example, when Vernon went into a place, really hitting them hard with a lot of teachings, and in the end he didn't get a single person because the people there just couldn't buy what he was saying. In Hawaii they did excellent. In Wisconsin they tried to get Steve Schneider's parents and sister, but it didn't work out. He got a bunch of people out of England though.

Erwin   Was there different geographical areas that he liked?

David   California. They liked California. Hawaii. Australia was a wonderful place for him to go until the "new light" came and Marc went to Australia and basically shut Australia and New Zealand down for him.

Erwin   Why do you think he did well in some places and flopped in other places?

David   It must have something to do with the mood of Adventism in these different places. Ultimately, that's where he's going. He's going to Adventists.

Debbie   And Adventists can be very different.

David   If you go around and visit different Adventists in different parts of the world you're going to find different attitudes that Adventists will have. So, if he goes to South Carolina and doesn't get any Adventists, but goes to Hawaii, and Australia and gets a bunch, and goes to Great Britain, and out there gets entire families, women and children, just a whole slew of people, it's whatever's going on there so far as what Adventism is teaching. They're not being fed spiritually. They don't know the gospel. They don't have the truth. So, somebody comes along with something else that seems better than what they have which isn't the truth anyway, then, "Hey, let's do it!"

Debbie   They don't seem to have anything to fight with.

Erwin   There's a receptive mind-set to begin with?

David   Right. This is the thing too. Adventists are having a large fallout from the church. The young people in the church do not stay. It's like a revolving door kind of thing. You've got old people dying, young people leaving in droves. That's why a lot of people that Vernon got were younger people, mid to late twenties, early thirties, people who had joined Adventism based on the premise, "I joined Adventism because I wanted more light." You always got this "new light" stuff, it's almost like a drug. These people have to sit down and get this like fix all the time. They want new, new, stuff so they can feel special. That's what I think motivates people to join him.

Erwin   Did he use testimonials of people to draw others in, and also to reinforce the fact that people should feel privileged and honored and good that they're part of this group?

David   Sure. Also, sometimes he'll start out very slowly with people and work them up. A lot of people he's done that to he'd reel in. But some people he tells them too much shocking stuff before he's got control of them. And that's pushed people away. Some of the people he's lost is because he told them too much, too soon.

David   Vernon had this funny idea that if he was giving people light or truth, if they didn't totally accept what he was saying, in other words, if they didn't totally drop what they were doing and say, "Oh, yeah you've got the truth," he'd brush them off. With Debbie's sister

and brother-in-law, because they rejected him, he left thinking they didn't know anything. That everything he had told them had just gone in one ear and out the other, when in fact, they had learned a lot of things about him, but they just rejected it. Like they found out he was a polygamist. When Vernon heard later that they knew he had more than one wife, he was like, "Well, who told them," thinking he never told them because they didn't accept him.

Debbie   He's very strange. He says things and tells people things, he gives permission for things and then he doesn't remember. Or he'd teach big things and then months or a year later, he would never remember that he said that. He would deny it, "I didn't say that!"

David   A good example of this was when Marc Breault came in because he allegedly had visions of Koresh and some people that were with him. When Marc met Perry Jones at Loma Linda, Perry started to tell Marc about the message and Marc thought he had to listen because of the vision. Well, Koresh was really excited about this vision. He thought this was neat that somebody actually had a vision about him. He went and met Marc and thought it was really God working. I remember I was there. We were in the meeting and Vernon was up front and he said, "Well, who else did you see in that vision, Marc?" And Marc said, "Well, I'd like to tell you later, not here." That happened. I saw it. I was there.

Debbie   Oh, we heard it.

David   We heard it. In 1990, when I had started listening to Marc Breault, and was starting to realize that Koresh was wrong, Koresh called me on the phone, and was trying to re-recruit me, he was trying to get me back. And he was talking to me for hours on the phone. I specifically mentioned that incident—the general vision that Marc had—and the specific happening in that building that day, and he said that it didn't happen, he didn't remember it, and that he didn't know what I was talking about. I'm serious. If Koresh has a piece of information in his brain that does not fit in with his thinking he just gets rid of it. He just throws it out. He can pull things in and out as he needs them. And if he doesn't have any use for it, he just chucks it.

Debbie But if it's something he has use for, boy, he keeps it right in the forefront of his mind.

David Something that he doesn't want to remember he just forgets it. So, all of a sudden Marc Breault who used to be Mr. Hero, now because he doesn't agree with him, he's Mr. False Prophet-Judas.

Debbie He's very good at remembering the horrible, bad, wrong, sinful things you've done, and he never remembers the good things.

David The whole time I was Vernon I never heard anything bad about Marc. Mostly Marc was just great; he was playing the keyboards with Vernon, he could teach, he could give studies, and actually teach things out of the Bible without having to hear it from Koresh first which was very privileged. He was like a minor prophet in the group. He had a lot of authority to actually tell people things from the Bible and it was accepted as authoritative.

Debbie And Vernon told him many, many things that he never told anybody else.

David And then, all of a sudden he's in the doghouse. He is a Judas. He is the worst. He was never anything. "Oh, he always watched TV," Koresh told me. He was so terrible. And Koresh was trying to convince me on the phone that I'm better than Marc because I was with him from very early on. Two years before Marc ever knew him, I knew Vernon. He's trying to build me up like I'm more superior to Marc in the sense of knowing Vernon better. He tried to pull me back in that way. And I'm hearing this

and thinking, "This guy's just playing games."

Erwin Describe the process you went through when you came out.

David When I got booted out, I believed I was lost and going to hell and everything. I believed he was the Lamb. And I stayed in that belief for a long time, about ten months. I even wrote him a letter right before I contacted Marc and I said, "I don't want to have to stand before you one day and hear you say, 'Depart from me, I never knew you.'" I believed it. I wrote him a letter telling him that. I believed that he was going to judge us. I believed I was going to stand before him and he was going to say "Depart from me, I never knew you."

Richard Because he was the Lamb?

David Sure. Yeah. And then, at the same time there was this curiosity in me because this "new light" thing was secret, secret, secret. Nobody knew what was going on. Nobody would tell. Nobody would talk about it, it was secret. I wanted to know what it was. What is this "new light" that made Marc Breault leave? I couldn't handle it.

Debbie I told you what it was.

David Yeah, we speculated that maybe he took all the women.

Debbie I speculated. David said, "No, he'd never do that."

David I said, "No way! He would never do that."

Debbie I said, "It's the only thing it could be."

Richard It was the only thing that was left.

Debbie Exactly.

David So then, I write Marc and I say, "Okay, I'm lost and you need to reconsider." And he sent me a tape. So then, at that point I have his information about what Vernon is doing. He is committing adultery with other men's wives.

Debbie [laughs] David was in the land of confusion.

David Yeah. You know, I've got to deal with this. I mean, this is serious. We're talking about marriage. An institution that I upheld very highly. I was married.

Debbie The very first day we got that tape I immediately sat down and found all the verses in the Bible that talked about marriage [laughs].

Erwin Debbie, at that point did it seem like you were more distant from Vernon? It seems you were more cynical and had already written him off by then, but David was still struggling through it?

Debbie Yeah. I was.

David I had to logically think it through more. It was such a radical thought, it almost hurt to think it—"Vernon is wrong." Those three words. To think that and to actually believe it was very painful. It was very difficult. But with the evidence that was presented to me I had no choice. That was the only conclusion that I could come to.

Debbie Whereas I was scared, at the same time I welcomed it. It was like, "YES!"

David Believing that he was wrong solved so many problems for me. It was amazing.

Richard At the same time that it hurt, it just made everything go into focus?

David Yeah. It was like, all those times where he seemed wrong—he was wrong. I mean, he was wrong. That's all there was to it.

Erwin What grabbed you?

David Well, the thing that grabbed me specifically was when I found out that the Lamb was Jesus Christ. And in my thinking at the time, I never ever confused the person of Jesus Christ with Vernon Howell. He never taught it when we were there.

Debbie He had to keep reading it at work all the time.

David I had to always go in the Bible. I would panic and think I was lost, and had to go and actually read it over and over again. "Is it still there?" You know, I had to read it, and analyze it, and break it down.

Debbie I grew up at Mt. Carmel. I saw those people lie, and use people over and

over again, and I can be a very cynical person. David is the kind of person, he doesn't like to see that about people, especially those people. And he didn't grow up there, so he didn't see that all the time. So, when he'd get on the phone and Vernon would lie to him, I would see it as a lie. I'd say, "He just lied to you David." And he'd say, "Well, I don't think he'd do that."

David Steve Schneider got on the phone and told me point blank, "Me and Judy are still together." And he was lying. But I didn't think the guy would get on the phone and just lie to me like that.

Debbie I told David if Vernon told Steve to lie he would.

David The only reason that I was considering going back at that point is because they were saying that Marc was lying about what Vernon was doing with the women. I thought, Well, if Marc's lying about that, then Marc's wrong, and Vernon must be because he's not taking married women. That's wrong. I was convinced of that. So, Vernon tried to get me back on a lie. He was thinking— this is how Vernon thinks—he was thinking (I found this out from my sister later) that he was going to have me come all the way out to Laverne [California].

Debbie We were in Texas.

David And I was going to sit down in front of him and then as he was able to teach me, then I would be able to believe and then I would be able to accept him. When in reality, what would have happened was when I heard and found out what he was doing, I would have had to leave. My sister told Vernon, "My brother, if you lie to him like that and get him out here on a false premise, you're not going to get anywhere."

Debbie Vernon wanted David to leave me, Jennifer, and Megan.

David Yeah, wanted me to leave her, and my job!

Debbie Just leave us and trash us. Leave us with

nothing, no money, nothing and go to Vernon. He expected David to do that. And I left it up to David—I was scared to death.

Erwin   Did you struggle with that David?

David   I had to think about it for a day. At the end of the day, I was going over his explanation of how he could still be the Lamb when the Bible clearly says Jesus is. And at the end of the day I'm going, "No."

Debbie   Oh, and I was so happy when he said that, 'cause I didn't want to influence him. So I just said, "Whatever you want to do." 'Cause I knew that if I begged and pleaded with him and cried, he wouldn't go. But I wanted it to be his decision.

David   And I just said, "Hmm, no that's not true. Vernon's wrong."

Debbie   And I was like, "Oh, God, thank you, thank you, thank you."

David   And at that point I vowed, "Look, whatever I do from now on, anything that I do is going to be based on a solid reason from Scripture. I'm not going to make any rash decisions anymore. Because I had made a rash decision to go out to be with Vernon. What actually happened was, he had talked to me on the phone the day before. When he first started talking to me, he wanted me to come out. Then he saw that I was resistant, so we had a long conversation. At the end of the conversation he didn't ask me to come out, he told me to think.

Debbie   And he was going to say yes if Vernon asked again!

David   The next morning I decided to go. And so I tried to call and I didn't get a hold of anybody—which was good. By the end of that day I had turned around again, "No, I'm not going because I don't believe what you told me." At that point I thought, now I'm not going to worry about Marc, or Vernon, or anybody. I'm gonna stick to the Bible and I'm going to figure this stupid thing out.

So I got all the accusations that Vernon was making against Marc and I said, "Okay Marc, you answer these accusations." See we were coming down off of this idea of a prophet thing and we thought Marc is gonna be the new prophet. I mean that's the way we were thinking.

Debbie   We even said, "Okay, what do we have to do to follow you?"

David   Yeah. What are the rules, you know? [David laughs]

Debbie   Marc could have used that big time, and he did not use it. And I admire him for that.

David   He could have, man.

Debbie   He could have used it.

David   And then from that point: "Okay, Vernon's wrong, now what?" And then I started going back. Well, Vernon's wrong today. And he was also wrong when he started polygamy in '86. Oh look, he was wrong here when he started doing this in '84. And pretty soon he was wrong when he first started.

Debbie   And it took a while to get to that.

David   And then, I found out, "Hey, Lois Roden was wrong." And Ben Roden was wrong, too. He was a false prophet. And Houteff was wrong. I'm reading his teachings on Hebrews and he's just totally mangling Scriptures all over the place. Then, Seventh-day Adventism was wrong. I remember reading Ken Samples' article talking about the Adventists' position on grace.

Debbie   He's the kind of person that he wants to study the stuff out and see it. I mean when he first started to study Roden and Houteff, he was shocked at what he found. He first started studying to find out where it went wrong. He didn't expect it to be wrong all the way back like that.

David   I'll show you what really shocked me. This is a chart that Ben Roden did in 1958 and here's a time-line, okay? At 1960 he's predicting these events here.

All listed down here. If you understand Branch Davidian eschatology, these are end of the world events. We're talking about Ezekiel 9, purification of the Seventh-day Adventist church where all the wicked in the Seventh-day Adventist church fall down dead, and all this major stuff happening here. This is a pre-1960 chart that was published by the Branch to Adventists: "Read this, look at my inspired chart, see how inspired I am, be impressed." And then look. This is the revised version after things happen and they didn't go the way they thought they would go. Now all of a sudden we have this: the only thing that happened was a Catholic President was elected. "Oh no, we have a Catholic in the White House, so that's the deadly wound being healed." And then in '61 the Supreme Court decided that it was okay for towns to enact Sunday closing laws. "Oh my God, they're going to make us keep Sunday. OH NO!" That's it. And I thought, "What in the world is this? Look at this change! What are they trying to pull?!" This is the kind of stuff we used to get all over the Jehovah's Witnesses for. I thought forget this. I had never taken the time to study the Branch materials because I had assumed that they were true. Everybody said they were true. My dad told me they were true. Ben Roden said they were true. His wife said they were true. Vernon said they were true. "Hey, they must be true." Then, when I actually read them. No, it's not true, it's false. So then, I just went back to the Bible itself in context. I got the expositor's Bible commentary just to see what it said. To see what others were saying and if it made any sense. It made a lot more sense than what Koresh taught. We also went to a Seventh-day Adventist church for a while. But then, I decided their prophecies were wrong cause I was reading like *Kingdom of the Cults* there, in the back section of the

book about the Seventh-day Adventist church.

Erwin   And you stumbled onto that in a Christian bookstore?

David   Well, I was aware of Walter Martin before, I just thought he was wrong.

Erwin   As a Branch Davidian?

David   Sure. I used to listen to the "Bible Answer Man" [radio program] in '86 when I was a Branch Davidian. I thought he was right on certain things, but I didn't think he was right in condemning Adventism. When he would talk about the Mormons, sure, yeah, they're wrong. And the Jehovah's Witnesses, "Oh yeah." He was right there too, but if he started attacking Adventism or the Sabbath, "Oh, well, then he's wrong." Like we had the *Maze of Mormonism*, this book right here was on the shelves in our house in Highland Park [California] in '86. In fact, some Mormons came to our door when we were living in Highland Park and Koresh was there. Now you know how Mormons are, they were doing their standard Mormon thing: "Well, I just believe the Book of Mormon, I believe it's true because I just feel it." And they're giving us their thing. Well Koresh is there, and he's got his thing. When they left, I pointed out the *Maze of Mormonism* and I said, "Hey, Martin's studied this maybe he knows something about Mormonism." And Koresh says, "Well, he attacked the Adventist church, so he doesn't know what he's talking about."

Erwin   Even Koresh was aware of Martin?

David   Oh yeah. He knew who Walter Martin was. He hated the guy. Steve Schneider hated Walter Martin too. He thought Walter Martin was the devil himself because he was against the Adventist church.

Erwin   It seems to me that now you're getting in touch with some alternative materials, how did that happen? How did you make the transition to non-Davidian resources?

Richard   Did you go to a Christian bookstore?

David   Yeah, sure.

Richard   And by then you had completely rejected Koresh's message?

David   Yeah.

Debbie   Oh yes.

Richard   If you could say one thing to someone who is right now in a cult, what would that one thing be?

David   I would say that you must critically analyze your beliefs. That is, you must not take anything for granted. That is a fatal mistake. You must examine and test what you believe to see if it's true. That may sound formal and boring, but you gotta do it. You just gotta get that Bible open and start reading it and try to understand what the Bible says *yourself*. If you can't do that, then you don't know what you believe. And if you're in a message being given by some central prophet or central teacher who is supposedly inspired and he gives this truth out (even if he uses the Bible to expound this truth) and when you look in your Bible and can see it, still take your Bible home later and read the text—just read the words and try to understand how the guy gets his teachings out of this Bible. If at that time you can't get it out yourself, if you can't read it and see it for yourself, you gotta stop right there and take a second look because that means you got a problem.

Richard   Debbie, how about you?

Debbie   Mainly this, don't fall into a group because you're afraid or because somebody's telling you that you should. That's why I followed. I followed because I was so afraid. If you're doing something out of fear, that's the wrong reason.

Richard   Okay. Thank you both for sharing so much.

Erwin   We really appreciate all the time.

David   Oh sure.

Debbie   No problem. Thank *you*.

David Thibodeau was present in the Branch Davidian compound throughout the entire siege. He is one of the nine survivors of the Davidian fire and is still a believer in David Koresh. Although he faces an upcoming trial, exactly what crimes he will be charged with is still pending. He is currently out on bail and living in Maine. Thibodeau was married to Michelle Jones, the girl whom David Koresh took as a "wife" when she was only twelve years old. She had two children by Koresh. Even after being legally married to Thibodeau, she remained Koresh's sexual partner (as did all women) up until the end. She never lived with Thibodeau as his wife in the same sense that the rest of married couples in society live. In other words, Thibodeau and Jones were married in name only. Thibodeau spoke with Richard Abanes on June 1, 1993. The conversation did not last very long.

Richard   David, I want you to know that I'm very sorry about the way everything has turned out. I know you lost some people that were precious to you and I really am sorry. How long have you been a Branch Davidian?

David   Well, I have a problem with "Branch Davidian." We didn't go around calling ourselves the Branch Davidians. We're just people studying the Book [the Bible]. Ever since the ATF raid we've been labeled a cult, Branch Davidians. I understand that I'm forever dubbed a Branch Davidian.

Richard   Well, I assumed from . . .

David   [Interrupting] I've known David [Koresh] for a couple of years, '91 I met him.

Richard   Let me put it this way. Why did you start studying the Book with David? What drew you to his views on the Book?

David   Cause he made a challenge out of the

David Book that nobody could make without some kind of understanding of Revelation 4 and 5 of the seals.

Richard Regarding his identity as the Lamb?

David Well, he didn't put it like that. Just what the Book said about someone to come and reveal the seven seals. And not only did he show you the challenge, but then he would show you the seven seals, where they're found. It was incredible. It was very conclusive.

Richard That's what attracted you to his message?

David Well, originally it was the music. I was looking for a good band. I was looking for a very progressive rock band and he was one of the most phenomenal guitarists up to that time.

Richard So when he started sharing his views with you on the Book it seemed to make sense?

David Definitely.

Richard Would you consider, then, the seven seals to be of primary importance out of everything in the Bible?

David Yeah. According to Revelation 4 and 5. Of all things in Revelation what stands out is the fact that the Lamb has a reward and he's given the Book and the Book is sealed with seven seals and no man can reveal it. And when you go to Revelation 22 where it says, "Behold I come quick and my reward is with me to give to every man according as his work shall be." You have to ask, "Well, what's the Lamb's reward?" The thing of significance that the Lamb gives is the Book sealed with seven seals.

Richard It is my understanding that the Lamb is equal to Jesus Christ. That's what the Scriptures seem to indicate. Would you agree with that? How would that fit into David being this "Lamb" who would open the seven seals?

David [extremely long pause] Well [pause], that's what the Book says you [mumbled words].

Richard If the Lamb equals Jesus, and David was the Lamb, then David was Jesus. That's just logical.

David Well, if he revealed the seven seals, then he obviously had a doctrine nobody else was presenting. You can put it how you like. I know what I know. Okay, I haven't agreed to anything and I'm answering a lot of questions and I want to know why.

Richard Well, I want to know what you want to say.

David I'd like to go over some of the FBI negotiation tapes.

Richard Okay.

David And try to pick apart some things that they were telling the media, some of the things from what I understand were actually being said from within. That's the thing I'd really like to do. I'd want to get together with you in person if I were to do this and spend a couple of days and go through some of these things.

Richard I want to give you an opportunity to now say what you want to say.

David What you fail to realize is that no matter what I say, if the seven seals are true, if the Book is true, if God did reveal the seven seals, then that won't be my job. That's God's problem. That's something that God is gonna make sure that every consciousness in the world is awakened to someday.

Richard How will that happen if Koresh is gone? That's what I don't see.

David Well, that's what a lot of people don't see.

Richard How will the rest of the world get the knowledge of the seven seals that came from him?

David You can't get it from me.

Richard Who will we get it from?

David Well look, if the Book of Revelation is true, then you can pretty much see what the Book says is going to happen in the final days. Now when are the final days. Like I said, I'm not going to get into this with you over the phone. The Book has to be opened and it has to be shown.

Richard   But who can open it now? *That's* the question I'm asking.

David   There's a lot of negotiation tapes. David and Steve spent hours, and hours and hours of days. Days and days actually during the siege just talking on the phone to FBI negotiators. He went over the first seal and the second seal all the way to the fifth seal, showed from the Scriptures where they're found, explained his side of the story, presented his cause. Do you realize that the FBI negotiators went through twenty-two different negotiators talking with David and Steve? They kept putting new people on just about every other day. That was a factor. Now, my rationale would be—why? Did they wear them? Were they becoming convicted? Were they seeing a lot of true points? How come we weren't allowed to have the media within the complex and have a forum? And a lot of people would say, "Well, he put himself in that position so he could get attention." The truth of the matter is we were just happy being alone and reading the Book. It wasn't us that initiated the fire-fight.

Richard   One thing that confuses everybody and is causing problems in everybody's mind is why there was fire directed toward the ATF? I mean, what happened? Why didn't David just allow the ATF to come in, do their search warrant thing, and let it blow over? Let the legal system work it out like it happened before in 1987?

David   If the sheriff's department would have come up and knocked on the door the way it was supposed to be done, served a search warrant, and then come in and checked it out, it probably could have been done differently.

Richard   But it was this armed assault that David felt like he was in danger?

David   This is where I have to be careful talking to you because I have a trial coming up and I'm not going to get into this. I want to answer your question and I can. And I can answer it very rationally, but now is not the time. I'm still facing a lot of crap.

Richard   Well, I don't want to get you in trouble. I'm just asking what everybody's wondering.

David   There's things I'm wondering. Not according to the message, but what's all being done and what's all being said.

Richard   You still believe in David and his message, then, at his point?

David   I believe that David showed me the seven seals.

At this point in the conversation David started becoming rather tense and began complaining about how the government was trying to find information to condemn him. After side-stepping a few more questions he terminated the conversation and said he would call me back. As of publication we have not been able to contact him to complete the interview.

Appendix C

A Brew of Controvesy

In their book, *Strange Gods*, sociologists David Bromley and Anson Shupe, Jr., recount the case of twenty-three-year-old Pam Fanshier and the ordeal she went through as her parents tried to have her deprogrammed from being a "Moonie," a member of Sun Myung Moon's Unification Church:

> The first part of the deprogramming consisted of three days of very strenuous and continuous verbal attack. I was mocked, degraded, accused of sexual crimes and prostitution. Bible verses were constantly being hurled at me plus lengthy and boring testimonies of individuals who had been deprogrammed from various other religious groups. Only twice during these entire three days did we carry on even a half-way intelligent conversation. . . . My brother screamed in my face that I was a prostitute and that I hated my parents and wanted to destroy them. When one group of "deprogrammers" and body guards got tired they simply called in a fresh group. When I would start to fall asleep someone would kick the bed or poke me to keep me awake. I lost track of the hours and no one would tell me what time it was. . . . The clothes and all personal possessions which I had were taken from me and my parents were ordered to burn them. For three days the intensive part of the deprogramming continued.

Pam managed to escape only to be violently abducted once again. Her parents were even more convinced that their daughter had been brainwashed. They had her committed as a mental patient at a clinic in Topeka, Kansas. The situation then took a turn for the worse, as Pam, her parents, and lawyers on both sides engaged in a bitter battle over the issue of her mental competence. The judge finally ruled her to be mentally sound.

Three years later, in 1978, Pam thought things needed to be patched up between her and her parents. She was about to graduate from the Union Theological Seminary in New York, and wanted to bring a harmonious resolution to the situation with her parents. She notified her parents of her arrival, and all went according to plan.

During the ceremonies, however, Pam was noticeably absent: she never made it back from her parents' home. Less than a week later her lawyer, accompanied by a sheriff, discovered that the Fanshier residence was empty. Pam was locked in a trailer undergoing yet another episode of deprogramming.

The Deprogramming Debate

The Fanshiers weren't very different from other concerned parents who were convinced that their children had been deceptively "programmed" to serve their gurus or masters. Many believed that the group their son or daughter joined employed sinister methods of brainwashing designed to enslave the innocent and unwary.

The term "deprogramming" was therefore used to describe the measures employed to counteract the effects of "programming" or brainwashing. Yet, like the word "cult," deprogramming had taken on a decidedly negative tone due, to a large extent, to the attention given those drastic and controversial means used by some early deprogrammers.

The type of deprogramming depicted by Bromley and Shupe can be more accurately called *involuntary* or *forcible* deprogramming. It is generally characterized by the physical detention of the person being deprogrammed and, at times, has included the abduction of the individual. The cost of deprogramming can run up to $10,000 or more and typically lasts three to five days.

Some say deprogramming was originally intended to allow parents the opportunity to speak with their children in a neutral setting, free from the negative influence of the group they have joined. Former members of the group often aided parents in snatching their adult children, keeping them detained at an isolated location, and presenting negative information about the group in question.

Involuntary deprogramming usually served as a final option for "rescuing" those believed to have been converted by means of unethical psychological and social manipulation. A move was also made by families of "cult" members to pass "guardianship" bills that would legally sanction the "extraction" of members from the group for psychiatric observation and deprogramming. To date no such bills have become law.

Deprogramming's coercive nature has resulted in a number of legal suits and criminal charges filed against parents and deprogrammers. The rulings, in most instances, have tended to favor the parents and deprogrammers, though there have been exceptions. It has been pointed out that the greater the danger posed by an individual's involvement with the group in question, the better the chances that deprogramming will be judged as a legally justifiable course of action.

A number of scholars and experts have voiced strong opposition to the practice of involuntary deprogramming, asserting that it involves kidnapping and the use of other violent measures to accomplish its intended purposes. They have questioned the legality of such actions altogether and have criticized the qualifications and ethical standards of professional deprogrammers.

Another concern is the psychological dangers of unsuccessful deprogramming. It is not at all difficult to see how a sense of betrayal and mistrust of one's family can result from being abducted and restrained when one expected nothing more than a congenial discussion. Observers have pointed to cases in which those who escaped from deprogramming sessions have become even further galvanized in their newfound beliefs and are driven even further from communicating with friends and relatives.

Deprogramming sessions are typically confrontational and take place within a confined space where the person being deprogrammed is physically detained by someone presenting a negative picture of a cherished belief system. For this reason, it is understandable how such an ordeal can exact a heavy emotional and mental toll on everyone involved.

Anticult observers have referred to various ways that groups accused of brainwashing have used their resources to wage misinformation campaigns against deprogramming. They allege that some groups have gone so far as to instruct members to act as though they have been victims of unlawful deprogramming, so as to sue parents and deprogrammers or file criminal charges against them.

A more moderate alternative to involuntary deprogramming is an approach called *exit counseling* or *voluntary deprogramming*. As the terms imply, many who opt for this method of intervention have as a central operating principle the invitation for the member to change his or her view about the group. This is accomplished mainly by the parents and exit counselors persuasively explaining why they believe the individual should leave the group.

Unlike involuntary deprogramming, exit counseling does not rely on the use of physical force like abduction or detention. A number of exit counselors believe that ends do not justify the means. Yet because the terms "exit counseling" and "deprogramming" are sometimes interchanged, there continues to be much confusion as to how they differ.

Even those critics who recognize the differences between the two approaches still charge that both exit counseling and deprogramming are based on a dubious theory of conversion known as "mind control," and are thus seen as false solutions.

Brainwash or Hogwash?

The term "mind control" is used synonomously with brainwashing, coercive persuasion, and thought reform—which a number of behavioral scientists believe is the primary tactic employed by "cults" to recruit and keep members. (Some prefer to distinguish mind control from brainwashing, which is said to include such physically coercive measures as assault and torture.)

In *Destructive Cultism: Questions and Answers* psychologist Michael Langone lists the following methods of mind control:

> a) extensive control of information in order to limit alternatives from which members may make "choices"; b) deception; c) group pressure; d) intense indoctrination into a belief system that denigrates independent critical thinking and considers the world outside the group to be threatening, evil, or gravely in error; e) an insistence that members' distress—much of which may consist of anxiety and guilt subtly induced by the group—can be relieved only by conformity to the group; f) physical and/or psychological debilitation through inadequate diet or fatigue; and g) the induction of dissociative (trance-like) states in which attention is narrowed, suggestibility heightened, and independent critical thinking weakened.

Langone comments that while many groups and individuals occasionally use such modes of influence, there are accountability structures to keep them in check. But in the case of "destructive cults" such actions are said to comprise the rule by which leaders exploit the members of the group. Furthermore, unlike the social conditioning employed by parents, schools, and other social institutions, which is designed to teach individuals independence, mind control trains members of "destructive cults" to become dependent on the leader and the group.

According to proponents of the mind control thesis, "destructive cults" dupe or manipulate vulnerable individuals into joining their ranks. The person may be going through a particularly trying moment in life, such as a recent family break-up or a change in jobs, which the group turns to its advantage in getting the individual to join. Or it may be that the individual was lured into a group as a result of participating in a seminar promoted as a workshop for improving personal skills.

In any case, the convert is generally regarded as the unwary victim whose personal circumstance was exploited by the group. Thus it is said that the convert was never given the opportunity to make a rational and informed choice. He or she was recruited under false pretenses.

It is also asserted that the techniques of mind control are so subtle that most individuals subjected to them don't even realize that they are being influenced. Once a person joins a group, a psychological change is said to take place; a secondary personality develops that reflects the attitude of the group. The inner tension caused by the two conflicting modes of thought and outlook creates further stress on the individual, which the leader of the group takes advantage of to further eradicate all traces of the individual's former personality.

Historically speaking, the mind control thesis is rooted largely in psychologist Robert J. Lifton's research and study, conducted during the Korean War; Lifton focused on communist thought reform programs employed by the Chinese Communists. In *Thought Reform and the Psychology of Totalism*, Lifton listed eight points that he believed comprised the program for ideological totalism used by the Communists to indoctrinate prisoners of war and the Chinese population at large. These points have been adapted to explain how "destructive cults" control those who fall prey to their influence. Lifton's research continues to be held up as proof positive that a person's attitude, beliefs, and behavior can be systematically overturned and recast to desired specifications.

Critics of the mind control thesis say Lifton's findings were not entirely revolutionary, interesting though they may be. According to these critics, lab experiments performed a decade before Lifton's research drew similar conclusions (i.e., that changing the outlook of individuals is more easily accomplished when done in a group setting). Moreover, such "voluntary" types of reform were considered to be longer-lasting and more efficient than "involuntary" measures that include abduction, sleep deprivation, the use of drugs, and physical abuse.

Anson and Shupe, opponents of the mind control thesis, point out that of the 3,500 U.S. prisoners of war who underwent "thought reform" during the Korean War, less than 1.5 percent made procommunist statements, and only half of those (.075 percent) refused repatriation after the war. They further note that the Confederate Army, which had no such elaborate program, experienced a higher success rate (2%) in getting captured Union soldiers to fight on the Confederate side during the Civil War.

Critics also charge that the mind control thesis fails to take into account several crucial factors that contribute to a person's decision to join a particular group. It is contended that the group may be meeting an individual's personal needs, whatever they may be. It has also been suggested that an individual more likely joined the group because he or she agrees with the values, ideals, and outlook expressed by the group. To fail to note such important factors, critics say, can only result in a distorted view of the situation.

Opponents of the mind control thesis say that the process that takes place when a person joins a "cult" is not very different (some say no different) from the conversion process associated with recognized religious traditions. Critics say the notion of mind control eradicates the idea of freedom of choice by failing to recognize the legitimacy of a person's conversion to a "cult"; that it may unjustifiably do away with personal responsibility as negative experiences are almost always blamed on the group rather than the individual; that it ignores the fact that many individuals leave "cults" voluntarily without the assistance of exit counselors or deprogrammers deemed necessary to diffuse the effects of mind control.

As the debate on this issue continues, primarily among behavioral and social scientists, readers are encouraged to consider further the arguments on both sides and contemplate the implications of each respective conclusion. Regardless of where one stands on the issue, there is no doubt that everyone is exposed daily to techniques of persuasion and influence—whether it be from friends, relatives, salespeople, television commercials, or newspaper ads.

When confronted by individuals or groups who are employing intensified forms of persuasion techniques, certain measures can be used to neutralize the situation. Persuasion is a normal and common activity among people that generally helps society function. The problem begins when persuasion is used for exploitative purposes.

In learning to recognize such techniques, a person can be better equipped to respond to what otherwise might be confusing and uncertain situations. Their applicability in dealing with individuals or groups that utilize high-pressure tactics is self-evident.

Bibliography

I. Primary Documentation

Breault, Elizabeth. "Personal letter from Elizabeth Breault to Debbie Bunds." 10/21/90.

Breault, Marc. "Personal letter from Marc Breault to Judy Schneider." 12/16/89.

Breault, Marc. "Personal letter from Marc Breault to David and Debbie Bunds." 05/22/90.

Breault, Marc. "Personal letter from Marc Breault to David and Debbie Bunds." 06/18/90.

Breault, Marc. "Personal letter from Marc Breault to Steve Schneider." 06/21/90.

Breault, Marc. "Personal letter from Marc Breault to Sherri Jewell." 10/17/90.

Breault, Marc. "Personal letter from Marc Breault to David and Debbie Bunds." 10/22/90.

Breault, Marc. "Personal letter from Marc Breault to David Bunds." 11/23/90.

Breault, Marc. "Open letter from Marc Breault to all Branch Davidians in America." 12/03/90.

Breault, Marc. "Personal letter from Marc Breault to David and Debbie Bunds." 02/20/91.

Breault, Marc. "An Explanation of My Actions, Studies, and Letters Since the So-called 'New Light' Taught by Vernon Wayne Howell." 03/16/91.

Breault, Marc. "Some Background on the Branch Davidian Seventh-day Adventist Movement from 1955 to the Early Part of 1991." 04/17/91 (revised ed. 05/27/91), unpublished manuscript.

Breault, Marc. "Personal letter from Marc Breault to David and Debbie Bunds." 04/30/91.

Breault, Marc. "Personal letter from Marc Breault to David and Debbie Bunds." 10/11/91.

Breault, Marc. "Personal letter from Marc Breault to David and Debbie Bunds." 10/14/91.

Breault, Marc. "Personal letter from Marc Breault to David and Debbie Bunds." 10/27/91.

Breault, Marc. "Personal letter from Marc Breault to Vernon Howell and Steve Schneider." 10/29/91.

Breault, Marc. "Personal letter from Marc Breault to David and Debbie Bunds." 11/12/91.

Breault, Marc. "Personal letter from Marc Breault to David and Debbie Bunds." 10/10/92.

Breault, Marc. "Personal letter from Marc Breault to David and Debbie Bunds." 11/09/92.

Breault, Marc. "Personal letter from Marc Breault to David and Debbie Bunds." 11/16/92.

Breault, Marc. "A History of My Involvement With The Branch Davidian Seventh-day Adventist Cult." n.d., unpublished manuscript.

Breault, Marc. "Story of Joel Andrew Jones." n.d., unpublished manuscript.

Bunds, David. "Personal letter from David Bunds to Jaydee Wendell." n.d.

"Choosing the Best Way of Life." *The Watchtower*, March 15, 1980, pp. 17–18.

"Church Universal and Triumphant News Release." March 11, 1993, p. 6.

Evans, David W. *Journal of Discourses by President Brigham Young, His Counselors, and the Twelve Apostles.* Liverpool, England: Albert Carrington, 1875.

Henry, Diana. "Personal letter from Diana Henry to Ian and Allison Manning." 6/18/91

Houteff, Victor T. *The Answerer No. 2.* Waco, TX: The Universal Publishing Assn., n.d.

Houteff, Victor T. *The Answerer No. 3.* Waco, TX: The Universal Publishing Assn., n.d.

Houteff, Victor T. *The Answerer No. 4.* Waco, TX: The Universal Publishing Assn., n.d.

Houteff, Victor T. *The Answerer No. 5.* Waco, TX: The Universal Publishing Assn., 1944.

Houteff, Victor T. *The Entering Wedge: The Genesis of Diet and Health.* Waco, TX: The Universal Publishing Assn., 1946.

Houteff, Victor T. *The Great Controversy Over The Shepherd's Rod.* n.s.: n.p., n.d.

Houteff, Victor T. *The Shepherd's Rod. Vol. 1.* n.s.: n.p., 1930.

Houteff, Victor T. *The Shepherd's Rod. Vol. 2.* n.s.: n.p., 1932.

Houteff, Victor T. *The World Yesterday, Today, Tomorrow*. Waco, TX: The Universal Publishing Assn., 1932.

Houteff, Victor T. *War News Forecast*. Waco, TX: The Universal Publishing Assn., 1943.

How Can Blood Save Your Life? New York: The Watch Tower Bible and Tract Society, 1990.

Howell, Vernon W. "Blow Ye the Trumpet in Zion" (an open invitation to visit Mt. Carmel). 12/12/83.

Howell, Vernon W. "Judge What I Say" (taped message). 02/4/85.

Howell, Vernon W. "Seven Eyes" (taped message). 02/04/86.

Howell, Vernon W. "Get Ready, Get Ready, Get Ready" (an open invitation to Passover 1986). 02/28/86.

Howell, Vernon W. "The Identity of the Ancient of Days" (taped message). 06/14/86.

Howell, Vernon W. "Study on the Assyrians" (taped message). 01/10/87.

Howell, Vernon W. "Confusion" (taped message). 07/18/87.

Howell, Vernon W. "Revelation 13" (taped message). 07/23/87.

Howell, Vernon W. "Study On Joel and Daniel 11" (taped message). 1987.

Howell, Vernon W. "Vernon's Dream" (taped message). 04/24/89.

Howell, Vernon W. "The Foundation" (taped message). 1989.

Howell, Vernon W. "Open letter to the Seventh Adventist Church." n.d.

Jewell, David. "Personal letter from David Jewell to Marc Breault." 01/11/92.

Jewell, Sherri. "Personal letter from Sherri Jewell to Marc Breault." 08/03/90.

"Keeping a Balanced View of Time." *The Watchtower*, July 15, 1976, p. 436.

Koresh, David. "Private telephone conversation between David Koresh and David Bunds" (taped). 02/21/91.

Koresh, David. "911 Emergency Call." 02/28/93.

Leahy, Frank X. "Personal letter from Frank X. Leahy to the FBI." 04/08/93.

The Lost Years and Lost Teachings of Jesus. "What Are Dictations?" (advertisement for Summit University Press), 1992.

Manning, Allison. "Affidavit of Allison Manning to the Consulate General of the United States of America." Melbourne, Australia, 08/20/90.

Manning, Ian. "Affidavit of Ian Manning to the Consulate General of the United States of America." Melbourne, Australia, 08/20/90.

"Questions From The Readers." *The Watchtower*, June 15, 1991, p. 31 (italics added).

Riddle, Myrtle. "Personal letter from Myrtle Riddle to Ian Manning." 08/29/90.

Roberts, B. H. *A Comprehensive History of the Church of Jesus Christ of Latter-day Saints*. Provo, UT: Published by the Church, Brigham Young University Press, 1965.

Roden, Ben L. *The Man On the White Horse*. 1958.

Roden, Ben L. "The Law of Moses in the Light of Revelation 14" (an open letter to all Davidian Seventh-day Adventists). n.d.

Roden, Ben L. "The New Name: Isaiah 62:2" (an open letter to all Davidian Seventh-day Adventists). 04/21/58.

Roden, Ben L. "The Branch in the Light of Zechariah 1 and 2" (an open letter to all Davidian Seventh-day Adventists). 05/07/58.

Roden, Ben L. "The Family Tree: Isaiah 11:1" (an open letter to all Davidian Seventh-day Adventists). 05/21/58.

Roden, Ben L. "THE BRANCH: Revelation 18:1" (an open letter to all Davidian Seventh-day Adventists). 05/25/58.

Roden, Ben L. "Details of the 430 year Prophecy According to Abraham & Ezek. 4" (an open letter to all Davidian Seventh-day Adventists). 07/10/58.

Roden, Ben L. "The Stone" (an open letter to all Davidian Seventh-day Adventists). 11/24/58.

Roden, Ben L. "THE ATONEMENT and PASSOVER FEAST" (an open letter to all Davidian Seventh-day Adventists). 04/14/59.

Roden, Ben L. *God's Holy Feasts: The Unrolling of the Scroll*. Waco, TX: The Universal Publishing Assn., 1965.

Roden, Lois. *SHEKINAH*, Vol. 1, No.1, 1980.

Roden, Lois. *SHEKINAH*, April 1981.

Roden, Lois. *SHEKINAH*, June 1981.

Roden, Lois. *SHEKINAH*, October–December 1982.

Schneider, Steve. "The Holy Spirit" (taped message). n.d.

White, Ellen G. *The Great Controversy*. Mountain View, CA: Pacific Press Publishing Association, 1927 (orig. 1888).

II. Books, Newspapers, Magazines, and Journals

Alnor, William M. *Soothsayers of the Second Advent*. Old Tappan, NJ: Fleming H. Revell Company, 1989.

Alnor, William M. and Ronald Enroth. "Ethical Problems in Exit Counseling." *Christian Research Journal* 14:3, Winter 1992, pp. 14–19.

Applebome, Peter. "Bloody Sunday's Roots In Deep Religious Soil." *The N.Y. Times*, March 2, 1993, p. A8.

Associated Press. "History Has Seen Many Apocalyptic Scenarios." *L.A. Times*, March 13, 1993, p. B8.

Associated Press. "Independent Pathologist supports Branch Davidian Autopsy Findings." *L.A. Times*, May 16, 1993, p. A17.

Associated Press. "Welfare worker says she was warned off Koresh investigation." *The Orange County Register*, October 11, 1993, p. 18.

Aynesworth, Hugh. "Defiant cult holds off lawmen." *The Washington Times*, March 1, 1993, p. A1.

Aynesworth, Hugh. "2 cultists leave: Feds foresee end of siege in days." *The Washington Times*, March 20, 1993, p. A4.

Aynesworth, Hugh. "Koresh's new tone gives FBI hope." *The Washington Times*, March 21, 1993, p. A3.

Aynesworth, Hugh. "7 more cultists emerge: FBI heartened by release pace." *The Washington Times*, March 22, 1993, p. A3.

Aynesworth, Hugh. "FBI turns up pressure on cult." *The Washington Times*, March 23, 1993, p. A6.

Aynesworth, Hugh. "Cultist's lawyer says members want out." *The Washington Times*, March 31, 1993, p. A7.

Aynesworth, Hugh. "Koresh attorney claims progress." *The Washington Times*, April 1, 1993, p. A5.

Bach, Alan W. "When they came for the Davidians." *The Orange County Register*, May 2, 1993, p. 1.

Baldwin, Dalton. "Experiences in Loma Linda." *Adventist Today*, May–June 1993, p. 11.

Barker, Eileen. *The Making of a Moonie: Choice or Brainwashing?* New York: Basil Blackwell, Inc., 1984.

Barker, Eileen. *New Religious Movements: A Practical Introduction.* London: Her Majesty's Stationery Office, 1989.

Barkun, Michael. "Reflections after Waco: Millennialists and the State." *The Christian Century*, June 2–9, 1993, pp. 596–600.

Bayles, Fred and Mitchell Landsberg. "Apocalyptic visions guide compound life." *The Orange County Register*, March 7, 1993, p. A4.

Beck, Melinda et al. "The Questions Live On." *Newsweek*, May 3, 1993, pp. 28–29.

Beck, Melinda et al. "Someone Dropped the Ball: How Authorities Missed the Child Abuse." *Newsweek*, May 17, 1993, p. 51.

Beckford, James E. *Cult Controversies: The Societal Response to the New Religious Movements.* London: Tavistock Publications, 1985.

Biskupic, Joan and Pierre G. Thomas. "Standoff Ensues at Texas site." *The Washington Post*, March 1, 1993, pp. A1, A6.

Bodine, Jerry and Marian. *Witnessing to the Witnesses.* n.p., n.d.

Boyer, Paul. "A Brief History of the End of Time." *The New Republic*, May 17, 1993, pp. 30–33.

Boyer, Paul. *When Time Shall Be No More: Prophecy Belief in Modern American Culture.* Cambridge, MA: Belknap Press/Harvard University Press, 1992.

Branson, Roy. "We Didn't Start the Fire, But the Tinder Was Ours." *Spectrum: The Journal of the Association of Adventist Forums* 23:1, May 1993, p. 2.

Braun, Stephen. "Koresh Sends Doom-Laden Letter to FBI." *L.A. Times*, April 11, 1993, p. A9.

Braun, Stephen. "Davidian's Key Weapon Was Their Unpredictability." *L.A. Times*, April 20, 1993, p. A12.

Brembeck, Winston Lamont and William Smiley Howell. *Persuasion: A Means to Social Control.* Englewood Cliffs, NJ: Prentice-Hall, Inc., 1952.

Briggs, David. "FBI played into Koresh fantasies." *San Louis Obisbo Telegram-Tribune*, October 2, 1993, p. E2.

Bromley, David G. and Anson D. Shupe, Jr. *Strange Gods.* Boston: Beacon Press, 1981.

Bromley, David G. and Anson D. Shupe, Jr., eds. *The Brainwashing/Deprogramming Controversy: Sociological, Psychological, Legal and Historical Perspectives.* New York: The Edwin Mellen Press, 1983.

Brooks, Juanita. *The Mountain Meadows Massacre.* Norman, OK: University of Oklahoma Press, 1962.

Brooks, Juanita. *John Doyle Lee: Zealot-Pioneer Builder-Scapegoat.* Glendale, CA: The Arthur C. Clark Company, 1973.

Brown, J. A. C. *Techniques of Persuasion: From Propaganda to Brainwashing.* New York: Penguin Books, 1963.

Bruno, Joel Bel. "Mother Mourns, 'It's All Over'." *The Orange County Register*, April 20, 1993, pp. 1–2.

Bull, Malcolm and Keith Lockhart. *Seeking a Sanctuary: Seventh-day Adventism and the American Dream.* New York: Harper & Row, 1989.

Bursey, Ernest. "In a Wild Moment, I Imagine ..." *Spectrum: The Journal of the Association of Adventist Forums* 23:1, May 1993, pp. 50–52.

Burton, Shirley. "News Release From the Seventh-day Adventist Church to the Media." Seventh-day Adventist Church, March 2, 1993.

Burton, Shirley. "News Release From the Seventh-day Adventist Church to the Media." Seventh-day Adventist Church, March 6, 1993.

Carol, Ginny et al. "Children of the Cult." *Newsweek*, May 17, 1993, pp. 48–50.

Cartwright, Robert H. and Stephen A. Kent. "Social Control in Alternative Religions: A Familial Perspective." *Sociological Analysis* 53:4, Winter 1992, pp. 345–61.

Cattau, Daniel. "Faith, in the wrong hands, is more dangerous than firearms." *Ashbury Park Press*, March 18, 1993, pp. E1, E4.

Cerio, Gregory and Lucy Howard. "Davidians: ID'd But Unclaimed." *Newsweek*, September 27, 1993, p. 10.

Cetnar, Bill and Joan. *Questions for Jehovah's Witnesses "Who love the truth."* n.p., n.d.

Chretien, Leonard and Marjorie. *Witnesses of Jehovah.* Video Tape. La Jolla, CA: Good News Defenders, 1988.

Chua-Eoan, Howard. "Tripped Up, By Lies." *Time*, October 11, 1993, pp. 39–40.

Church, George J. "The End Is Near?" *Time*, April 26, 1993, p. 32.

Cialdini, Robert B. *Influence: The New Psychology of Modern Persuasion.* New York: Quill, 1984.

Claiborne, William and Jim McGee. "The Making of David Koresh." *Spectrum: The Journal of the Association of Adventist Forums* 23:1, May 1993, pp. 18–25.

Clouse, Robert G. *The Meaning of the Millennium: Four Views.* Downers Grove, IL: InterVarsity Press, 1977.

Cochran, Mike. "Cult leader a deadly paradox." *The Orange County Register*, April 20, 1993, p. 12.

Cockburn, Alexander. "No Wimps, Just Janet Reno and the Dead." *L.A. Times*, April 20, 1993, p. B11.

Cohen, Daniel. *Not of the World: A History of the Commune in America.* Chicago, IL: Follett Publishing Co., 1993.

Cohn, Bob, Eleanor Clift, and Melinda Liu. "The Book of Koresh." *Newsweek*, October 11, 1993, pp. 26–30.

Collins, Jeff. "The law steps in after strife-torn religious sect's battle." *The Dallas Morning Herald*, November 24, 1987, n.p.

Cooper, Douglas. "Did David Die for Our Sins?" *Spectrum: The Journal of the Association of Adventist Forums* 23:1, May 1993, pp. 47–48.

Cottrell, Raymond. "History and Fatal Theology of the BRANCH DAVIDIANS." *Adventist Today*, May–June 1993, pp. 5–7.

Crumm, David. "CULTS: What's the allure? Are you at risk?" *Ashbury Park Press*, March 18, 1993, pp. E1, E4.

Damsteegt, P. Gerard. *Foundations of the Seventh-day Adventist Message and Mission.* Grand Rapids, MI: William B. Eerdmans Publishing Company, 1981.

Dart, John. " 'New' Concepts in Christianity Revive Ancient Ideas: Is Holy Spirit Best Seen As Female?" *L.A. Times*, April 10, 1982, n.p.

Davidson, Joe and Christi Harlan. "Texas Devastation: As Waco Crisis Ends, Clinton's Leadership Comes Under Scrutiny." *Wall Street Journal*, April 20, 1993, pp. A1, A6.

Davis, Deborah with Bill Davis. *The Children of God: The Inside Story.* Grand Rapids, MI: Zondervan Publishing House, 1984.

Deans, Bob. "House Panel will study Waco tragedy." *The Orange County Register*, April 24, 1993, p. 6.

Decker, Cathleen and Mike Ward. "Koresh, Bright and Dark: The Bizarre Charmer." *L.A. Times*, April 2, 1993, pp. A1, A14.

DeMar, Gary. *Last Days Madness.* Brentwood, TN: Wolgemuth & Hyatt, Publishers, Inc., 1991.

Dubrow-Eichel, Steve K. "Deprogramming: A Case Study, Part I: Personal Observations of the Group Process." *Cultic Studies Journal* 6, 2 (1989): 1–117.

Dubrow-Eichel, Steve K. "Deprogramming: A Case Study, Part II: Conversation Analysis." *Cultic Studies Journal* 7, 2 (1990), pp. 174–216.

England, Mark. "Lawman: group tried to deceive." *Waco-Tribune Herald*, April 14, 1988, pp. 1C, 4C.

England, Mark. "Families gather at trial." *Waco-Tribune Herald*, April 18, 1988, pp. 1B, 10B.

England, Mark. "7 Davidians found innocent." *Waco-Tribune Herald*, April 26, 1988, pp. 1A, 8A.

England, Mark and Darlene McCormick. "The Sinful Messiah – Part 1." *Waco Tribune-Herald*, February 27, 1993, pp. 1A, 10A–11A.

England, Mark and Darlene McCormick. "The Sinful Messiah – Part 2." *Waco Tribune-Herald*, February 28, 1993, pp. 1A, 8A.

England, Mark and Darlene McCormick. "The Sinful Messiah – Parts 3, 4, 5, 6, 7." *Waco Tribune-Herald*, March 1, 1993, pp. 1A–9A.

England, Mark. "4 Dead, 18 Hurt." *Waco Tribune-Herald*, March 1, 1993, pp. 1A, 3A–9A, 16A.

Enroth, Ronald M. *Youth, Brainwashing, and the Extremist Cults.* Grand Rapids, MI: Zondervan Publishing House, 1977.

Estrich, Susan. "The Waco Legacy." *L.A. Times*, April 25, 1993, pp. M1, M6.

Fair, Susan and Kathy Fair. "Well-known pathologist summoned for independent autopsy of Koresh." *The Orange County Register*, May 8, 1993, p. 4.

Fair, Kathy and Charles Saul. "Koresh quietly buried in Texas cemetery." *The Orange County Register*, June 5, 1993, n.p.

Fiddleman, Theodore H. and David B. Kopel. "ATF's Basis for the Assault on Waco Is Shot Full of Holes." *Insight*, June 28, 1993, pp. 21–22.

Frantz, Douglas. "Poor Leadership Doomed Waco Raid on Davidians, Probe Finds." *L.A. Times*, October 1, 1993, pp. A3, A18.

Frantz, Douglas. "Justice Dept. Report Absolves FBI, Blames Koresh for 75 Waco Deaths." *L.A. Times*, October 9, 1993, p. A17.

Franz, Raymond. *Crisis of Conscience*. Atlanta, GA: Commentary Press, 1983.

Franz, Raymond. *In Search of Christian Freedom*. Atlanta, GA: Commentary Press, 1991.

Freedman, Dan. "Federal officials didn't expect fire suicide, Reno defends plan." *The Orange County Register*, April 20, 1993, p. 10.

Froom, Leroy Edwin. *The Prophetic Faith of Our Fathers*. Washington: Review and Herald Publishing Association, 1954.

Galloway, Joseph L. "The woe outsiders brought to Waco." *U. S. News & World Report*, October 4, 1993, pp. 73–76.

Gardner, Noel. "David Koresh: Narcissistic Personality or . . ." *Adventist Today*, May–June 1993, p. 10.

Gaustad, Edwin Scott, ed. *The Rise of Adventism: Religion and Society in mid–19th Century America*. New York: Harper & Row, 1974.

Gelman, David. "From Prophets to Losses." *Newsweek*, March 15, 1993, p. 62.

Gelman, David. "An Emotional Moonscape." *Newsweek*, May 17, 1993, pp. 52–54.

Goleman, Daniel. "Experts Say Hostage Approach Led to Bloodshed." *The N.Y. Times*, April 21, 1993, p. A11.

Gregory, Sophronia Scott. "Children of a Lesser God." *Time*, May 17, 1993, n.p.

Grenz, Stanley J. *The Millennial Maze: Sorting Out Evangelical Options*. Downers Grove, IL: InterVarsity Press, 1992.

Grigg, William Norman. "Christianity as a 'Cult'." *The New American*, August 23, 1993, pp. 33–35.

Haliburton, Rita. "Centexan: Holy Spirit Female." *Waco Tribune-Herald*, April 26, 1980, p. 5B.

Haloviak, Kendra. "One of David's Mighty Men." *Spectrum: The Journal of the Association of Adventist Forums* 23:1, May 1993, pp. 39–42.

Hancock, Lee. "Treasury study blasts ATF's Davidian raid." *The Orange County Register*, October 1, 1993, pp. A1, A4.

Hanson, Eric and Stephanie Asin. "Tunnel could have saved cult members." *The Orange County Register*, May 1, 1993, p. 4.

Harper, Brian. "God, Guns, and Rock 'n' Roll." *Spectrum: The Journal of the Association of Adventist Forums* 23:1, May 1993, pp. 26–29.

Harper, Charles L. and Bryan F. Le Beau. "The Social Adaptation of Marginal Religious Movements in America." *Sociology of Religion* 54:2, Summer 1993, pp. 171–92.

Hassan, Steven. *Combatting Cult Mind Control*. Rochester, VT: Park Street Press, 1988.

Hedges, Michael. "Leader's messianic mirage mesmerized cult." *The Washington Times*, March 1, 1993, p. A10.

Hedges, Michael and Jerry Seper. "Lawmen fault ATF assault on cult's fortress." *The Washington Times*, March 2, 1993, p. A1.

Heinerman, John and Anson Shupe. *The Mormon Corporate Empire*. Boston, MA: Beacon Press, 1985.

Henig, Karl. "Apocalyptic Rock: My Days With David Koresh." *Liberty*, July–August 1993, pp. 10–15.

Henig, Karl. "Where Everybody Knows Your Name." *Liberty*, September–October 1993, pp. 12–14, 27–31.

Henneberger, Melinda. "At the Whim of Leader: Childhood in a Cult." *The N.Y. Times*, March 7, 1993, p. E6.

Hexham, Irving and Karla Poewe. *Understanding Cults and New Religions*. Grand Rapids, MI: William B. Eerdmans Publishing Company, 1986.

Hinds, Michael deCourcey. "A Believer Says Cult in Texas Is Peaceful, Despite Shootout." *The N.Y. Times*, March 6, 1993, pp. A1, A8.

Hinds, Michael deCourcey. "Texas Cult Membership: Many Lives, Shared Fate." *The N.Y. Times*, April 20, 1993, p. A12.

Hinds, Michael deCourcey. "Emerging From Smoke, A Tale of Blind Loyalty." *The N.Y. Times*, April 21, 1993, p. A11.

Hines, Michael deCourcy. "Arson Team Says Members of Cult Started Fatal Fire." *The N.Y. Times*, April 27, 1993, p. A9.

Hines, Michael deCourcy. "For Experts, Fire Tapes Provide Rare Evidence." *The N.Y. Times*, April 28, 1993, p. A9.

Hines, Michael deCourcy. "Toll is Lowered For Sect Dead to Around 72." *The N.Y. Times*, April 30, 1993, p. A9.

Hoekema, Anthony A. *The Four Major Cults*. Grand Rapids, MI: William B. Eerdmans Publishing Company, 1963.

Hokama, Dennis. "Koresh on Ellen White." *Adventist Today*, May–June 1993, p. 12.

Holmes, Michael. "FBI spokesman calls cult leader in Waco an ego-tripping liar." *The Orange County Register*, April 17, 1993, p. 16.

Hudson, Winthrop S. *Religion in America*. 3d ed. New York: Charles Scribner's Sons, 1981.

Hurtz, Howard. "Cult Leader Rambles About God, Bible In Live CNN Interview During Standoff." *The Washington Post*, March 1, 1993, p. A6.

Irvine, William C. *Heresies Exposed*. Neptune, NJ: Loizeaux Brothers, Inc., 1955.

Isser, Natalie and Lita Linzer Schwartz. *The History of Conversion and Contemporary Cults*. New York: Peter Lang, 1988.

Jackson, Robert L. "ATF Chief retires days before Waco raid report." *L.A. Times*, September 28, 1993, p. A10.

Jarboe, Jan. "Manacles of the Mind." *The N.Y. Times*, April 21, 1993, p. A19.

Jemison, T. Housel. *A Prophet Among You*. Mountain View, CA: Pacific Press Publishing Association, 1955.

Johnson, Benton. "Presidential Address—1987, On Founders and Followers: Some Factors in the Development of New Religious Movements." *Sociological Analysis* 53:S, Supplement 1992, S1–S13.

Johnson, Dirk. "40 Bodies of Cult Members Are Found in Charred Ruins." *The N.Y. Times*, April 22, 1993, p. A12.

Johnson, Dirk. "Head Agent Is Haunted, but Unbowed." *The N.Y. Times*, April 23, 1993, p. A10.

Johnson, Dirk. "Inside the Cult: Fire and Terror on Final Day." *The N.Y. Times*, April 26, 1993, pp. A1, C10.

Johnson, Linda. "Waco Home Base for Adventists' Sect: New Mount Carmel Center Residents Watch for Signs of World's End." *Waco Tribune-Herald*, May 18, 1978, p. 8A.

Johnston, David. "Federal officials saw tear-gas assault as best option." *The Orange County Register*, April 25, 1993, p. 29.

Johnston, David. "Panel Hears Tape of Koresh Screaming to Police." *The N.Y. Times*, June 10, 1993, p. A8.

Kantrowitz, Barbara et al. "Thy Kingdom Come." *Newsweek*, March 15, 1993, pp. 52–58.

Kantrowitz, Barbara et al. "Was It Friendly Fire?" *Newsweek*, April 5, 1993, pp. 50–51.

Kantrowitz, Barbara et al. "Day of Judgment." *Newsweek*, May 3, 1993, pp. 22–27.

Kennedy, J. Michael. "4 Federal Agents Killed in Shootout With Cult in Texas." *L.A. Times*, March 1, 1993, pp. A1, A10–A11.

Kennedy, J. Michael. "Cult Arsenal—How Much Is Legal?" *L.A. Times*, March 12, 1993, pp. A3, A32.

Kennedy, J. Michael. "Doctors Get Clearer Picture of How Cult Children Lived." *L.A. Times*, April 4, 1993, p. A24.

Kennedy, J. Michael. "Lawyers for Cult Predict Passover Exodus." *L.A. Times*, April 5, 1993, n.p.

Kennedy, J. Michael. "Cult's World Ends in the Eye of a Firestorm." *L.A. Times*, April 20, 1993, pp. A1, A16.

Kennedy, J. Michael. "Inferno: Fire is reportedly set. . . ." *L.A. Times*, April 20, 1993, pp. A1, A13.

Kennedy, J. Michael et al. "Will Smoke in Waco Ever Clear?" *L. A. Times*, April 23, 1993, pp. A1, A26–A27.

Knight Ridder News Service. "Waco man foretold how and when it would end." *The Chicago Tribune*, April 23, 1993, n.p.

Knoll, Erwin. "The Tragedy After Waco—Public Response." *The Christian Science Monitor*, April 27, 1993, p. 19.

Komarow, Stephen. "Wisdom of attack on cult questioned." *The Orange County Register*, April 20, 1993, p. 11.

Krauthammer, Charles. "Apocalypse, With And Without God." *Time*, March 22, 1993, p. 82.

Kyle, Richard. *The Religious Fringe: A History of Alternative Religions in America*. Downers Grove, IL: InterVarsity Press, 1993.

Labaton, Stephen and Sam Howe Verhovek. "U.S. Agents Say Fatal Flaws Doomed Raid on Waco Cult." *The N.Y. Times*, March 28, 1993, pp. A1, A11.

Labaton, Stephen. "U. S. Agency Head Defends Tactics in Assault on Sect." *The N.Y. Times*, March 30, 1993, p. A13.

Labaton, Stephen. "Reno Sees Error In Move On Cult." *The N.Y. Times*, April 20, 1993, pp. A1, A13.

Labaton, Stephen. "Officials Contradict One Another on Rationale for Assault on Cult." *The N.Y. Times*, April 21, 1993, pp. A1, A11.

Labaton, Stephen. "U.S. Opens Up to Avoid Backlash on Cult Attack." *The N.Y. Times*, April 22, 1993, p. A13.

Labaton, Stephen. "Reno Wins Praise At Senate Hearing." *The N.Y. Times*, April 23, 1993, p. A10.

Labaton, Stephen. "Inquiry Will Not Examine Final Assault On Waco Cult." *The N.Y. Times*, May 16, 1993, p. 17.

Labaton, Stephen. "ATF boss to quit as Waco report nears release." *The Orange County Register*, September 28, 1993, p. 3.

Labaton, Stephen. "Report on Initial Raid on Cult Finds Officials Erred and Lied." *The N.Y. Times*, October 1, 1993, pp. A1–A10.

Labaton, Stephen. "Report on Assault on Waco Cult Contradicts Reno's Explanations." *The N.Y. Times*, October 9, 1993, pp. 1, 10.

Labaton, Stephen. "Firearm's Agency Struggles to Rise From the Ashes of the Waco Disaster." *The N.Y. Times*, November 5, 1993, p. A7.

Labaton, Stephen. "Outside Review Criticizes FBI On Raid on Cult." *The N.Y. Times*, November 16, 1993, p. A7.

Lacayo, Richard. "Cult of Death." *Time*, March 15, 1993, pp. 36–39.

Lambert, Pam, and Joe Treen, et al. "Waco: 13 Who Died." *People*, May 3, 1993, pp. 44–49.

Lamy, Philip. "Millennialism in the Mass Media: The Case of *Soldier of Fortune* Magazine." *Journal for the Scientific Study of Religion* 31:4, December 1992, pp. 408–24.

Land, Philip, ed. *Adventism in America*. Grand Rapids, MI: Eerdmans Publishing Company, 1986.

Langone, Michael D. *Destructive Cultism: Questions and Answers.* Weston, MA: American Family Foundation, 1982.

Langone, Michael D. "Social Influence: Ethical Considerations." *Cultic Studies Journal* 6:1, 1989, pp. 16–24.

Langone, Michael D., ed. *Recovery from Cults: Help for Victims of Psychological and Spiritual Abuse.* New York: W. W. Norton and Company, 1993.

Langone, Michael D. and Paul Martin. "Deprogramming, Exit Counseling, and Ethics: Clarifying the Confusion." *Christian Research Journal* 15: 3, Winter 1993, pp. 46–47.

Lee, Robert W. "Truth and Cover-up: Sorting Out the Waco Tragedy." *The New American,* June 14, 1993, pp. 23–30.

Lewis, Anthony. "After the Buck Stops." *The N.Y. Times,* April 23, 1993, p. A19.

Libit, Howard. "ATF Chiefs Testify on Cult Raid." *L.A. Times,* April 23, 1993, p. A26.

Lifton, Robert Jay. *Thought Reform and the Psychology of Totalism.* New York: W. W. Norton and Company, 1961.

Lightner, Robert P. *The Last Days Handbook.* Nashville: Thomas Nelson Publishers, 1990.

Lindell, Chuck. "Mass suicide shows how deeply Koresh dominated Branch Davidians." *The Orange County Register,* April 20, 1993, p. 12.

Lindell, Chuck. "Vengeance, sorrow among reactions." *The Orange County Register,* April 20, 1993, p. 11.

Lindelof, Bill. "Recalling horror of deaths in Guyana." *The Sacramento Bee,* March 2, 1993, pp. A1–A12.

Liu, Melinda. "Hard Lessons in the Ashes." *Newsweek,* May 3, 1993, p. 31.

Loe, Victoria. "Researcher predicted fiery tragedy." *The Sacramento Bee,* April 22, 1993, p. A14.

Lynch, Dalva with Paul Carden. "Inside the 'Heavenly Elite': The Children of God Today." *Christian Research Journal,* Summer 1990.

Martin, Paul R. "Dispelling the Myths: The Psychological Consequences of Cultic Involvement." *Christian Research Journal* 11: 3, Winter–Spring 1989, pp. 8–14.

Martin, Walter R. *The Kingdom of the Cults,* revised and expanded edition. Minneapolis: Bethany House Publishers, 1985.

Martin, Walter R. *The Rise of the Cults.* Grand Rapids, MI: Zondervan Publishing House, 1955.

Mattingly, Terry. "Koresh's cult evolved from peaceful offshoot." *Rocky Mountain News,* March 20, 1993, p. 99.

McGiffert, Michael, ed. *Puritanism and the American Experiences.* Reading, MA: Addison-Wesley Publishing Company, 1962.

McGraw, Dan. "A Place To Hang Their Hats." *U.S. News & World Report,* August 23, 1993, n.p.

Melton, J. Gordon. *Biographical Dictionary of American Cult and Sect Leaders.* New York: Garland Publishing, 1986.

Melton, J. Gordon. *Encyclopedia of American Religions.* 4th ed. Detroit: Gale Research Inc., 1993.

Melton, J. Gordon. *Encyclopedic Handbook of Cults in America.* New York: Garland Publishing, 1986.

Melton, J. Gordon and Robert L. Moore. *The Cult Experience: Responding to the New Religious Pluralism.* New York: The Pilgrim Press, 1982.

Milloy, Ross E. "My God . . . It's Horrific." *The Orange County Register,* April 20, 1993, p. 10.

Montgomery, John Warwick. *The Shaping of America.* Minneapolis: Bethany House Publishers, 1981.

n.a. "4 Federal Agents Die in Shootout While Trying to Seize Cult Leader." *The N.Y. Times,* March 1, 1993, pp. A1, A11.

n.a. "At The Present Moment." *Church and Society,* May–June 1990, p. 54.

n.a. "Cult Children Tell of Abuse in Compound." *L.A. Times,* March 4, 1993, p. A16.

n.a. "God to avenge raid on cult, member says." *The Orange County Register,* March 27, 1993, p. A4.

n.a. "FBI fears Koresh may relish follower's death." *The Washington Times,* March 28, 1993, p. A3.

n.a. "Koresh now wants to finish book before surrender." *The Orange County Register,* April 15, 1993, p. 8.

n.a. "Visitor says Davidians didn't plan suicide." *The Orange County Register,* April 20, 1993, p. 14.

n.a. "A Fire Carried by the Wind Through Matchstick Walls." *The N.Y. Times,* April 21, 1993, p. A10.

n.a. "3 victims found in Waco were shot, officials say." *The Sacramento Bee,* April 22, 1993, pp. A1, A14.

n.a. "Workers Pick Through Cult's Compound." *The N.Y. Times,* April 23, 1993, p. A10.

n.a. "Finding Cult Leader's Remains: Delicate but Doable Task." *The N.Y. Times,* April 28, 1993, p. A9.

n.a. "Cult siege cost: $6.6 million." *The Sacramento Bee,* May 2, 1993, p. A5.

n.a. "Koresh's Body Found With Bullet Wound." *L.A. Times,* May 3, 1993, p. A4.

n.a. "Texas Officials Identify Bodies of Cult Lieutenants." *The N.Y. Times,* May 12, 1993, p. A8.

n.a. "Koresh Tape Blasts Mass Suicide Idea." *L. A. Times,* May 29, 1993, p. A24.

n.a. "Koresh burial small, private." *The Sacramento Bee,* June 6, 1993, p. A17.

n.a. "Koresh's unsigned will left estate to children." *The Orange County Register,* June 19, 1993, p. 31.

n.a. n.t. *The New Republic,* June 21, 1993, p. 11.

n.a. "Cult members gather at ruins of compound." *The Orange County Register*, July 3, 1993, n.p.

n.a. "Autopsies show three cultists were shot in head at point-blank range." *The Orange County Register*, July 15, 1993, p. 3.

n.a. "Texas still monitoring 12 Branch Davidian kids." *The Orange County Register*, September 28, 1993, p. 7.

n.a. "Religious group's smoldering dispute erupts in gunfire." *The Dallas Morning News*, November 15, 1987, pp. 45A, 47A.

n.a. "The Jehovah's Witnesses Are a 'Killer Cult,' Says a Defector." *Christianity Today*, November 20, 1981, p. 70.

Nelson, Alan and Sandra Gines. "Crying in the Wilderness." *Waco-Tribune Herald*, January 17, 1988, pp. 1A, 8A.

Neufeld, Don F., ed. *Seventh-day Adventist Encyclopedia*. Washington: Review and Herald Publishing Association, 1966.

Noll, Mark A. *A History of Christianity in the United States and Canada*. Grand Rapids, MI: William B. Eerdmans Publishing Company, 1992.

Numbers, Ronald L. *Prophetess of Health: Ellen G. White & the Origins of Seventh-day Adventist Health Reform*. Knoxville, TN: University of Tennessee Press, 1992.

Numbers, Ronald L. and Jonathan M. Butler. *The Disappointed: Millerism and Millennarianism in the Nineteenth Century*. Indiana: Indiana University Press, 1987.

Ofshe, Richard. "Coerced Confessions: The Logic of Seemingly Irrational Action." *Cultic Studies Journal* 6:1, 1989, pp. 1–15.

Ostling, Richard. "A Sinister Search for 'Identity.'" *Time*, October 20, 1986, p. 74.

Ostrom, Carol M. "Edge of Dread: Preparing for the Worst in Montana Hills." *Seattle Times/Seattle Post-Intelligencer*, April 22, 1990, p. 10.

Ostrow, Ronald J. "Clinton Supports Reno in Waco Attack." *L.A. Times*, April 21, 1993, pp. A3, A12.

Ostrow, Ronald J. "Reno Believed a Mass Suicide Was Unlikely." *L.A. Times*, April 21, 1993, pp. A1, A14.

Ostrow, Ronald J. "No Recriminations Over Cult Children, Reno Says." *L.A. Times*, April 29, 1993, pp. A1, A22.

Ostrow, Ronald J. "Reno, FBI Officials Cleared In Assault On Branch Davidian Compound." *L.A. Times*, October 3, 1993, p. A22.

Pareles, Jon. "It's Got a Beat and You Can Surrender to It." *The N.Y. Times*, March 28, 1993, p. 2E.

Paxton, Geoffrey. *The Shaking of Adventism*. Grand Rapids, MI: Baker Book House, 1977.

Pennock, J. Roland and John W. Chapman, eds. *Coercion*. Chicago: Aldine/Atherton, Inc., 1972.

Pérez-Peña, Richard. "U.S. Braces For A New Test By Branch Davidians, In Court." *The N.Y. Times*, April 30, 1993, p. B16.

Perry, Bruce. "Brainwashing or Socialization." Lecture delivered at 1993 Cult Awareness Network National Conference, Bloomington, MN.

Pitts, Bill. "The Mount Carmel Davidians: Adventist Reformers, 1935–1959." *SYZYGY: Journal of Alternative Religion and Culture* 2:1–2, Winter–Spring 1993, pp. 39–54.

Potok, Mark. "Cult kid's stories of horror." *The Sacramento Bee*, May 5, 1993, p. A8.

Pratkanis, Anthony and Elliot Aronson. *Age of Propaganda: The Everyday Use and Abuse of Persuasion*. New York: W. H. Freeman and Company, 1991.

Prejean, Lisa Tedrick. "What drew them to the cult?: David Koresh uses complex Bible verses to hook his followers." *The Daily Mail*, 1993, April 1, 1993, p. C1.

Price, Debbie M. "It never should have happened." *The Orange County Register*, April 21, 1993, p. 9.

Rainie, Harrison et al. "The Final Days of David Koresh." *U.S. News & World Report*, May 3, 1993, pp. 25–34.

Ramstad, Evan. "'Religious fanatic' enters cult compound." *The Orange County Register*, March 26, 1993, p. A21.

Rea, Walter T. *The White Lie*. Turlock, CA: M & R Publications, 1982.

Reid, Daniel G., Harry Stout, and Robert Linder, eds. *Dictionary of Christianity in America: A Comprehensive Resource on the Religious Impulse That Shaped a Continent*. Downers Grove, IL: InterVarsity Press, 1990.

Reid, George W. "Sorting the Messiahs." *Liberty*, July–August 1993, pp. 16–19.

Reiterman, Tim. "Parallel Roads Led to Jonestown, Waco." *L.A. Times*, April 23, 1993, p. A26.

Religious News Service. "Groups Warn Against Using Waco Tragedy to Define a Valid Religion." *L.A. Times*, May 8, 1993, p. B8.

Richardson, James T. "Definitions of Cult: From Sociological-Technical to Popular-Negative." *Review of Religious Research* 34:4, June 1993, pp. 348–56.

Rimer, Sarah. "Cult's Surviving Children: New Lives, New Ordeals." *The N.Y. Times*, April 27, 1993, pp. A1, A9.

Risen, James. "Independent Panel Will Probe ATF Raid." *L.A. Times*, May 2, 1993, p. A22.

Rivenburg, Roy. "When Worlds Collide: For Some, Cults Hold All the Answers." *L.A. Times*, March 10, 1993, pp. E1, E8.

Rosado, Caleb. "Lessons From Waco." *Ministry: International Journal for Clergy*, July 1993, pp. 6–11.

Rosado, Caleb. "Lessons From Waco II." *Ministry: International Journal for Clergy*, August 1993, pp. 14–19.

Ross, Joan Carol and Michael D. Langone. *Cults: What Every Parent Should Know*. Weston, MA: American Family Foundation, 1988.

Rowley, James. "Koresh planned for cult to attack Waco, U.S. says." *The Orange County Register*, October 3, 1993, p. 30.

Ryan, Patricia. "Are Other Wacos Waiting to Happen?" *L.A. Times*, May 13, 1993, p. B11.

Safire, William. "Waco, Reno, Iraqgate." *The N.Y. Times*, October 14, 1993, n.p.

Sahagun, Louis and Michael J. Kennedy. "Custody Efforts Begin in Waco Siege." *L.A. Times*, March 10, 1993, pp. A3, A18.

Sahagun, Louis. "FBI'S Tactics Seen Not Weakening Sect's Resolve." *L.A. Times*, March 16, 1993, p. A10.

Sahagen, Louis and J. Michael Kennedy. "FBI Says Koresh Entirely to Blame." *L.A. Times*, April 21, 1993, pp. A1, A13.

Samples, Kenneth R. "From Controversy to Crisis: An Updated Assessment of Seventh-day Adventism." *Christian Research Journal*, Summer 1988, pp. 9–14.

Samples, Kenneth R. "The Truth About Seventh-day Adventism." *Christianity Today*, February 5, 1990, pp. 18–21.

Sandeen, Ernest R. *The Roots of Fundamentalism: British and American Millennarianism, 1800–1930*. Chicago: The University of Chicago Press, 1970.

Sandefur, Joel and Charles Lu. "Apocalypse at Diamond Head." *Spectrum: The Journal of the Association of Adventist Forums* 23:1, May 1993, pp. 30–33.

Saul, Charles and Kathy Fair. "Koresh's mother likens his death to Crucifixion." *The Orange County Register*, June 27, 1993, p. 10.

Scarborough, Rowan. "Reporters called a hindrance." *The Washington Times*, March 2, 1993, pp. A1, A7.

Schein, Edgar H., Inge Schneier, and Curtis H. Barker. *Coercive Persuasion*. New York: W. W. Norton and Company, 1961.

Schwarz, Richard W. *Lightbearers to the Remnant*. Mountain View, CA: Pacific Press Publishing Assoc., 1979.

Serrano, Richard A. "Cult Leader Also Led '88 Shootout At Church Camp." *L.A. Times*, March 2, 1993, p. A16.

Shea, William H. "How Should SDA's Respond?" *Spectrum: The Journal of the Association of Adventist Forums* 23:1, May 1993, pp. 43–45.

Singer, Margaret Thaler and Richard Ofshe. "Thought Reform Programs and the Production of Psychiatric Casualties." *Psychiatric Annals* 20:4, April 1990, pp. 188–93.

Smith, Robert W. and Elisabeth A., compilers. *Scriptural and Secular Prophecies Pertaining to The Last Days*. n.p., 1948.

Sobran, Joseph. "Applying the cult label." *The Washington Post*, March 22, 1993, p. E4.

Stammer, Larry B. "Cult's Believers Waiting for Judgment Day." *L.A. Times*, March 1, 1993, pp. A1, A11.

Stammer, Larry B. "Cult's Path to Violence Is Well Traveled." *L.A. Times*, March 2, 1993, p. A16.

Stapleton, Arnie. "Two in Koresh group fatally shot in head." *The Orange County Register*, April 25, 1993, p. 3.

Steinfels, Peter. "Promise of the Millennium Has Long Driven Cults." *The N.Y. Times*, March 3, 1993, p. A11.

Steinfels, Peter. "Beliefs: Other Davidians want it to be known they're not like the outlaw sect besieged in Texas." *The N.Y. Times*, March 6, 1993, p. A8.

Stephenson, Neal. "Blind Secularism." *The N.Y. Times*, April 23, 1993, p. A19.

Sykes, Charles J. "Bonfire of the Vanities." *The Wall Street Journal*, April 21, 1993, p. A14.

Tabor, James D. "Apocalypse At Waco: Could the Tragedy Have Been Averted?" *Bible Review*, October 1993, pp. 25–33.

Tanner, Gerald and Sandra. *The Mormon Kingdom*. 2 vols. Salt Lake City, UT: Utah Lighthouse Ministry, 1971.

Taves, Ernest H. *This Is The Place: Brigham Young and the New Zion*. New York: Prometheus Books, 1991.

Taylor, Thomas F. "Why Doesn't Somebody Stop That Cult?" *Christianity Today*, October 25, 1993, pp. 25–27.

Teel, Charles. "Kissing Cousins or Kindred Spirits?" *Spectrum: The Journal of the Association of Adventist Forums* 23:1, May 1993, pp. 48–49.

Terry, Don. "Standoff in Texas Goes On After Cult Chief's Broadcast." *The N.Y. Times*, March 3, 1993, p. A1.

Terry, Don. "Federal Agents Set For Long Standoff With Cult in Texas." *The N.Y. Times*, March 4, 1993, pp. A1, A11.

Times Wire Services. "Family Buries David Koresh in An Unmarked Grave." *L.A. Times*, June 6, 1993, p. A20.

Treen, Joe et al. "Zealot of God." *People*, March 15, 1993, pp. 38–43.

Van Zandt, David E. *Living in the Children of God*. Princeton, NJ: Princeton University Press, 1991.

Verhovek, Sam Howe. "'Messiah' Fond of Rock, Women and Bible." *The N.Y. Times*, March 3, 1993, pp. A1, A11.

Verhovek, Sam Howe. "Children of the cult: they wait in limbo." *The Orange County Register*, March 8, 1993, pp. 1, 7.

Verhovek, Sam Howe. "In Shadow of Texas Siege, Uncertainty for Innocents." *The N.Y. Times*, March 8, 1993, pp. A1–A10.

Verhovek, Sam Howe. "6 Women and Man Leave Texas Cult's Compound." *The N.Y. Times*, March 22, 1993, pp. A7.

Verhovek, Sam Howe. "Decibels, Not Bullets, Bombard Texas Sect." *The N.Y. Times*, March 25, 1993, n.p.

Verhovek, Sam Howe. "FBI turns Koresh cult's fortress into a prison." *The Orange County Register*, April 13, 1993, p. 6.

Verhovek, Sam Howe. "Apparent Mass Suicide Ends A 51-Day Standoff in Texas." *The N.Y. Times*, April 20, 1993, pp. A1, A12.

Verhovek, Sam Howe. "FBI Cites Fresh Evidence That Cult Set Fatal Fire; U.S. Strategy Questioned." *The N.Y. Times*, April 21, 1993, pp. A1, A10.

Verhovek, Sam Howe. "FBI Saw the Ego in Koresh But Missed Willingness to Die." *The N.Y. Times*, April 22, 1993, pp. A1, A13.

Verhovek, Sam Howe. "Investigators Puzzle Over Last Minutes of Koresh." *The N.Y. Times*, May 5, 1993, p. A10.

Verhovek, Sam Howe. "Criticism of Raid Heartens Cult Members." *The N.Y. Times*, October 1, 1993, p. A10.

Waite, Albert A. C. "The British Connection." *Spectrum: The Journal of the Association of Adventist Forums* 23:1, May 1993, pp. 34–38.

Wall, James M. "Eager for the End." *Christian Century*, May 5, 1993, pp. 475–476.

Wattenburg, Daniel. "Gunning for Koresh." *The American Spectator*, August 1993, pp. 31–40.

Weiseltier, Leon. "The True Fire." *The New Republic*, May 17, 1993, pp. 25–27.

Wessinger, Catherine. "Annie Besant's Millennial Movement: Its History, Impact, and Implications Concerning Authority." *SYZYGY: Journal of Alternative Religion and Culture* 2:1–2, Winter–Spring 1993, pp. 55–70.

West, Louis Jolyon. "Milieu Control: Sleep Deprivation." Lecture delivered at 1993 Cult Awareness Network National Conference, Bloomington, MN.

———. "Persuasive Techniques in Contemporary Cults: A Public Health Approach," *Cultic Studies Journal* 7:2, 1990, pp. 126–49.

Witkin, Gordon and Ted Gest. "G-men of the Nineties." *U.S. News & World Report*, May 3, 1993, pp. 36–40.

Witkin, Gordon. "ATF: Agency under the gun." *U.S. New & World Report*, October 4, 1993, pp. 56, 73.

Woodward, Kenneth L. et al. "Cultic America: A Tower of Babel." *Newsweek*, March 15, 1993, pp. 60–61.

Woodward, Kenneth L. and Kendall Hamilton. "Children of the Apocalypse." *Newsweek*, May 3, 1993, p. 30.

Quotes Cited

everal quotes in *Prophets of the Apocalypse* were not given directly to the authors, but taken from already existing material. The following is a list of both the quote and source from which it was taken.

Marc Breault

To have the guts to blatently say something that people might see as weird, knowing how people would react, he had to have some sort of conviction. . . . The way I was looking at it then was that your TV evangelists pretend to be average, normal people. They keep the bad things in the closet. When they come out, they fall. But this guy was saying it straight out. (England, Mark. "The Sinful Messiah—part 2," *Waco-Tribune Herald*, February 28, 1993.)

So Marc, how does it feel now that I'm stuck with Elizabeth? (England, Mark. "The Sinful Messiah—part 5," *Waco-Tribune Herald*, March 1, 1993.)

Sometimes, to illustrate what hell would be like, how the people would scream, he'd start screaming. He once said it would be worse than someone flaying off your skin with nail clippers. It was certainly graphic. It got your attention. (England, Mark. "The Sinful Messiah—part 3," *Waco-Tribune Herald*, March 1, 1993.)

Once, [Vernon] Howell ordered followers not to eat any fruit except bananas. Then Howell would not let anyone eat oranges and grapes at the same meal. They could, however, eat oranges and raisins. It was hard to keep up with the changes. (England, Mark. "The Sinful Messiah," *Waco-Tribune Herald*, March 1, 1993.)

First, he was the only one allowed to eat meat. Then he was the only one allowed to drink Coke. Then he was the only one allowed to drink beer. The thing I noticed about Vernon is that whatever he was tempted with, eventually God would get around to saying it was all right for him to do. (England, Mark. "The Sinful Messiah—part 3," *Waco-Tribune Herald*, March 1, 1993.)

Lisa Gent

It's like he cooks women. He prepares them for the fire by the way he gives his studies. It's mind manipulation. (England, Mark. "The Sinful Messiah—part 3," *Waco-Tribune Herald*, March 1, 1993.)

Nicole Gent

Vernon wants me to be his teddy bear for the night. Will you give me your permision? (England, Mark. "The Sinful Messiah—part 3," *Waco-Tribune Herald*, March 1, 1993.)

Bruce Gent

Nicole had spent four days with him being convinced of the message. It wasn't for me to say yes or no. . . . She was going to have children for the Lord. I shudder when I say that now. (England, Mark. "The Sinful Messiah—part 3," *Waco-Tribune Herald*, March 1, 1993.)

Robyn Bunds

You know when an animal's scared, how its heart just pounds? That's how Vernon said her heart sounded. Like when you're hunting something is how he put it. (England, Mark. "The Sinful Messiah—part 4," *Waco-Tribune Herald*, March 1, 1993.)

It's not like he says that you're his favorite. It's just obvious. He isn't with anyone else. He's always with you. It' more like a flavor-of-the-month thing. (England, Mark. "The Sinful Messiah—part 3," *Waco-Tribune Herald*, March 1, 1993.)

It was like a beauty contest—all of us battling against each other to be this woman that God thinks is the greatest. It was like a fairy tale. . . . Back then, I was still dreany-eyed. I wasn't into reality. (England, Mark. "The Sinful Messiah—part 5," *Waco-Tribune Herald*, March 1, 1993.)

His bottom was hit so much that the skin was raw. It's not like a scrape. It's just where the skin is hit so much that it bruises and can't take anymore and bleeds. (England, Mark. "The Sinful Messiah—part 4," *Waco-Tribune Herald*, March 1, 1993.)

Yeah, I spanked him [Wisdom]. I'm not proud of it. . . . I'm sorry I did that. There's no way to take it back. But I was told to. . . . All I can say is I was in a certain frame of mind. Vernon said that even if a child died from a spanking they would go to heaven. (England, Mark. "The Sinful Messiah—part 4," *Waco-Tribune Herald*, March 1, 1993.)

Lisa Gent

We managed to get to bed at 11:00 P.M. At 1:00 A.M. Vernon ran through the camp ringing the food bell, making an awful racket. We had to come and eat, as he himself had not had food that night. We then were compelled to study with him unti 5 A.M. (England, Mark. "The Sinful Messiah—part 2," *Waco-Tribune Herald*, February 28, 1993.)

Jeanine Bunds

I wanted to be in the House of David. He made it sound so wonderful. I did, I did believe. I couldn't tell you why now. The children in the group are so beautiful. You think, these must be God's children. They're so beautiful. (England, Mark. "The Sinful Messiah—part 6," *Waco-Tribune Herald*, March 1, 1993.)

George Roden

They didn't come here to get a picture. They come here to kill me. (Collins, Jeff. "The Law steps in after strife-torn religious sect's battle," *The Dallas Times Herald*, November 24, 1987.)

Vernon Howell

I figured if he could see . . . that we have just as much fire power as he has, he'd back off. (Collins, Jeff. "The Law steps in after strife-torn religious sect's battle," *The Dallas Times Herald*, November 24, 1987.)

Lt. Dickeron

They had more ammunition than a patrol would have in Vietnam in their possession at the time of their arrest. (Collins, Jeff. "The Law steps in after strife-torn religious sect's battle," *The Dallas Times Herald*, November 24, 1987.)

Anonymous ex-Davidian

When I was there . . . guys were in tears about it, that God wanted them to give up their wives. (England, Mark. "The Sinful Messiah—part 5," *Waco-Tribune Herald*, March 1, 1993.)

Anonymous ex-Davidian

You don't have time to think. He doesn't give you time to think about what you're doing. It's just bang, bang, bang, bang, bang!